MORE BURS UNDER THE SADDLE

UNIVERSITY OF OKLAHOMA PRESS : NORMAN

More Burs
Under the Saddle

BOOKS AND HISTORIES OF THE WEST

by Ramon F. Adams

Foreword by Wayne Gard

Cowboy Lingo (Boston, 1936)

Western Words: A Dictionary of the Range, Cow Camp, and Trail (Norman, 1944)

Charles M. Russell, the Cowboy Artist (with Homer E. Britzman) (Pasadena, 1948)

Come an' Get It: The Story of the Old Cowboy Cook (Norman, 1952)

The Best of the American Cowboy (compiler and editor) (Norman, 1957)

The Rampaging Herd: A Bibliography of Books and Pamphlets on Men and Events in the Cattle Industry (Norman, 1959)

A Fitting Death for Billy the Kid (Norman, 1960)

The Old-Time Cowhand (New York, 1961)

Burs Under the Saddle: A Second Look at Books and Histories of the West (Norman, 1964)

From the Pecos to the Powder: A Cowboy's Autobiography (with Bob Kennon) (Norman, 1965)

The Legendary West (Dallas, 1965)

The Cowman and His Philosophy (Austin, 1967)

The Cowboy and His Humor (Austin, 1968)

Western Words: A Dictionary of the American West (Norman, 1968)

The Cowman and His Code of Ethics (Austin, 1969)

Six-Guns and Saddle Leather: A Bibliography of Books and Pamphlets on Western Outlaws and Gunmen (Norman, 1954; revised and enlarged edition, 1969)

Wayne Gard (Austin, 1970)

The Cowman Says It Salty (Tucson, 1971)

The Language of the Railroader (Norman, 1977)

More Burs Under the Saddle: Books and Histories of the West (Norman, 1979)

Library of Congress Cataloging in Publication Data

Adams, Ramon Frederick, 1889–1976.
    More burs under the saddle.

    "Books by Ramon F. Adams": p. iv
    Includes index.
      1. Crime and criminals—The West—History—Bibliography. 2. The West—History—Bibliography. 3. Frontier and pioneer life—The West—Bibliography. I. Title.
Z1251.W5A29   1978 [F596]   016.978   77–18606

Dedicated to my friend David Grossblatt, who is deeply interested in true history and who acted as a volunteer book scout to discover and bring me a number of books to examine that I would not otherwise have seen.

FOREWORD

****

By Wayne Gard

Does history consist solely of military exploits and political races, with an occasional glance at economics? Some of our academic historians have seemed to think so. They have looked down their noses at those who wrote of ordinary people and how they lived and worked and died. This has been glaringly true in a superior attitude toward historians of the western cattle country and of the development of order and law on the frontier.

Partial justification for this attitude comes from the fact that, with notable exceptions, most of those who have written about cowboy life and about outlaws and law officers have been amateurs with little learning and no real conception of historical research. They recorded hearsay without checking and perpetrated the errors of earlier writers.

As a result, one hardly can pick up a book on the American West without finding factual errors that the authors could have avoided if they had spent a little time in research. For example, when John Wesley Hardin, the notorious gunman, wrote his autobiography, he was in prison and did not have at hand all the records he needed. After he set down, from faulty memory, the date of his capture in Florida as July 23, 1877, dozens of other writers accepted and used that date. But Walter P. Webb and at least one other historian looked up the adjutant general's papers in Austin, found the telegrams of the Texas Ranger who had captured Hardin, and corrected the month to August.

Likewise, many frontier biographers, in interviewing their subjects, failed to check fading memories and swallowed without question erroneous boastings. Stuart N. Lake took the word of Wyatt Earp on scores of misstatements, including one that Earp had been chief deputy marshal of the frontier Kansas town of Wichita. But if Lake had looked up the official records in Wichita, he would have found that Earp had been only an ordinary patrolman, the bottom one on the list.

Finally this field attracted some serious and painstaking historians, such as Edward Everett Dale, Everett Dick, J. Evetts Haley, Ernest Staples Osgood, Joseph G. Rosa, and Don Russell. Yet many lazy writers continued to copy the errors of careless predecessors.

In time the constant finding of errors in books and pamphlets about the Great Plains cattle country, especially about the bad men and their exploits, got under the skin of the Texan best qualified to correct them—Ramon F. Adams. From his youth Adams had been fascinated by cowboy lore, and over the years he had made an amazing collection of cowboy words and sayings. He published those, along with enlightening works on various aspects of cowboy life, rangeland narratives, and bibliographies of books and pamphlets on cowmen and western outlaws.

By the time he turned to exposing the multitude of errors in books on the West, Adams had sold his business and was giving all his time to writing. He had become familiar with almost every book and pamphlet written on the cowboy life of the plains and on the outlawry that often prevailed in the frontier era. So he took up the formidable task of separating fact from legend.

In his *Burs Under the Saddle* (1964), Adams ran his fine-toothed comb through more than four hundred books and pamphlets, pointing out their errors. Some of those authors still living must have winced, but they deserved to have their errors brought to light and corrected. This work made it easier for later historians to avoid making the same mistakes. Yet some went on with their careless habits.

More than two hundred additional western books and pamphlets are put under the spotlight here in *More Burs Under the Saddle*. Some of their errors could have been avoided if the authors had read and heeded the preceding listing of burs. From now on, there will be even less excuse for passing off legends as facts.

In these corrective works Adams was motivated not by any kind of jealousy or malice but rather by a desire to set the historical record straight and to provide guidelines for future writers. His own historical writing has been meticulous and exact, and readers have a right to expect the same from other writers.

Ramon Adams traveled from one side of the continent to the other to run down historical facts, often digging deep into faded documents and public records. He corresponded with historians and librarians who did research in many states. Each project seemed to spawn others, and his field of history broadened over the years.

Adams never took time to retire. Even in his last years, when he was in his eighties, he spent part of each day in research and writing, turning out new books and updating earlier ones. Yet he always had time to give a hand to another writer who might need help. Many will remember him as one who swept some of the cobwebs from the history of the American West and who set a fine example in telling the story of the frontier as it really happened.

INTRODUCTION

****

In the first paragraph of the introduction of my *Burs Under the Saddle*,[1] I made the statement that "just as burs under the saddle irritate a horse, so the constant writing of inaccurate history irritates the historian. And nowhere has research been so inadequate or writing so careless as in accounts of Western outlaws and gunmen. Indeed, many chroniclers seem to delight in repeating early sensational and frequently untrue stories without any real attempt to investigate the facts." This book, which is a supplement to *Burs* is an effort to set history straight by examining the accounts closely and critically side by side with fact.

For instance it is somewhat surprising to find in the book *The Overland Stage to California*, by Frank Root and William Elsey Connelley, such errors as "Doc Brink was at Rock Creek Station with Wild Bill when the bloody fight took place with McCandless [sic] gang, when no less than *five outlaws* were killed." They have Wild Bill "dying with his boots on in *Wyoming* while at a game of cards." They misspell Reni's name as Beni, and of Joseph Slade they say that he "soon was the head of a notorious gang of highway robbers and murderers that ever infested a civilized community." This is not true. He was never a robber, but a general nuisance, because of his heavy drinking and shooting up saloons. They are also mistaken in having someone ride for Slade's wife when the vigilantes had Slade in custody and having her arrive in time to rescue him "under a fierce fire." The truth is that he was hanged before his wife arrived.

These statements are surprising because Root was a stage driver at

[1] Norman, University of Oklahoma Press, 1964.

the time and should have known the truth, and Connelley, as the secretary of the Kansas Historical Society, with access to the wonderful library of the society and all the contemporary newspapers, had the truth at hand if he had only used it. Yet one is not too surprised, for Connelley's book *Wild Bill and His Era* is filled with errors.

It is surprising, though, to find such books as *Cowboy Capital of the World*, by Samuel Carter III, published in 1973, so full of errors (see item 33 of this work). It is discouraging indeed to learn that so many would-be historians refuse to believe the truth. Again I repeat from the introduction to *Burs Under the Saddle*:

> The special weakness of authors writing about outlaws is following time-worn legends. An early writer wrote that Billy the Kid had "killed twenty-one men by the time he was twenty-one years of age," and practically every writer on Billy the Kid since then has repeated the statement, apparently never questioning its truth. Many writers think that Buel, Emerson Hough, Fred Sutton, Frank Harris, and the like are authentic historians, although all of them are unreliable and follow one another blindly, without any effort to verify what their predecessors wrote, most of them never having seen contemporary newspaper accounts or court records. These followers were and still are gullible, evidently believing that if they see it in print it is so.
>
> When one continues to read even now that Wild Bill Hickok fought and killed from eight to ten men at Rock Creek Station, that Billy the Kid killed twenty-one men by the time he was twenty-one years of age, that Jim Murphy committed suicide, that Jesse James was not killed in 1882, and other such nonsense, it makes him lose patience. As an avid follower of Western history and as a writer, I felt called upon to do something about the situation, and thus began my long years of research. . . .
>
> Granted, it is easy to make mistakes when writing about Western outlaws because men living outside the law seldom left a clear-cut trail; yet that does not excuse the historian for merely parroting old legends and refusing to investigate those records which are available.

It has been many years since my *A Fitting Death for Billy the Kid* was published (1960) and *Burs Under the Saddle* appeared (1964). From their reception it is obvious that they made some sort of impression—though perhaps not upon writers who prefer legend to history. Soon after publication of *A Fitting Death for Billy the Kid* I received a letter saying: "These stories about Billy the Kid are part of our heritage. Why change them now?" Such an attitude is indeed discouraging to one who wants to see truth prevail.

As I wrote in 1964, I still believe that

the real facts are dramatic enough without the embellishment of absurd melo-drama. But, for three-quarters of a century and more, authors have picked out what they liked from the dime novels, from the faulty recollections of old-timers or purported old-timers, and even from the accounts of some of the participants themselves who were not averse to appearing larger than life. Fabulous tales grew up about Hickok in his own lifetime which he never troubled to deny, and Wyatt Earp himself promoted his own image as the faultless hero—after everyone who could deny his stories of his exploits was dead and gone. Too many writers have made the outlaw and gunman a hero: Billy the Kid a lovable and misunderstood young man; Sam Bass a latter-day Robin Hood; Wild Bill Hickok a super-gunman and conqueror of wicked men; Jesse James the eternal savior of the widow harassed by the villainous mortgage-holder; and Wyatt Earp the stalwart guardian of peace and law in frontier towns.

All in all, a great mass of absurdities has been written about most of the gunmen, and one writer has repeated another, compounding the glaring errors until they have become legends which refuse to die. And when one tries to correct these figments of the dime novelists' imagination, he surely makes an enemy of the romanticist. In spite of all this, however, I hope writers will begin to seek the truth behind the fictitious tales that have been so tenaciously re-corded, and I hope this truth will receive proper emphasis and wide circulation.

Since those words were written, I have found more than two hundred books to be added to those discussed in *Burs*. They are covered in these pages. The comments show how hard it is to teach some writers the difference between history and legend. It is most discouraging to the honest historian, but I'll keep trying.

RAMON F. ADAMS

Dallas, Texas

CONTENTS

* * * * * * * * * * * * * * *

Foreword, by Wayne Gard   vii

Introduction   xi

200 Books and Histories of the West   3

Afterword   169

Index   171

MORE BURS UNDER THE SADDLE

BOOKS AND HISTORIES OF THE WEST

****

1. ALLSOPP, FRED W. Folklore of romantic Arkansas, by Fred W. Allsopp. Illustrated. ₁N.p.₁, Grolier Society, 1931. Cloth. 2 vols.

The last chapter of Volume 1 is about outlaws from Murrell to Bill Doolin and Henry Starr. There is a section on the James boys and their robbery of the stagecoach on the Hot Springs run. The author also tells of some of Quantrill's activities in Arkansas. There is a story about Wild Bill Hickok that I had not read before. The author then writes: "A long time afterward he [Hickok] went to Deadwood, Dakota, and became the comrade of Buffalo Bill." But Hickok's association with Cody occurred before he went to South Dakota. There is also a section about Judge Parker's court and the many men he condemned to hang.

The author is mistaken in saying that Belle Starr was shot three times by a jealous wild man "as she rode her thoroughbred horse, 'Venus' home from a dance." She was only shot twice, from ambush, and she had not been to a dance. The author has Bill Tilghman capturing Bill Doolin in Eureka Springs "after a desperate struggle," and the author says that this happened "early in the morning of December the 5th, 1895,"

but it happened on the morning of January 15, 1896. There was no desperate struggle. He is also mistaken in calling Doolin's baby son "presumably the child of Rose of Cimarron"; he was his son by his wife, Edith Ellsworth Doolin.

2. [ARIZONA] Outlawry and justice in old Arizona. A collection of reports published by the history club, Sunnyside High School. Tucson, Arizona, 1965. Tucson, Arizona, Printed by L. A. Printers, 1965. Stiff wrappers.

This is a collection of essays, mostly about outlaws, by teenage students. There are many errors and misspelled proper names. The information was obtained from many untrustworthy sources. In the first chapter the author calls the Harpes the Harpers and says that they "were two mulatto brothers," which is untrue. Most of her information on the early trace outlaws of the Mississippi River is unreliable. She jumps from the outlaws of the trace to those of California, and her information on the latter is just as unreliable.

The author of the second chapter has Billy the Kid in Tombstone, but he was never there. In another chapter, on Luke Short, the author says that Short was born in Arkansas, but he was born in

Mississippi. She says that he "grew up near Grainsville [sic], Texas, but he spent his boyhood in Grayson County, Texas. He says that Wyatt Earp managed the Oriental gambling house at Tombstone, but that is false.

In a chapter on the Clantons the author gives a very poor description of the O K Corral fight. He does not mention Wyatt Earp being there. All these authors spell the McLaury boys' name Mc-Lowery. In another chapter, about Johnny Ringo, the story of an attempt by a mob to lynch Johnny-Behind-the-Deuce O'Rourke is all wrong.

In a chapter about Bat Masterson the author has him sheriff of Dodge City, but that was a county job. In a chapter on Wyatt Earp the author has him saving the life of Johnny-Behind-the-Deuce, which is an error. She is also mistaken when she says that Wyatt spent his life as a United States deputy marshal, and also that after the O K Corral fight Morgan and Virgil Earp "disappeared into the desert never to be seen again." We know that Virgil was crippled for life by a would-be assassin and that Morgan was killed by another assassin.

In a chapter on Pat Garrett the author is mistaken in saying that Billy the Kid was fourteen when his father died, that Olinger was killed by the Kid from a balcony, and that J. W. Bell was a sheriff. The Kid was much younger when his father died, he shot Olinger from an upstairs window, and Bell was only a deputy. I fail to see why Garrett and Billy the Kid are included in a book about Arizona, except that most writers about the West feel that they must bring these two characters into their stories. A typographical error spells "Foreword" as "Forward."

These young writers were attempting to write history, and it is too bad their editor did not guide them to reliable information and assist them in writing true history.

3. ASKINS, Col. Charles. Texans, Guns & history, [by] Col. Charles Askins. [New York], Winchester Press [1970]. Cloth.

There are many errors throughout this book; I will attempt to point out some of them. The author has Bat Masterson a city marshal of Dodge City, Kansas, but he was sheriff of Ford County. The author writes as though the killing of Bill Sutton and Gabe Slaughter were the real start of the Taylor-Sutton feud, but the feud had been going on for some time when the two were killed. He says that Sam Bass was twenty-six when he was killed, but he died on his twenty-seventh birthday. He says there was bad blood between Ben Thompson and King Fisher, but that is untrue, for they were friends when they went to San Antonio, where they were both killed. He says that Ben Thompson was an Englishman but intimates that he was born in Lockhart, Texas. Thompson was born in Knottingley, Yorkshire, on November 11, 1842. He relates that Thompson shot a man named Adams Brown three times but did not kill him and that for that crime he was sentenced to serve two years in the penitentiary. I have never seen this story before. His statement about the killing of Phil Coe by Wild Bill Hickok is also unreliable. He writes that Coe died before morning, but Coe lived for three days in agony. He says that Thompson did not take up the fight with Hickok over Coe's death because he was laid up with a broken leg caused by falling off a horse. But his leg was broken at the same time his wife and son were injured in Kansas City, when the buggy in which they were riding hit a hole and was overturned.

He also says that after Thompson killed Jack Harris in San Antonio he was fired from his job as city marshall of Austin, but that is incorrect. Thompson did write a letter of resignation, but the city council refused to accept it. The author is also mistaken in saying that Thompson went back to the Variety Theater with Fisher "to finish off Joe Foster and Billy Simms as he had done to their partner." He returned there to patch things up. The author is also mistaken in saying that King Fisher was indicted by the grand jury for being "in cahoots with Ben Thompson" for killing "a man named Amos Wilson in Austin." He also says that Matthews, Wilson's bartender, whom Thompson shot, lingered three weeks before dying.

He writes that at the age of fifteen John Wesley Hardin killed "a black state policeman," but the first man he killed was a Negro named Mage, a former slave who had belonged to his uncle, Judge Clabe Holshouven. He also says that at the age of sixteen Hardin became a professional gambler. He has a poor opinion of Hardin, who "was most likely to shoot from ambush and was a cattle rustler and a horse thief," but Hardin cannot be accused of those crimes. He says that Hardin's ambition was to "add another notch to his gun." He is wrong in saying that, after killing Webb, Hardin "ducked over to Louisiana and stayed there." He spells Mannen Clements' name as Manning, a common error.

He is mistaken in saying that Ranger Armstrong captured Hardin by "bending his gun barrel over his head." In his autobiography Hardin does not give his capture in this manner. The author is also mistaken in saying that Hardin "remained in custody of the Lone Star State

for twenty long years." He was convicted in the spring of 1878 and was pardoned February 17, 1894, thus serving only sixteen years. He also says that Hardin was a model prisoner, but during his first years in prison he made many attempts to escape.

The author is also mistaken in saying that Hardin was born in 1848; he was born May 26, 1853. He also credits Hardin with some killings that never took place. He misspells Jack Helm's name as Helms. He has Jim Miller a brother-in-law of Mannen Clements, but they were cousins. On page 201, Ira Aten's name is spelled Iran, but that is evidently a typographical error; it is spelled correctly elsewhere. He also says that Aten had been in the Ranger service for eight years, but in his own book Aten states that he served five and a half years.

The author is also mistaken in saying that Wild Bill Hickok killed men to enforce the city ordinance that no guns were to be fired in the city limits—unless he is referring to the killing of Phil Coe and, by accident, his own deputy, Mike Williams.

In his tale about a Mexican named Pablo Gutiérrez murdering a Texas rancher named James Roundtree, I think he is confusing the story of the killing by a Mexican named Juan Bidino of William Coran, his boss and a cattleman from Texas. Of the two Negro policemen who tried to capture Hardin in Gonzales, Hardin says that he killed one and shot the other off his white mule, but the author says that Hardin shot at the latter, which "only served to speed him down the dusty road."

He is mistaken in saying that Jim Miller was hanged in Bartlesville, Oklahoma. He was hanged in Ada. Again, he is mistaken when he writes that Bass Outlaw killed Ranger Joe McKidrict in "Tillie Howard's sporting house." The shooting took place in her back yard. He also claims that when Selman killed Hardin he "strode up behind Hardin, walking catlike on the balls of his feet. When he was at arm's length he whipped out his .45 and shot Hardin in the back of the head." But Selman shot Hardin from the doorway of the saloon. He says that Hardin had just bought Henry Brown, the bartender, a drink, but they were shooting dice.

The author writes that "Joel Collins was a Texas cowboy who had a good reputation. He was not a gunfighter, did not headquarter in the saloons and gambling halls, and the most of his friends were ranchers and their hands." Collins was no cowboy but a bartender when Bass first met him in San Antonio. The author is also mistaken when he says that Collins had been up the trail with cattle herds several times. He claims that Collins shipped his herd by train to Sydney, Nebraska, and then drove them to Deadwood. Actually he drove the cattle over the trail to Kansas, where he sold them. The author claims a great change came over Collins between Uvalde and Abilene, and he was no longer the honest man he had been.

The author has the Collins-Bass robbery of the Union Pacific on September 19 at 10 o'clock at night, but it occurred on the 18th, and the train arrived at 10:48 P.M. He also says that Jim Berry was captured "after a gun fight" in an alley, but he was shot in the woods near a friend's home trying to escape, and there was no fight. He did not die for several days. The author is mistaken in saying that Bass and Davis went to Waco, Texas, when they got back to Texas. They went to Fort Worth, where Davis left Bass for good.

The author has Bass's first Texas train robbery at Allen on February 18, but it took place on the 22d. He also says that the Bass gang robbed the same train at Hutchins a month later, but it was slightly less than a month, on March 18. He is also mistaken in writing that Frank Jackson was a cousin of Jim Murphy and that Sheriff William C. Everheart (whom the author calls Jennings Everheart) was in on the deal whereby Murphy was to play the traitor to the gang. He has the battle at Round Rock wrong and misspells Koppel's name Kopperel, and he is another who mistakenly claims that Jim Murphy committed suicide. He is also mistaken in saying Frank Johnson was rumored to be "deeply mixed up with Billy the Kid in the Lincoln County War." That too is incorrect.

In his first chapter the author has the trail cowboy a regular devil of disaster when he hits the end of the trail. The book is a rehash of events already familiar to readers of this kind of literature, which is, as we see, very untrustworthy.

The author misspells many proper names, such as Ellie Grimes for "High" W. Grimes, Everts Haley for J. Evetts Haley, Rafe Perry for Rufus Perry, and Seiker for Sieker. The caption under the photograph of Jack Harris reads "Jack Harris in whose theater Thompson killed Fisher," but Thompson did not kill Fisher. They were both killed by theater employees. A picture of a building is captioned "The old building in Round Rock where Sam Bass met his death." This leaves the impression that Bass was killed in this building, but he was shot on the street. The caption under a photo of a group of four men with guns reads "Frank A. Hamer, the man who captured Bonnie and Clyde." Hamer did not capture Bonnie and Clyde; he killed them. He misspells Lon Oden's name as Odom and Jim Putman's name as Putnam, and he writes

G. Tucker for T. F. Tucker and Indianolo for Indianola. The entire book shows careless proofreading, as well as careless writing, for there are still more mistakes than one cares to mention.

4. AXFORD, JOSEPH MACK. Around western campfires, by Joseph Mack Axford. New York, Pageant Press, [1964]. Cloth.

I met Axford in Tombstone, Arizona, where he autographed his book for me and took me on a personally guided tour through the old courthouse museum, showing me the gallows in the yard where five men were hanged, the cell where the women were kept, and the old courtroom itself with its uncomfortable benches. Like most of the old-timers of Tombstone, he has little use for the Earps and claimed that the O K Corral fight was "murder." He misspells Emilio Kosterlitsky's name as Koskalisky, Rurales as Ruallas, and Burt Alvord's name as Bert. He is also mistaken in saying that the Eighth Cavalry was Negro.

He claims that, according to old-timers, the so-called fight between Wyatt Earp and Curly Bill Brocius at Iron Springs never took place. He is mistaken in saying that McGinnis, Carver, and Sam Ketchum tried to rob a Santa Fe train; it was a Colorado and Southern train. He is also mistaken in saying that Russian Bill was hanged in Galeyville, Arizona. He was hanged with Sandy King in Shakespeare, New Mexico.

He writes that the McLaury boys had sold their ranch and were leaving the Tombstone country because they had witnessed the stagecoach robbery in which Bud Philpot was killed, that Ike Clanton had been foolish enough to claim that Doc Holliday was among the robbers, and that now they were afraid of the Earps. As they were leaving the country, they approached Tombstone, and the Clantons wanted to stop there, but the McLaurys did not. Yet when the McLaurys were shamed about their fears, they agreed to have a last fling in Tombstone—and a last fling it was for three of them.

The author seems to think that Buckskin Frank Leslie killed Johnny Ringo and claims that Billy Claiborne, whose hero was Ringo, attempted to kill Leslie for this deed. He tells a story of the O K Corral fight that I have not seen before and admits that this story has not been verified when he says that Tom McLaury (whom he repeatedly spells McLaura) was shot in the belly by Doc Holliday and "was down when a prostitute, living in a cabin in front of which the fight was taking place, rushed to the door and threw a Winchester toward McLaury in the street. McLaury, kneeing his entrails, crawled to the Winchester and drove the Earps and Holliday off the street before he died." He admits, however, that that might be a tale started by some old-timer who wished that such a thing had happened. I think the author is mistaken when he says that "John Slaughter had very little to do as sheriff and spent most of his time sitting in his office" because when the Earps were run out of Arizona crime practically ceased. According to the records Slaughter had plenty to do, for crime did not cease with the passing of the Earps.

The author tells about Albert Jennings Fountain and his son being murdered in the White Sands of New Mexico and says that nothing was ever found of them except the buckboard and horses; but they were not found either, and the whole affair remains the great mystery of New Mexico. He misspells Longabaugh's name as Longbaugh and seems to have too little respect for Pat

Garrett. Except for these and other mis-statements, the book is very readable.

5. BAGGS, MAE LACY. Colorado, the queen jewel of the Rockies ..., by Mae Lacy Baggs. With a map and fifty-four plates, of which six are in color. Boston, Page Company, MDCCCCXVIII. Cloth.

The author is mistaken when she writes that "the route from Trinidad to the San Juan was one periodically visited by the stage coach robbers while 'Billie the Kid,' the famous outlaw, plied his trade here with more or less success." Billy the Kid never operated in Colorado, nor was he ever a robber of stagecoaches.

6. BAILEY, ROBERT G. River of no return, by Robert G. Bailey. Lewiston, Idaho, [n.pub.], 1947. Cloth.

This author has Calamity Jane born in 1850, but she said that she was born in 1852. He has her dying at Terraville, Wyoming, but she died in Terryville, South Dakota. He is also mistaken in saying that she made her last public appearance in Buffalo, New York, in a wild West show for the Buffalo Exposition, and he claims that it was a moot question whether she ever married.

He also says that Boone Helm was killed by a "tribe of Sheepeaters" in August, 1878. Helm was hanged by vigilantes in 1864. He quotes a long letter that he received from W. H. Latta correcting him on this mistake, but he adds no comment. His account of Henry Plummer is also very unreliable.

7. BAKER, ELMER LEROY. Gunman's territory, by Elmer Leroy Baker. San Antonio, Texas, Naylor Company ..., [1969]. Cloth.

The author tells much about the out-laws and marshals of Oklahoma, but he is mistaken in having Sam Bass join a cattle drive in West Texas as an expert cowboy, roper, and cook. Bass's experience with cattle was very limited, and the only cattle drive in which he took part was the one to Kansas with his friend Joel Collins, and there is no record that he was ever a cook or a roping expert. The author has Bass with the outfit when they were dodging the Rangers "for the holdups of stage coaches, banks and railroad trains." Bass never robbed a bank; he was preparing to do so when he was killed. The author has Bass killed on July 21, 1878, but he was shot on the 19th and died on the 21st.

This author seems to settle the argument about who killed Belle Starr; he states that it was Jim July. I think he is mistaken in saying that the people of Coffeyville knew that the Daltons were going to rob the banks there. The entire book is filled with conversation, but who recorded it?

8. BAKER, PEARL. The Wild Bunch at Robbers Roost, by Pearl Baker. Los Angeles, Westernlore Press, 1965. Fabrikoid.

This author claims that "a new technique" of train robbery was invented by the Wild Bunch, that is, "the one of uncoupling the engine and express car and moving them away from the rest of the train." This trick was used back in the days of Jesse James. She is also mistaken in having Orion Logan, one of the Logan brothers, going by the name Kid Curry. Harvey Logan assumed the name Kid Curry. She also errs in placing George Curry and Harvey Logan's activities in Utah and Nevada in 1898. According to contemporary newspaper accounts they were in Wyoming. She has the loot from the robbery of the Colorado and Southern train $30,000, but that is greatly exaggerated.

The author has Elza Lay taking part in the third robbery, when Black Jack Ketchum's arm was nearly shot off. Lay participated in the second Folsom robbery (July 11, 1899). In the third robbery (August 15, 1899) Tom Ketchum was alone, but this author writes: "The rest of the gang was battling a posse in the rain and darkness and Sheriff Farr of Walsenburg, Colorado, was killed, as was Black Jack's brother, Sam Ketchum." She intimates that all this took place at the same time and place, but these were separate robberies, and in neither was Sam Ketchum killed, though he was wounded after the second robbery and died from his wound soon afterward.

She is also mistaken in saying that the WS Ranch in New Mexico was a partnership adventure owned by "an Australian named Wilson and Montague Stevens, a one-armed Englishman." The ranch was owned by Harold G. Wilson, an Englishman, and its first manager was James H. Cook, the author of *Fifty Years on the Frontier*. Stevens owned the SU Ranch, forty miles away. When Cook married and left the WS Ranch, management fell to Captain William French, an Irishman from Dublin, and it was during his reign that several members of the Wild Bunch found work there. She is also mistaken in saying that, "when the WS sold out, Butch Cassidy and the others drifted into Fort Worth where the famous picture with them in derby hats was taken."

She has the killing of Pike Landusky all wrong according to all other accounts, having him killed at his own ranch during a Christmas party instead of at Jew Jake's saloon. She also repeats that threadbare tale of the outlaw loaning a widow money to pay off her mortgage and then robbing the collector. This time it was Tom McCarty, though the story was told originally of Jesse James and later of other outlaws. It seems to have been a favorite story about the modern Robin Hoods. Though conversation makes more interesting reading, in my opinion the author uses too much of it in a book of this nature. I always wonder who recorded it for future historians. Despite these errors, the book is interesting and has some heretofore untold history.

9. BARKLEY, MARY STARR. A history of central Texas, by Mary Starr Barkley. [Austin, Austin Printing Company, 1970]. Cloth.

This author has one of her characters saying that Frank James, in his later years, worked as a janitor in Fort Worth, Texas, but that is not true, nor is the statement she makes that James died there in 1914. James worked as a shoe salesman in Dallas, never in Fort Worth as a janitor, and he died on the old James farm in Clay County Missouri on February 18, 1915. The author is also mistaken in saying that, when the Bass gang rode into Round Rock to look over the bank they proposed to rob, a Ranger stopped them. Two deputy sheriffs, Grimes and Moore, stopped them, and that caused the battle in which Bass was wounded, dying two days later.

10. BENNETT, EDWIN LEWIS. Boom town boy in old Creede, Colorado, by Edwin Lewis Bennett. Chicago, Sage Books, [1966]. Cloth.

This book contains an account of the killing of Bob Ford by Ed O. Kelly, whom the author, like so many others, calls Ed O'Kelly. He is also mistaken when he writes that Kelly "was killed by a law officer in Texas." The killing took place in Oklahoma City.

11. BLACKER, ERWIN R. (ED.). The old West in fact, edited by Erwin R. Blacker. New York, Ivan Obolensky, Inc., 1962. Cloth.

Among other western subjects this book has two chapters on outlaws: an excerpt from Pat Garrett's book on Billy the Kid and one from Gillett's *Six Years with the Texas Rangers* on the killing of Sam Bass. In the editor's introductory remarks about the latter he repeats some of the false statements made by Teddy Blue Abbott. In this chapter he, of course, makes the same mistakes Gillett made, such as saying that Frank Jackson returned to Denton and that Jim Murphy committed suicide. In one chapter, entitled "The Cattlemen," he quotes the complete text of Charlie Siringo's book *A Texas Cowboy* and perpetuates many mistakes about the life and death of Billy the Kid.

12. BLYTHE, T. ROGER (ED.). Tombstone, Arizona, edited by T. Roger Blythe. [Tombstone, Tombstone Epitaph, n.d.]. Wrappers.

This editor is mistaken in saying that Wyatt Earp's brothers, Morgan, James, and Warren, and Doc Holliday went to Tombstone with him. It is also disappointing that the editor repeated many of the false legends about Wyatt, such as having him a deputy U.S. marshal when he arrived in Tombstone; having Wyatt the man who hit Curly Bill Brocius over the head and took him to jail for killing Fred White; having Wyatt hold off a mob trying to lynch Johnny-Behind-the-Deuce O'Rourke. All these statements are incorrect.

I very much doubt the author's state-ment that Russian Bill paid $25,000 for a box at the Bird Cage Theater every night for two years. Where did he get such money? He was just a would-be outlaw and horsethief. The author also says that Russian Bill stole a horse and was hanged for it the same day, but that did not happen. It is true that he stole a horse, and it is true that he was hanged, but not on the same day.

13. BOND, MARSHALL, JR. Gold hunter. The adventures of Marshall Bond, by Marshall Bond, Jr. Albuquerque, University of New Mexico Press, 1969. Cloth.

A most interesting book written from the letters and records of an adventurous father by his equally adventurous son. In Chapter 8, entitled "Billy the Kid," the author makes the usual mistakes when writing about the young outlaw. He appears to have got most of his information from Miguel A. Otero, and he is mistaken when he writes that Dolan sent Sheriff Billy Matthews "to get Tunstall on a trumped-up charge." Matthews was not a sheriff, only a deputy. He has Tunstall "herding a bunch of horses" when the mob caught up with him, but Tunstall was driving them to Lincoln, not herding them. He is also mistaken in having the battle at the McSween home a "three-day battle." It lasted five days.

He has McSween killed as he "started across the yard," but he was killed on the porch of the house. He also has Buckshot Roberts "discovering" Billy the Kid and his friends at Blazer's Mill. Roberts was hunting them for the reward that had been offered. He has Charlie Bowdre killed "in April, 1881," but he was killed at Stinking Springs just before Christmas, 1880.

He claims that Buckshot Roberts got

his nickname "from his numerous gun-fights," but he was named for just one fight, which filled him full of buckshot. The author also has the wrong amount for the reward for the killing of Sheriff Brady and George Hindman. He has the date of Billy the Kid's killing July 13, which is incorrect; he was killed on the night of July 14.

14. BOWMAN, HANK WIEAND. Famous guns from famous collections, by Hank Wieand Bowman. New York, Fawcett Publications, 1957. Stiff pict. wrappers.

In a chapter entitled "Outlaw Guns" the author makes many mistakes in his accounts of western gunmen. He is mistaken in having Bat Masterson killing the men who had shot his brother Ed. Bat was not present at the time. He has Luke Short a marshal of Dodge, but Short was never an officer of the law. He is also wrong in having Billy Brooks a marshal "who did away with fifteen troublemakers his first month in office." He follows that legend about Billy the Kid having killed twenty-one men by the time he was twenty-one years of age, "by his own admission." He also says that among those killed by the Kid were "two sheriffs," but the only sheriff I ever heard of him killing was Sheriff Brady, and there is no proof that the Kid killed him, because others were shooting at him, too, though the Kid was tried for the crime.

The author is also greatly mistaken in stating that Morgan Earp "was killed in a famous gun fight with the McLowery [sic] gang." As we know, Morgan was killed in Hatch's Billiard Parlor while playing pool with Hatch. In one place the author says that Wyatt "felled Mc-Lowery [sic] with his gun butt," but no westerner would ever use the gun butt,

and Wyatt was noted for striking his opponents with the gun barrel. His account of the battle at the O K Corral is unreliable, and he says that "all four of the McLowery [sic] gang were dead." Only three were killed in this fight, Tom and Frank McLaury and Billy Clanton. He says that George Scarborough challenged John Selman to a duel after Selman killed John Wesley Hardin because he had been "convinced of Hardin's changed outlook on life" and "was incensed by Selman's cowardly action."

He is mistaken in having Wild Bill Hickok, while marshal of Hays City, killing three soldiers and wounding nine others. Not that many were involved. He then has Hickok moving to Abilene to become marshal and says, "He continued his law enforcement approach by killing offenders." Hickok killed only two men while in Abilene, Phil Coe and, by mistake, his own deputy, Mike Williams. He also says that Belle Starr killed a sheriff from Dallas, Texas, but Belle never killed anyone.

15. BREIHAN, CARL W., and CHARLES A. ROSAMOND. The bandit Belle, by Carl W. Breihan and Charles A. Rosamond. The story of the notorious Belle Starr combined with other tales of almost legendary characters. The life story of Henry Starr (written by himself while in prison). True facts about "Hanging Judge Parker" and his hangman George Maledon, Cherokee Bill and others. Seattle, Washington, Hangman Press as presented by Superior Publishing Company, [1970]. Col. pict. imt. leather.

On the very first page the authors make the mistake of saying that Belle Starr "joined forces with Henry Starr, a distant relative of her husband [Sam Starr]." Henry was a mere boy when Belle was murdered, and he was Sam's first cousin, not a distant relative. As in some of Breihan's earlier books the authors insist upon calling Belle by the name Bella. They also insist upon calling Jim Reed by the name Read, as they say, "erroneously spelled Reed by some accounts." They evidently believe that old *Police Gazette* book about Belle.

On another page the authors state that Belle "usually signed her name with an 'a', Bella and not Belle." Wrong again, and they cite no evidence that she signed her name thus. These authors also claim that Carthage, Missouri, was burned after the Shirleys left. They left because of the fire that had burned Shirley's tavern to the ground. They also have the killing of Sam Starr by Frank West taking place in a room of Lucy Surrat's home, but it happened outside in her yard during a country dance. They state that after Sam's death Belle "threw in her lot with Henry Starr," but Henry was only sixteen years old when she died in 1889, long before he started robbing banks.

The authors are wrong in saying that in 1887 Pearl Starr "married a Cherokee Indian named Nilly or Jim July, but the vicious-tempered Bella [sic] refused his admittance until he changed his name to Starr." Jim July was the lover of Belle, not of her daughter, Pearl. Of Belle's death they write: "While [she was] lying there unconscious, her assassin walked up beside her, took her own revolver from its holster and shot her in the head. The weapon was then replaced." This is untrue, for she was shot with a shotgun, one barrel loaded with buckshot and the other with birdshot.

The book contains a facsimile printing of Henry Starr's rare little book of his life. If the authors read it, they should have known that Henry had nothing to do with the crimes of Belle and her gang. The authors also intimate that Pat Garrett was killed by Mannen Clements (whose name they spell Manning) as a hired killer. They say that when Cherokee Bill Goldsby was captured he was hit over the head with a pistol barrel, but the weapon was a stick of stovewood.

They are certainly wrong when they write: "Soon after the Grayson robbery, Read [sic] drifted to Paris, Texas, where he met John Morris. Read, always willing to help a friend in trouble, loaned Morris $600 after his friend lost all his money in a high-stake poker game." In the first place, Morris was no friend of Reed, but a deputy sheriff who had been trailing Reed for three months. They also say, "Morris claimed $1700 in rewards, but the money did him little good." Morris never received any reward because Belle refused to identify her husband as Jim Reed. They repeat that old legend about Blue Duck losing $2,000 of Belle's money in Dodge City and her holding up the gambling hall to retrieve her money.

Their chapter on Black Bart seems strangely out of place in a book supposedly devoted to the Starrs and the outlaws of Indian Territory. They have Black Bart being commissioned a first lieutenant in the Union Army during the Civil War, but he was a first sergeant.

Perhaps the book written by Henry Starr while in the Colorado penitentiary is the most valuable section of the book. The book is profusely illustrated, though many of the illustrations are irrelevant to the text. Though the book's title is *The Bandit Belle*, Belle is given less attention than Henry Starr and other outlaws.

16. BREIHAN, Carl W., and Marion BALLERT. Billy the Kid. A date with destiny, by Carl W. Breihan with Marion Ballert. Seattle, Washington, Hangman Press as presented by Superior Publishing Company, [1970]. Col. pict. imt. leather.

These authors have the Kid illegitimate, but his parents were married before his birth. They also have Joe McCarty a half brother, but he was a full brother, older than the Kid by two years. They have the father, whom they call William H. Bonney, murdered in New York City in 1862, something I have not seen before. They make the statement that the stepfather, William H. Antrim, was a bad influence on the Kid, turning him "to outlawry and Mrs. Antrim to her grave." They have Joe born as the result of a rape of the mother and claim that "the name of Joe's father has never been determined."

They have the battle at the McSween home "the beginning of a civil war in New Mexico," but the war started with the murder of John Tunstall. As in one of his earlier books, Breihan has the Murphy crowd celebrating with a dance in the streets of Lincoln after their victory over the McSween party, but the only celebrating was the looting of the Tunstall store. They have Bob Beckwith killed by the Kid at the battle at the McSween home, but that is not correct. Like so many others too, they have the Kid carrying a gun when he was killed by Pat Garrett, but the records do not show that to be true.

Most of the accounts of the killing of Sheriff Brady and Deputy Hindman say that they were going to the courthouse to post a notice when they were killed, but these authors say that Henry Brown was sent "down the road" to pretend he was drunk and shoot up the town to get the sheriff on the street. They are also mistaken in saying that "people blamed McSween for the killing."

The authors write: "It would be difficult to find anyone about whom so many lies have been told and so much fiction written," and "Billy no doubt contributed to this state of affairs by saying he had killed 21 men." It has been the would-be historians who have made such claims. They misspell Widemann's name as Windenmann and misname Joshua Webb as John. Instead of having Rudabaugh killing the jailer at Las Vegas, as it happened, they have a desperado named Allen doing the killing.

These authors have the shooting of Bowdre and the surrender of the Kid, Rudabaugh, Pickett, and Wilson on December 22, but they surrendered on December 23. They are also mistaken in saying that Garrett, though he had been elected sheriff, had not been sworn in and was serving as a deputy sheriff. They are also slightly confused about the date the Kid's gang left Stinking Springs for Las Vegas after their capture.

They leave the impression that Olinger's shotgun was left in the Kid's cell: "Billy hobbled quickly down the hall [after he had shot Bell] and into his cell-room, grabbed Olinger's shotgun which was leaning against the wall and moved swiftly to the east corner room." They write that Billy himself said that Olinger was the first to shoot Tunstall, but no other account has this information. They continue: "Olinger dismounted and walked to the body with a cocky swagger and gave it a kick in the head with a heavy boot which was followed by a couple more shots at the body." This statement is ridiculous. The authors say that, when this happened,

"Billy was paralyzed. He was dizzy and his stomach felt twisted." How do they know that?

They also tell a wild tale about Rudabaugh escaping and going to Montana, marrying and having three daughters and living to be an old man, dying in 1928. That is a fairy tale. They are also wrong in having the Kid carrying a gun the night he was killed. They admit that Garrett was shot from a thicket but say that when he reached for his own gun "Brazil's [sic] gun spouted flame and Garrett fell forward with a bullet through his head." They are also mistaken in having Sam Bass the trail boss of a herd of cattle being driven north.

17. BREIHAN, CARL W. The complete and authentic life of Jesse James, by Carl W. Breihan. New York, Frederick Fell, Inc., Publishers, [1953]. Boards.

Though this is a "new revised edition," I fail to find many changes except that the introduction of the original edition was written by Homer Croy and the introduction of this revised edition is written by the author of the book. There are some changes in dates. For example, on page 109 of the original edition the author has the bank at Corydon, Iowa, robbed on June 28, 1873, and in the revised edition he has it occur June 3, 1871. On page 113 the original edition has "the first robbery of a train credited to the James group (and one of the first train holdups in the nation) took place on the night of July 20, 1873, . . . about 14 miles from Council Bluffs, Iowa." The new edition reads: ". . . July 21, 1873, . . . about two miles from Adair, Iowa." And the Renos had been robbing trains for some time before the James gang attempted it.

The author has the Hot Springs stage-coach robbery taking place in January, 1874, in the original edition, but says specifically January 15 in the new edition. In the first edition he says that the little station at Muncie, Missouri, was robbed on December 13, 1875; the new edition says December 13, 1874. Except for these few changes of dates the two books are much the same.

The author writes: "It is now doubtful if any of the Missouri robbers participated in the train robbery at Ogallala, Nebraska." Certainly none of the James gang was in this robbery; and, of course, he means the Union Pacific robbery at Big Springs by the Joel Collins–Sam Bass gang. Again he repeats that worn-out legend about Jesse James paying off the widow's mortgage, this time in Tennessee. Of the Gad's Hill robbery he writes: "Of course many people believed that the Jameses and the Youngers were responsible for this new outrage also. Some thought they might have combined with Jim Reed [sic], John Wesley Hardin and other noted outlaws." John Wesley Hardin was never a robber of any kind.

He continues to spell Reed's name as Read, Belle Starr's name as Bella, and Ed O. Kelly's name as Ed O'Kelly. He also makes many of the same mistakes that I pointed out in Burs Under the Saddle.

18. BREIHAN, CARL W. The escapades of Frank and Jesse James, by Carl W. Breihan. New York, Frederick Fell, Publishers, Inc., [1974]. Cloth.

The author makes some statements that I have not seen before, such as having Frank James joining the Big-Nose Parrott gang, and the suspected robbers of the Liberty Bank being arrested and placed in the Liberty jail, where they were "lynched by an angry mob." That never happened. His account of the James boys in Mexico is also very questionable. This book is largely a repetition of his former books, containing the same errors.

19. BREIHAN, CARL W. Great lawmen of the West, by Carl W. Breihan. London, John Long, [1963]. Cloth.

Like the author's other books, this book is full of inexcusable errors. On the dust jacket his publishers tells us that the author "has studied the American gunfighter (as outlaw and lawman) for more than 30 years and has covered nearly 40 states and many thousands of miles researching him." They also state that "he lived in St. Louis, Missouri, the home of Jesse James." Jesse never lived in St. Louis; he lived for a time in St. Joseph, where he was killed. If the author had stayed home and read the better biographies of the various men he wrote about, he would have got more reliable information on his subjects.

He has chapters on Wyatt Earp, Pat Garrett, Burton Mossman, Tom Smith, Commodore Perry Owens, Billy Breakenridge, Bill Tilghman, and Chris Madsen—and also Ranald Mackenzie, though why that army officer is classed with law officers is beyond me. He is mistaken in saying that Doc Holliday went to Dodge with Wyatt Earp and in saying that Ed Masterson was killed immediately when he was shot by Jack Wagner. Masterson lived to walk across the street to Hoover's Saloon before he died.

The author is rather careless with his dates throughout. He says that Earp shot George Hoy (whom he calls Hoyt) "in August, 1879," but Hoy was shot on July 26, 1878. He lived until August 21.

Such minor errors as Nellie Cushman's Russ House being at Sixth and Toughnut streets in Tombstone instead of Fifth and Toughnut are frequent. He writes of Doc Holliday telling Wyatt Earp how he could capture Dave Rudabaugh, who had escaped from the Las Vegas jail, but he was writing of 1877. He also tells about an incident that I have never seen in print before: he says that Big Nose Kate "could be seen chasing Doc up the street [of Dodge], firing at his buttocks with a shotgun loaded with mustard seed and rice."

The author writes: "In Dodge City Wyatt Earp was smart enough not to surround himself with the bunch of killers he used in Tombstone." Wyatt had Doc Holliday and his own brothers in both places, and they were about the only "killers" he "used." He has Wyatt arriving in Tombstone a month before his brothers, Morgan and Virgil, but Virgil met Wyatt in Prescott, and they went to Tombstone together. He says that before this time Morgan had been marshal in Butte, Montana, but that is news to historians. He says that Wyatt married Josephine Sarah Marcus after the death of his wife, Bessie, but Wyatt deserted Bessie when he left Arizona and did not wait long to marry Josephine since Bessie had been his common-law wife.

The author seems to think that Buckskin Frank Leslie died in a San Diego hospital, but Leslie took his boss's revolver and disappeared sometime in 1925 when he was over eighty, never to be heard of again. The author says that Wyatt Earp declared that the killing of Fred White by Curly Bill Brocius was deliberate, while Curly Bill maintained that he had killed the man in self-defense. White himself, before he died, said that it was an accident. The author names White as "the former sheriff of Tombstone," but he was town marshal.

He has Virgil Earp dying in Goldfield, Arizona, but he died in Goldfield, Nevada. The author says that the Benton stage was robbed on March 18, but it happened on the 15th. Breihan has Morgan Earp playing pool with his brother, Wyatt, when he was killed. Morgan was playing with Hatch, the owner of the billiard parlor. He has Wyatt "confronting" Frank Stillwell just before he was killed, but Stillwell was more likely killed from ambush. Phin Clanton was sent to prison in 1887 and lived for several years after his release, but Breihan has him killed in 1882. He says that the reason Earp and Holliday left Arizona was because John Behan kept "hounding" them with warrants.

The author writes that Billy the Kid was killed by Garrett "the night of July 13th," but it was the 14th. He has the Kid going to visit his sweetheart, Chelsa, when he was killed, but it common knowledge that he went to Maxwell's to get some meat for his evening meal. He also says that Garrett was killed on February 28, but he was killed on the 29th—more near misses.

The author has Tom Smith on the wrong side of the Bear River riots in 1868. He has Ben Thompson telling two of his gunmen to kill Smith, and when Smith was actually shot at, the author says, "everyone knew Ben Thompson was responsible for the shots." He has Smith running Thompson out of Abilene, but the two never had any trouble there. Though the author says that Thompson tried to kill Smith several times, Thompson was not that poor a shot. The author has Calamity Jane going into Abilene to try to get Smith's job for Wild Bill Hickok, and he is in error in having Smith killing the son of the publisher of the *Abilene Chronicle*. Historians will wonder where he got this information. There is no record that Smith killed anyone in Abilene, though Breihan has him killing a man called Ace. He has General Miles appointing Smith to the post of U.S. marshal and at one time has a detachment of troops from Fort Leavensworth going to Abilene to keep the peace, but according to the records Smith alone was keeping the peace in good fashion, and Miles never entered the picture, nor was there any detachment of soldiers. Besides, a military man had no authority to appoint anyone U.S. marshal.

The author has Commodore Perry Owens and old Mart Blevins shooting it out, Blevins being killed in March, 1887, but Blevins disappeared from his ranch in July of that year, and his fate was never known. In a battle at the Tewksbury Ranch the author says that "Hampton Blevins and a man named Duchet were the only two to escape with no injuries," but Blevins was killed in the battle. He has Blevins killed by Owens a few pages farther on. He writes, "The real showdown came in February, 1887, when the Tewksburys brought sheep into the valley," but that happened early in the fall of 1886.

He writes: "The Grahams and the Tewksburys of Pleasant Valley were accused of holding up and robbing the bank at St. Johns, and later getting into a fight over the spoils, which culminated in the terrible Pleasant Valley or Tonto Basin War." That is ridiculous. A page or two later he writes: "The cause of their enmity has never really been determined." At the same time he has a war going on between the Hashknife Ranch and its Texas cowboys, who were angry because they had been replaced by cowboys from Montana. The war broke out because one side was attempting to run sheep in cattle country.

Breihan says that Little Bill Raidler

was sent to the Ohio State Penitentiary, where he met O. Henry, "whose influence over Little Bill prevailed even in the young man's later life," and he has Raidler becoming a well-known writer, something no one else has reported. He tells about many things that Mrs. Bill Tilghman did not seem to know about her husband, for she did not mention them in her splendid biography of him.

According to the author, while Wyatt Earp was an officer in Wichita, Mayor Dog Kelly wired him to come to Dodge. According to all other accounts, this telegram was sent by Mayor George Hoover, whom the author calls "Major." He writes that Earp brought Neal Brown and Ed Masterson with him. That never happened, nor did Wyatt ever serve Dodge as marshal, only as deputy marshal. He says that Bill Tilghman was with Bat Masterson when he caught the train robbers at Lovell's camp, but that is untrue. He states that Tilghman married the widow Flora Robinson in 1877, but her name was Flora Kendall. He is also wrong in saying that the Kiowa renegades under Dull Knife invaded the area in 1881; the raid was in 1878. He states that "in the following years [1882] Pat Sughrue was elected sheriff"; he was elected on November 6, 1883, and took office January 14, 1884. He states that Tilghman "was called to run the marshal's office at Oklahoma City in 1911," but Tilghman was chief of police, not marshal.

The chapter on Chris Madsen is also full of errors. The author states that Madsen led a posse after Kid Lewis and Tom Foster, trailed them to Wichita Falls, Texas, and caught them robbing a bank. They were not caught until later that night, about ten o'clock, and they were captured by Rangers McDonald, McCauley, and McClure.

The author states that during this robbery the president of the bank and the cashier were killed. The president was J. A. Kemp, whom I knew personally many years later. The cashier, Frank Dorsey, was killed, and the bookkeeper, H. H. Langford (whom I also knew) was wounded. The author says that an hour or two after the capture Madsen and his posse started back for El Reno, but Madsen had nothing to do with this capture. The author further states that when the posse got back to Wichita Falls a mob had lynched Lewis and Foster. They were lynched, it is true, but not until after McDonald and his Rangers had turned them over to a guard of twenty-five men selected by the judge to protect the jail. There are many other errors in this chapter.

The author says that Tombstone was founded in 1879, but it was founded in 1878. He says that Wyatt Earp was a deputy sheriff when he arrived in Tombstone, having been appointed by Sheriff Shibel of Pima County, and adds that "someone must have pressured Sheriff Shibel to dismiss Earp and appoint John Behan in his place, for this change occurred not long after Earp had received his commission." Behan was made sheriff, not deputy. The author is prejudiced against Behan, calling him "the white-livered sheriff."

He says that Wild Bill Hickok assumed his father's name, William, when he joined the Red Legs and that that is how he got the name Bill. Many men of that period were nicknamed Bill, and thus it was with Hickok. He says that Hickok chased and struck Jack McCall's younger brother with a hoe and that Jack declared he would kill Hickok when he grew up. That is pure fiction. When McCanles was shot, according to the author, he called to his son, "Run, son, run! Your life's in danger here. I'm a goner! Hurry—get goin' now!" But in later years the son said that his father died without speaking a word.

20. BREITENBAUGH, DOLLY. Pioneer days in Jackson County, Missouri, during the Civil War, [by Dolly Breitenbaugh, n.p., n.d. Typed, not published. Mimeographed on one side of paper with spiral binder]. Rare.

This unique account of the pioneer people of Jackson County contains some information on the James and Younger outlaws, and the author repeats the old legend about Jesse paying off the mortgage for the widow and then robbing the collector to get his money back. But in this version it was Frank James instead of Jesse. She says of the Northfield bank robbery: "Frank James miraculously escaped from Minnesota, bringing in a wagon his wounded brother, Jesse, who recovered." The James boys did not escape in a wagon, nor was Jesse wounded. She is also mistaken in saying that Jesse was shot in the back by Bob Ford; he was shot in the back of the head. She says that Frank was tried but not convicted. Frank voluntarily surrendered to Governor Crittenden, and was pardoned and never tried for his crimes.

21. BRENT, WILLIAM. The complete and factual life of Billy the Kid, [by] William Brent. New York, Frederick Fell, Inc., [1964]. Boards.

This book corrects some of the errors in many of the legends about Billy the Kid, but the author makes quite a few mistakes himself. In the Foreword he writes: "The rash of books, stories and narratives written over the years about Billy Bonney have, for the most part, two basic faults, (1) Distortion of facts, events and situations, gross inaccuracies and bald-faced fiction, masquerading as truth. (2) The narrators have missed the Kid's character completely. They have made him an impossible caricature, without rhyme or reason, omitting, or distorting, the motivations behind his actions." We shall see that Brent's book has quite a few "distortions" and "gross inaccuracies" of its own.

The author has Mrs. Antrim giving Ash Upson all the untrue information about the Kid's birth, moving to Kansas in 1862, Billy having a younger brother, and the mother moving to Colorado, where she married Antrim. None of this is true. He has the Kid at an early age rolling drunks, committing petty thefts, and constantly fighting. He claims that Pat Garrett was very much embarrassed when he read the draft of the book he had Ash Upson ghost-write about the Kid, but I doubt that, for he evidently failed to make any changes of importance.

Brent seems to believe everything that Upson wrote about the Kid's early life, though records to the contrary have been unearthed. He believes that Billy had a younger brother and that his mother married in Colorado and lived in Santa Fe for four years before moving to Silver City. Though all of this has been proved false, he says that these facts have been substantiated by the Kid himself, Garrett, Upson, and Mrs. McSween and also states that they "must be accepted at face value." He has a version of the Kid's escape from the law after stealing some shirts from a Chinese that is different from any other account that I have seen.

Although it has been proved that Henry Brown's name was misspelled Hendry solely because of a typographical error that once appeared, Brent says, "There is a *d* in Brown's first name, not Henry, as most writers erroneously call it."

Early in the book he makes the statement that "so much pure and unadulterated hokum has been written about the Kid, that he was born here, there and everywhere; that his name wasn't Billy Bonney, but Henry McCarty, or McCartney, or something else; that such facts have been 'proven by extensive research.'" He questions the research, but he has no evidence to support Mrs. Antrim's statement or the Kid's own account. He seems to be unaware that there are civil and religious records of the marriage of Mrs. McCarty to Antrim, both revealing that her two sons, Joseph and Henry, were witnesses. There are newspaper records showing that the Kid's name was Henry McCarty, and his schoolmates called him by that name. The name Bonney was not heard until after Billy got into serious trouble and took the name on his own account.

The author claims there is no record of the Kid killing a blacksmith in Arizona, but he will find an account of it in the August 23, 1877, issues of the *Tucson Arizona Citizen* and the *Arizona Weekly Star* and later papers.

He has the Kid the only one shooting at Baker and Morton when they were killed, but I will never believe that all the others sat idly by without taking action. He makes the statement that "Billy Bonney had notched his first killing of actual record" with these killings, but his killing of Cahill in Arizona was recorded in the newspapers much earlier. He does not have Peppin with Sheriff Brady and deputies Hindman and Matthews when they were ambushed by the Kid's gang, and he has the battle at Blazer's Mill different from any I have read before when he says that Buckshot Roberts had "stashed an old Sharp's buffalo gun inside the adobe shack and a handful of ammunition, for just such a possible contingency." That I doubt very much, for Roberts had no idea that he would meet the Kid and his gang at that place. He says that the Kid swore his first shot got Roberts, but it was Bowdre's shot that did the damage. He also says that Roberts shot Coe through the hand, but Coe lost his finger when a bullet ricocheted off Bowdre's cartridge belt. He is also mistaken when he says, "Next day he [Roberts] was buried along with Brewer." Brewer was buried the day he was killed, and Roberts did not die until the next day.

As for the Kid's killings in Arizona and his wanderings in Mexico, Brent writes: "Naturally these tales were Billy's own and he made sure to give himself the best of it," but these tales were from the pen of Ash Upson. Although he writes on one page, "I'll concede that the Kid did go to Mexico [and] that he spent several years there," on the next page he says, "I'm afraid I'm going to have to string along with Jim Brent, my father. Dad always contended they were only tall tales—big windies— told by the Kid."

This author is also mistaken when, writing of the Brown-Wheeler bank robbery at Medicine Lodge, Kansas, he says: "The robbers were pursued and overtaken by a posse. Two men in Brown's gang were killed, Hendry [*sic*] was captured and it was not until they had been put in jail that a mob took them out and hanged them." Brown was killed when he ran, and Wheeler was also shot trying to escape. After that they were all hanged, the dead, the wounded, and the living.

The author admits that there were three bullet holes in Carlyle's body but gives the Kid credit for killing him. He writes: "Thus another cold blooded and unwarranted killing could be chalked up against William Bonney."

When O'Folliard was killed, Brent writes, "Garrett, Chambers and the Mexican deputy were under the porch, partially concealed by some harness against the wall." This information I have never seen before, and there was no Mexican deputy in the party. I imagine that it would be rather difficult to be shooting from beneath a porch during such a snowstorm as occurred that night, and why would harness be stored under a porch (unless he means under the porch cover)? He describes Tom Pickett as "a loudmouth and yellow at heart."

The author says that the Las Vegas mob broke up when the station agent told them that they would get in trouble for detaining the United States mail. "The train then slowly got underway," he writes, and "the mob danger was over." That is not the way it happened.

The author is also in error on some dates. He writes that Mrs. Antrim rushed to the Silver City jail when Billy got into trouble, but that was a year after her death. He has Tom Hill and George Davis hanging around the saloons long after the Lincoln County War was over, but Hill was killed March 9, 1878, and Davis was killed July 3, 1880.

He gives the Kid credit for killing Morton, Baker, Brady, and Hindman and writes that the Kid himself said that his first shot got Roberts. Then he gives Billy credit for killing Bernstein and Beckwith. Though he does say that there is some doubt of that, he says that the Kid himself "claimed Bernstein." Kid was not even present when Bernstein was killed. He credits the Kid with Joe Grant and Carlysle and finally with Bell and Olinger, which brings the total to eleven.

Also, like so many others, this author has the Kid attending Tunstall's funeral, but Billy was being detained by the Murphy crowd at the time. He mis-spells Gauss's name as Geiss as many others do, and he says that after Bell and Olinger were killed "Geiss [sic] arrived with a heavy file and the Kid ordered him to cut the chains between the leg irons." But that never happened either. Gauss merely tossed a small miner's pick to the Kid so that he could free himself.

He has the Kid entertaining Bell by slipping his handcuffs off and on, but such an act would soon have been stopped. After Bell had taken the Kid downstairs to an outdoor privy, the author says, the Kid went "bounding" back upstairs. How was that possible when he had on heavy leg irons? He is also mistaken in having the Kid pushing open a locked door of the arsenal and grabbing a loaded six-shooter. He had already retrieved one placed in the privy by a friend.

Just before the killing of Olinger (whose name he misspells as Ollinger throughout), he has him "taking some prisoners across the street to what is now the Wortley Hotel." It was the Wortley Hotel at that time too. Of course, we know that Olinger rushed back to the jail when he heard the shot that killed Bell, only to meet his own death. This author has the horse the Kid escaped on returning with the saddle smeared with jackrabbit blood to make people think he had been killed or wounded. This must be original with Brent and is quite unlikely.

On the night the Kid was killed, Brent has him "shifting his knife to his left hand" and "drawing his gun as he stepped into the doorway." But those who examined him after his death found no gun, though the author says that "his pistol was still clutched in his right hand, the butcher knife on the floor a few feet away" when he was examined after his death. On the next page he writes: "Then they examined the Kid's revolver. Four live shells were in the cylinder with the hammer down on an empty."

"Certainly the Kid was armed," Brent writes. "He was always armed. He'd have been a damned fool if he hadn't been—a man hunted, with a death sentence hanging over his head." He seems to forget that the Kid had taken off his boots and arms to relax when he suddenly decided that he wanted some meat. Why would anyone think at that time of night (midnight) there would be enemies in a friend's house? There was no reason to suspect any danger. "Another sore spot among Garrett's old timer friends," the author continues, "was the indignant wailings of these same story-tellers that the Kid was unarmed when he met his death that night. This, of course, is a vicious and outright untruth which, however, still persists among these self righteous bleeding-hearts."

At the end he claims that the Kid's name was undoubtedly William Harrison Bonney; yet it seems strange that the Kid, his father, and his stepfather would all be named William Harrison. Throughout the book there is conversation that cannot possibly be known to have occurred, with no one to record it. However, in the Foreword the author excuses this when he writes: "The writer has also taken the liberty of using conversation throughout the book, which he hopes the reader will bear with indulgence. This is to bring the story and characters to life, so a better picture of the people involved might be obtained." Was he writing history or fiiction?

22. BRENT, WILLIAM, and M. BRENT. The hell hole, by William Brent and M. Brent. Yuma, Arizona, Southwest Printers . . ., 1962. Pict. wrappers.

This little book tells something of the life and crimes of Buckskin Frank Leslie and other Arizona outlaws. The authors' account of Leslie's prison life is not accurate. Instead of trying to disprove some of the fiction written about him, they perpetuate it. They are certainly mistaken in saying that he was released from prison in 1907. He was pardoned by Governor Benjamin J. Franklin on November 17, 1896. They list Phin Clanton as one of the prisoners, but they are mistaken in saying that "Phin was one of the notorious Clanton-McLowery [sic] outlaws of Cochise County who engaged in that memorable gun fight in Tombstone against the Wyatt Earp clan at the O K Corral." The only Clantons in this fight were Ike and Billy. They say that Mike Killeen was a barber in Tombstone, but he was a bartender. They have the killing of Killeen all wrong. It was much more of a fight than they describe it: "Frank Leslie . . . pulled his pistol and shot Killeen dead."

They misspell Doc Holliday's name as Halliday, but that could be a typographical error. They intimate that Leslie killed Johnny Ringo while he was sleeping off a drunk. They say that Mollie Bradshaw, Leslie's girl friend, was shot by Leslie and died instantly, but the shooting took place on the front porch, and Mollie lived long enough to run around the house and fall at the back door. They also say that the wounded Jimmy Neal crawled to Cy Bryant's ranch, but Colin Rickards, who has made a thorough study of Frank Leslie, writes that he went to William Reynolds' ranch.

Concerning the disappearance of Leslie these authors write: "Then one day

Buckskin failed to show up for work [at the saloon where he got a job as a swamper after his pardon]. The day bartender sent someone to look for him to see if he was sick. In a small, dirty room on the Barbary Coast, they found him dead. Fully clothed in bed—a bullet hole in his right temple." What really happened was that one day Leslie asked for his pay and disappeared, taking the manager's six-gun with him. He was never seen again, and it was supposed he had committed suicide, but his body was never found.

23. BRITT, ALBERT. The boys' own book of frontiersmen. By Albert Britt . . . . New York, Macmillan Company, 1926. Cloth.

Written for teenage boys, this book has a chapter on Wild Bill Hickok. Early in the chapter the author writes: "Around Wild Bill's name has grown up a body of romance, of tradition, of fiction and plain lies, so that to separate the true from the false is beyond the power of the student of frontier records." As a historian writing for impressionable boys, he should have sought the truth.

The author writes that, after Wild Bill's fight with the bear, the company moved him to Rock Creek Station to serve as a station keeper, but he was only a stable boy. The author has the McCanles brothers (?) leaders of a gang of outlaws, but there were no brothers, and David McCanles had no gang but was a respected citizen. He has Hickok alone at the Rock Creek Station when "the McCanles brothers rode up to take over the stage company's horses for the Confederate army." No such thing happened.

He calls the battle that followed "Homeric." He follows the old legend of Wild Bill fighting ten men. Like Buel, he has Hickok killing six men and wounding two others so badly they soon die. He has Hickok receiving seven bullet wounds, a fractured skull, and knife wounds too numerous to mention. All this when only three men approached the station, one collecting an honest debt and two companions. McCanles was shot from behind a curtain by Wild Bill, and then he, with the help of Wellman, murdered the other two in cold blood.

This author calls Phil Coe by the name Phil Cole. He has not only Coe but also his friend Haney (whoever he was) killed. He claims that Coe made the "declaration that no marshal named Bill could stay in the same town with him." Jack McCall is called John, and the author claims that McCall went to Cheyenne and bragged about shooting Hickok, but that happened in Laramie.

24. BROWN, DEE. The gentle tamers; women of the Old West, [by] Dee Brown. New York, G. P. Putnam's sons, [1958]. Cloth.

This author is mistaken in writing that Belle Starr's brother was "killed while riding with Jim Lane's Red Legs bushwhackers." Starr was a loyal southerner. Brown also says that Belle was sentenced to a six-month term in prison, but she was sentenced to nine months. He says that conditions became so bad that Belle's parents *fled* to Texas. They did not flee but went to Texas after Carthage, their home town, was burned, and they had nothing left to stay for.

He says that Belle was seduced by Cole Younger and that she then turned to a life of crime, but that was not the cause and Younger denied fathering her child. He further writes: "She was involved in enough robbings and holdups to fill a large catalog," but she did very little robbing. That was left to the members of her followers, and their crimes were mostly stealing horses. He spells Calamity Jane Cannary's name as Connorray and is mistaken in calling Rose of Cimarron and Cattle Kate outlaws.

25. BROWN, GEORGE ROTHWELL (ED.). Reminiscences of Senator William H. Stewart, of Nevada, edited by George Rothwell Brown. New York and Washington, Neale Publishing Co., 1908. Cloth.

This author tells of the O K Corral fight and says that he "witnessed it from a distance." He must have been quite a distance, for he claims that six of the Clantons were killed. Only two Clantons and two McLaurys were in the fight, and only one Clanton and two McLaurys were killed. He spells the Earp brothers' name Erp.

26. BRUCE, LEONA. Banister Was There, by Leona Bruce. Fort Worth, Branch-Smith, Inc., 1968. Fabrikoid.

In telling of the Union Pacific robbery by Joel Collins and his gang, the author quotes James Gillett's false statement that John Underwood was in the gang. The sixth member was actually a man named Nixon. She says that this Underwood was a brother of Henry Underwood, who later joined Bass in his new gang at Denton, Texas. That is incorrect.

The author quotes from a letter to a Mr. Williams: "Berry, one of the robbers, decided to take it alone, but was soon captured in Mexico, Missouri; he confessed and named other robbers, telling as much as he knew of their destination." Berry was killed and made no confession, nor did he tell of the others' destination, for he did not know it.

The author misspells Koppel's name as Copprel. She is also mistaken in saying that Bass and her subject (Banister) had gone up the trail to Kansas twice in the same year, though not together. Bass only made the trip once, and that was with the herd of cattle that Joel Collins drove up the trail. She also has Banister assisting in the capture of Bass, but that is not true. Banister wrote his mother about Bass's death and quoted him as saying on his deathbed, "This world is but a bubble—trouble wherever you go." What he said was "The world is bobbin' around," and Banister was not there.

27. BURTON, JEFF. Dynamite and six-shooters, [by] Jeff Burton .... [Santa Fe, New Mexico], Palomino Press. An Imprint of the Press of the Territorian [1970]. Stiff wrappers and imit. leather.

This is a good and well-researched account of Black Jack Ketchum and his gang, but the author makes one or two errors. He writes that the Black Jack gang robbed the Santa Fe train near Folsom, New Mexico, but it was a Colorado and Southern train. He is also mistaken in saying that a Nick Grider was the man with Ben Kilpatrick in the train robbery near Sanderson, Texas. The man was Ole Beck, an old cellmate of Kilpatrick's.

28. BUSHICK, FRANK H. Glamorous Days, by Frank H. Bushick, San Antonio, Texas, Naylor Co., 1934. Cloth.

This book touches upon many western outlaws and gunmen, with chapters on King Fisher, Ben Thompson, and John Wesley Hardin. The author claims that his is the first account of the killing of Thompson and Fisher. "The actual facts were not made public at the time," he writes, "nor for many years afterward, for reasons that can be readily understood." He proceeds to name McLaughin, a bartender, Canada Bill, a gambler, and Harry Tremaines, an English variety actor, as the men who shot Thompson and Fisher from a nearby box in the theater. The killers immediately left town, according to this account.

He is mistaken in having Bat Masterson sheriff of Dodge City, a county job. He has Thompson born in Nova Scotia, another error. He misspells Hickok's name as Hickock and has the killing of Phil Coe all wrong. "Coe," he writes, "opened up on Bill [Hickok] one day as the marshal was leaning against a table in a saloon, but in an instant Wild Bill had out both his pistols. Shooting from the hip, as was his fashion, he dropped Coe with a mortal wound and also killed another man whom he mistook for a Texan." This killing took place in the street, not in a saloon. He also says that Thompson was in St. Louis at the time and missed the fight, but he was laid up with a broken leg in Kansas City.

The author is also mistaken in having Wyatt Earp city marshal of Ellsworth, Kansas, and, with Sheriff Whitney, trying to arrest the Thompson brothers. He adds, "Ben submitted to arrest [after he got his brother, Bill, away] by Marshal Earp and went to jail for a day or two and paid a fine." As we know, Earp was not even in Ellsworth at the time, nor was he a marshal of the town. The author has the capture of John Wesley Hardin in Florida all wrong: "Hardin was found standing by a wall, and Armstrong [Texas Ranger] suggested that Wes draw up a bucket of water, as he was thirsty. Hardin set his gun down at his right, caught the well rope in both hands and commenced to lower the bucket. While he was leaning over the well, Armstrong poked two pistols under Hardin's nose, as he kicked the rifle to one side. Hardin was handcuffed and marched to the railroad depot." This makes an interesting story, but, as we know, Hardin was captured on the train with some of his pals.

The author has Joel Collins running a variety show and gambling hall with Rowdy Joe Lowe in San Antonio, but he was just a bartender. He writes that after the Union Pacific robbery Bass "and his companions [there was only one, Davis] returned to Denton and robbed the fair in broad daylight." That never happened. He then continues: "After a fight with a posse, they headed for Austin." That never happened either. He is also wrong in having Arkansas Johnson with Bass at Round Rock; Johnson had been killed in a battle with the Rangers at Salt Creek. He has the Bass gang riding into Round Rock on July 21, but that was the day he died after having been shot a few days earlier. He is another who mispells Koppel's name, here as Copprell, and says that Bass was killed by Dick Ware, but that has never been proved. He also says that Jackson escaped to Mexico, but he went to Arizona. The author is another who is mistaken in having the James and Younger boys cousins. They were no kin. Mention is made of many other outlaws, and there are more errors, but as a whole, it is an interesting book.

29. CALDER, JENNI. There must be a Lone Ranger. The American West in film and in reality, [by] Jenni Calder . . . . New York, Taplinger Publishing Company, [1974]. Cloth and boards.

This book is different from other books

dealing with the West. It compares western history with the movie films, pointing out some of the historical errors of the films. The author makes a few mistakes herself, saying that Granville Stuart was a Wyoming cattleman. He was a Montana cattleman. Of the Johnson County War she writes: "It is all the more disturbing, for the fact that the real truth of this strange affair still escapes careful historians." But this conflict has been well covered by able historians.

On page 55 she makes reference to a "Grant-Tewksbury feud of Arizona." This was the Graham-Tewksbury feud. I thought that this might be a typographical error, but it is repeated in the index. She says that Bob Ford shot Jesse James "in the hope of a two thousand dollar reward," but the reward offered was much larger. She also says that John Chisum was married "and produced a tough-looking daughter," but he never married. The girl living under his roof was his niece, and she was far from tough-looking. The author misspells Longabaugh's name as Longbaugh and has Tunstall's given name Henry, but it was John.

30. CALLON, MILTON W. Las Vegas, New Mexico. The town that wouldn't gamble, by Milton W. Callon. Las Vegas, New Mexico, Published by Las Vegas Daily Optic, 1962. Cloth.

A history of Las Vegas in its early days, with some material on Billy the Kid and his gang, as well as Bob Ford and the James boys. The author is mistaken, however, in saying that the Kid was captured at Stinking Springs "on the afternoon of December 24, 1880." He was captured on the morning of December 23. Of the capture he writes: "In the

battle that followed Charlie Bowdre was killed and Dave Rudabaugh, Tom Pickett, Billy Wilson and Billy the Kid surrendered to the posse." There was no battle, for Bowdre was killed as he stepped out of the little stone house to feed the horses.

After the Kid was killed and buried, the author writes, a Russ Kistler, of the *Las Vegas Optic*, who told a story about a friend of his bringing the Kid's index finger to the *Optic* office and about a "fearless skelologist" who during the night after the fifth day of the burial dug up the Kid's body and carried it off in a wagon. That sounds like some of the earlier tales printed in the *Las Vegas Optic*.

31. CARLSON, ROBERT E. (ED.). Nebraska folklore. (Book Two), written and compiled by the Nebraska Writers' Project Work Projects Administrations Federal Works Agency. Sponsored by the State Superintendent of Public Instruction. Lincoln, Nebraska, Woodruff Printing Company, 1940. Stiff pict. Wrappers.

In a chapter on the personal reminiscences of George W. Streeter, the book tells some ridiculous stories about Cattle Kate Watson. In one she held up a poker game in which her foreman was getting fleeced. Kate had no ranch or foreman, though the author says that he sold a bunch of her steers, got drunk, and was letting the gamblers fleece him of her money. Cattle Kate was no holdup but a prostitute who traded her favors to the cowboys for a calf or two.

The author says that he later joined a herd of cattle "near the north boundary of Indian Territory, known as the Staked Plains." The Staked Plains are in Texas. He says that one of the herders of these cattle was Calamity Jane, but she was never a trail driver. He writes: "She derived her peculiar appellation from her habit of telling a hard luck story to nearly every stranger she met, and, after gaining his sympathy, prevailed upon him to give her a few dollars." That, too, is incorrect, but as the little book's title reveals, this is only folklore.

32. CARSON, JOHN. The Union Pacific: Hell on wheels! by John Carson. [Santa Fe, Press of the Territorian, 1968]. Wrappers.

The author's information on the Union Pacific robbery at Big Springs is unreliable. He has "Joel Collins, Sam Bass and six other Texas cowboys" holding up this train. There were only six men, and none were real Texas cowboys; in fact, the only ones from Texas were Collins and Bass. He says, "Collins had delivered a herd of cattle to the Black Hills and had lost the proceeds in a poker game." The cattle were sold in Kansas, and the money was spent in a session of general debauchery. He has M. F. Leech paying more attention to chasing outlaws than to minding the store where he worked.

33. CARTER, SAMUEL, III. Cowboy capital of the world. The saga of Dodge City, by Samuel Carter III. Garden City, New York, Doubleday & Company, Inc., [1973]. Cloth.

A history of Dodge City, Kansas, most of which has been written before. Though published in 1973, after several books (including two of my own) have pointed out the errors commonly committed by would-be historians, this book is filled with the same errors and distorted legends. Early in the book the author calls the Kansas Pacific Railroad the "Katy," but the Katy was the Missouri, Kansas and Texas, an entirely different railroad. He is also wrong in having Wichita "ruled by one of the earliest of western marshals, Wild Bill Hickok." Hickok was never marshal of Wichita. He also exaggerates the facts when he says that Billy Brooks "killed or wounded fifteen men" during his first thirty days as marshal of Dodge.

He says that Mayor Hoover had heard of Wyatt Earp's "success as marshal of both Wichita and Ellsworth" and wired him to accept a job in Dodge. Earp was only a city policeman in Wichita and was never any kind of officer in Ellsworth in spite of what he told Stuart Lake, his biographer. He repeats the legend of Wyatt arresting Ben Thompson in Ellsworth, after Bill Thompson had killed Sheriff Whitney. Earp was not in Ellsworth at that time. He has Earp serving three terms as marshal of Dodge and absolutely running the town. When Bat Masterson's brother, Ed, was killed, this author says that Bat came upon the scene and shot both Walker and Wagner, but the contemporary papers do not have Bat at the scene. The author is another who seems to believe in the miraculous shooting of Wild Bill Hickok—having him splitting a bullet on the edge of a dime and driving a cork through the neck of a bottle without nicking the rim of the neck.

His statement that "no high-spirited Texan would think of entering an unfamiliar town without blasting the skies with both his six-guns, just to let the people know he had arrived." In the first place, the cowboy did not carry two guns, and not all Texans were so rambunctious. He tells a preposterous tale about Rose of Cimarron who he says "went through a blizzard of bullets . . . in a desperate attempt to join her exiled lover." He says that there was a basis of truth in this story, for she was *riding* to smuggle some ammunition to her sweetheart "who had holed up on the prairie." The original legend has her going on foot to take a Winchester to Bitter Creek Newcomb during the battle at Ingalls, not out on the prairie. But that is not true either.

The author is greatly mistaken when he has Belle Starr going to Dodge with "her renegade paramour *Tom Starr*." Her paramour was Sam Starr, Tom's son, and the legend has it that it was Blue Duck who went with her to Dodge and lost two thousand dollars of her money gambling. That never happened either. He has all this taking place in the Long Branch Saloon, but legend (and it too is just a legend) has it that the incident took place in an upstairs gambling hall. He is also wrong in saying that the dance-hall girl, Alice Chambers, has "the distinction of being the only woman to be buried in Boot Hill." He also says that Bat Masterson owned the Lady Gay Saloon, but I find no record of this, though his brother Jim did own an interest in this establishment.

The author says that Billy the Kid shot his first man at the age of twelve and that he usually shot his victims in the back. He repeats that well-worn legend about the Kid killing twenty-one men by the time he was twenty-one years of age, and he is wrong in having him killed while visiting his Mexican sweetheart. He has Bill Thompson in Abilene "punching cows by day and gambling by night." Bill was never a cowboy. He has the two Thompson brothers running a Bull's Head Tavern, from which emporium Ben virtually ruled the twon." This, too, is untrue; Ben's partner was Phil Coe, a fellow Texan, and all this happened in Abilene. He repeats that legend about Wyatt Earp arresting Ben

Thompson in Ellsworth. Added to his many errors is the statement that Ben Thompson held off the crowd in Sweetwater, Texas, after Bat Masterson had killed Sergeant Melvin King, and again he has Ben killed in Austin, Texas, instead of in San Antonio and adds that "it took nine bullets to bring him down." I had not read that before.

His account of the killing of Chunk Colbert by Clay Allison is all wrong. He does not call Chunk by name but merely says that when Allison saw a Mexican at an adjoining table who "had once bad-mouthed" him "without leaving his chair, Clay shot the Mexican through the head then went back to eating." He also repeats the legend about Wyatt Earp running Allison out of Dodge. He says that before Earp left for Tombstone, Arizona, he had tamed Dodge, but history does not agree with that statement. He leaves the impression that, as soon as Wyatt arrived at Tombstone, "the town engaged Wyatt's services as marshal." That we know is untrue. He also says that Doc Holliday followed Wyatt to Arizona to escape the "irascible Big Nose Kate," but she went with him.

When Doc was accused of robbing the stage at the time Bud Philpot was killed, the author has Doc denying the charge in court, "explaining to the judge that the holdup was not on a par with his professional capacities," and the judge letting him off. He says "Marshal" Earp loaned Doc a thousand dollars, "with which the latter bribed Kate to leave Arizona. His account of the O K Corral fight is also unreliable, and he has the Clantons sending word to the Earps to come and fight, but they were saddling up to leave town. Like so many others, too, he misspells the McLaury boys' name as McLowery. "The quartet of marshals," he writes, "descended on the outpost in formation," but the only marshal in the group was Virgil Earp.

He has Wyatt Earp owning the Oriental Saloon and Gambling Hall, but Wyatt was given a small interest in the gambling department by the owner for protection, and he has Luke Short working for Wyatt as a gambler. Throughout the years many writers have followed that well-worn legend about a dentist pulling the wrong tooth for Clay Allison, but this author is the first, to my knowledge, to say that the dentist was Doc Holliday. He is also mistaken in having Ben Hodges a half-blood Mexican. He was a Negro.

This author is also mistaken in saying that Joel Collins was hired by cattlemen to drive a herd of cattle "to Dodge." The cattle were merely assigned to Collins to sell with his own small herd. He is also mistaken in saying that Collins "recruited some footloose souls in Dodge to form his gang. Except for the members of his trail crew the men were recruited in South Dakota. He is also mistaken in saying that Sam Bass was recognized by the Texas Rangers from his pictures in the Kansas papers. Bass's picture did not appear in any paper. He also repeats that legend about Clay Allison sending word to Wyatt Earp asking Wyatt to let him come into Dodge to complete a cattle deal. That never happened either. He is wrong in having Wild Bill Hickok marshal of Wichita and having his office in the Bull Head Saloon. In the latter part of his book the author is determined to have Wyatt Earp the owner of the Oriental Saloon. On page 232 there are some misplaced sentences.

In telling the story of the baby contest in Dodge, the author has Bat Masterson a deacon in the church and leaves the impression that the prize-winning baby was white and the offspring of a white woman of the red-light district, but it was the baby of a Negro woman. To climax his many mistakes, the author has the killing of Ben Thompson entirely wrong. He says that Foster shot him in the head five times after Thompson offered to shake hands. He also has the death of Clay Allison wrong: "Clay stole the heavily loaded freight wagon of a friend. The wagon struck a pothole. Clay was thrown from his seat, and a wheel passed over him, breaking his neck." Allison did not steal a wagon but offered to drive it for a friend. A wheel struck a large clump of grass, and Clay lost his balance, striking his head on a front wheel and fracturing his skull. The author says that Wild Bill Hickok and Buffalo Bill Cody "spent their later years touring the country in Ned Buntline's Wild West Show, then having Hickok going blind. Buntline had no Wild West Show; he had a company playing western dramas that he wrote. They were not very successful.

Though the book is of interest, it is but a repetition of books that have gone before, full of legends that have been exposed by historians and are thus of little value historically.

34. CHILTON, CHARLES. The book of the West, by Charles Chilton. New York, Bobbs-Merrill Co., 1962. Cloth.

In his chapter on outlaws and gunmen the author makes many mistakes, misspells many proper names, and gives some wrong dates. He calls Big Nose Kate Fisher "one of the most famous gunwomen of the West," but she was not a gunwoman at all, just a soiled-dove common-law wife of Doc Holliday. According to the author, when she rescued Doc from a mob in Fort Griffin, Texas, she and Doc escaped "to Arizona on a pair of fast horses." They escaped to Dodge City, Kansas. He calls Calamity Jane "perhaps the most famous of all women outlaws," but she, too, could not be classed as an outlaw. He is also wrong in having her the wife of Wild Bill Hickok and says that she acquired the name Calamity "from the fact that where ever she went trouble usually followed." He claims that the West was full of gunwomen.

Of Wyatt Earp he says, "He did more to help turn the Southwest into a civilized, law-abiding community than any other peace officer on record." That is quite a record. Actually, he did more to cause trouble in Tombstone than anyone else. The author is also wrong in calling Ben and Bill Thompson cowboys. Neither of them ever had anything to do with cattle but were saloonkeepers and gamblers. He says the Thompsons killed more than twenty men between them, but that also is not true. Another mistake he makes is having Bill Thompson killing Sheriff Whitney on purpose. It was a drunken accident.

The author follows that old legend about Earp arresting Ben Thompson in Ellsworth, Kansas, when Sheriff Whitney was killed. Earp was not in Ellsworth at the time. He has Earp not only arresting Thompson but cowing the whole crowd of tough Texans. He repeats Lake's version of this imaginary incident. When will writers quit repeating such legends as history?

The author is also mistaken in having Earp marshal of Wichita. He was only a city policeman, and he did not hold that position long. He has Earp marshal of Dodge instead of deputy marshal, and a United States Marshal at Tombstone. He writes that when Dodge was completely tamed Earp headed for Tombstone. He has six men in the Clanton gang at the O K Corral fight, and he repeats that tale about them sending word to the Earps to come to the corral and fight it out. He follows the Lake account in Sheriff Behan a coward, and the Clanton gang "heavily armed." He also says the battle of the O K Corral "virtually ended organized lawlessness in Tombstone." He places the fight inside the corral, but it took place on the street outside. Like so many others he misspells the name McLaury as McLowery.

He has Wild Bill Hickok sheriff of Hays City and has him living in Abilene when he was appointed marshal by Joseph McCoy (which he spells McKoy), but Wild Bill went to Abilene to assume that office, and was not already there "making his living at the gambling tables." The author makes no mention of Hickok's trouble with Phil Coe nor of his killing of his own deputy.

"In 1876," writes the author, "[Hickok] turned up in Deadwood, where he offered his services as a guide to the would-be miners flooding into the Black Hills in search of gold. He intended, also, to do some prospecting on his own account." What did Hickok know about the Black Hills? Then he says that a rumor soon went around that he was to be made marshal; the lawless of the camp wanted none of his interference, and that was why he was killed.

He has Jesse James leading his "gang of ruffians on a raid into Liberty," but Jesse was home suffering from a lung wound. At this point he has a newly elected sheriff arresting Jesse "for the first and only time in his life." That never happened either. In the following year he has another raid on Liberty when the bank was robbed and says this was the first bank robbery to take place in the United States. "It seems almost certain," he writes, "that Jesse and Frank James were the leaders of the gang though the fact was never definitely established." He is also mistaken in saying that Frank James stood trial "but after much litigation was acquitted." Frank was pardoned when he gave himself up. The author seems to think that Jesse had only one child, and he has the train robbery at Council Bluffs, Iowa, the first large train robbery in the United States, but that is untrue.

He has Bat Masterson a reporter on the New York *Morning Telegraph* for seventeen years, but Masterson did not go to New York until 1909, and he died there in 1921.

He calls Sam Bass "a typical cowboy who went wrong," and says that he helped drive a herd of cattle "from Texas to Deadwood," but the cattle were driven to Kansas and sold there. The drovers later went to Deadwood with the money, not all of which belonged to them. He says that Joel Collins was a professional trail driver, but he was a bartender when they started. He says that Leech was an agent of the express company, though he was only a clerk in a store in Ogallala. He further says that "no one knows what happened to Davis" after he separated from Bass at Fort Worth, but we know that Davis went to South America and was never caught. He lists five men in the Union Pacific robbery, but there were six, and he is wrong when he dates the Allen Station train robbery as February 23. It was February 22. He says that Major Jones, of the Ranger force, went in pursuit of Bass after he was wounded at Round Rock, but that is not true. Yet this author makes fewer mistakes about Bass than many others do.

He follows the many legends about Billy the Kid's early life, such as having his family moving to Coffeyville, Kansas, and his mother moving to Colorado where she married Antrim, then to Santa Fe, and later to Silver City. He has the Kid killing a man when he was twelve and says the Kid left New Mexico "and lived a wandering vagabond life." He is mistaken in having Murphy heading the posse that killed Tunstall, and later has him dying several days before the battle of the McSween home. He repeatedly misspells Chisum's name as Chishum. He has that the battle in Lincoln lasted three days, but it lasted five. He says that Charlie Bowdre fell dead when he was shot as he came out the door at Stinking Springs, but he lived long enough to return inside and then come out again.

He has the mob at Las Vegas composed of the whole Mexican population, and he says that they were attempting to lynch the prisoners, but they were only after Dave Rudabaugh, who had killed a jailer at Las Vegas earlier. He has Olinger going to have his supper, but he was taking some prisoners to supper. He has the Kid playing cards when he killed Bell and says that no one will ever know how he got Bell's gun. He did not use Bell's gun, but a gun a friend had left in the outdoor privy the Kid visited. Later he has the Kid killing Olinger with Bell's gun, but Olinger was killed with his own shotgun, with which he had so often threatened the Kid. He spells Gauss's name Geiss, as so many others have done, and says the Kid was killed on July 13, but it was the 14th. He is also mistaken in saying that the Lincoln County War "was a struggle between the small ranchers of New Mexico and the great cattle kingdom of John Chisum." All such errors are examples of careless history.

The author says of the figures 3-7-77, "No one seems to know quite why the figures were used but on seeing them

most desperadoes took the hint and left."
They knew that these figures meant a
grave 3 feet wide, 7 feet long, and 77
inches deep.

35. CHISHOLM, FANNIE G. The four
    state Chisholm Trail. A pastural ac-
    count of the origin of the Chisholm
    Trail and other stories of the Chis-
    holm family in early days of Texas,
    by Fannie G. Chisholm. [N.p.,
    Munguia Printers, Publishers,
    1966]. Pict. cloth.

This author claims the Chisholm Trail
was named after her relative Thornton
Chisholm, whom she claims was the
first man to drive cattle over this trail.
But, as we know, the original Chisholm
Trail was named after Jesse Chisholm,
an Indian trader. This is the same claim
made by the Artrips in their book
*Memoirs of Daniel Fore (Jim) Chis-
holm.*" But the trail this author's relative followed, if he followed the route
she lists, was a later and more westward
trail. She has this trail going through
Fort Worth, Doan's Crossing, Oklahoma City, and Tulsa. In her map she
shows this trail going to St. Joseph, Missouri, but its main destination was
Dodge City, Kansas. This was known
as the Western Trail, which had been
moved farther west from Abilene when
the railroad was extended westward and
the nesters crowded the trail to Abilene.
   In one place she writes: "The drive as
near as can be traced today went by way
of Gonzalas, San Marcos, Austin, Round
Rock, Georgetown, Gatesville, Glen
Rose, Mineral Wells, Graham, Olney,
Seymour, Viernon [sic], across the Pecos
River and on to Red River Crossing."
Of course, the Pecos River was much
farther west and not on this trail, and
Red River Crossing was much farther
east than Vernon. The crossing was

known as Doan's Store, or Doan's Crossing.
   She has her narrator telling about
Pat Garrett killing Billy the Kid but saying he does not believe that happened.
She frequently has herds of five thousand head being driven up the trail, but
that would be a rather unwieldly herd.
She misspells John Chisum's name as
Chisholm and misspells John Selman's
name as Selmon. She also claims that
naming the Chisholm Trail for Jesse
Chisholm is erroneous.

36. CHRISMAN, HARRY E. Fifty
    years on the Owl Hoot Trail. Jim
    Herron, the first sheriff of No
    Man's Land, Oklahoma Territory,
    by Harry E. Chrisman from an
    original manuscript by Jim Her-
    ron. Introduction by Edward
    Everett Dale. Chicago, Sage Books,
    [1969]. Cloth.

An interesting story of a rancher in No
Man's Land who had to follow the Owl
Hoot Trail for fifty years because of a
frameup by a powerful cattlemen's association.
   The author is mistaken in saying that
the Dalton boys were related to the
James boys through the Youngers. They
were related to the Youngers but were
no relation to the Jameses. He has Frank
James wintering in the Indian Territory while he was recovering from "a
bullet in his leg acquired in a Dakota
bank robbery." This is the first time I
have read that the James boys robbed a
bank in Dakota. He also says that when
Bob and Grat Dalton were deputy marshals in the Indian Territory their job
was to ride the trains and keep off robbers, but that is not correct.
   He is mistaken in having the Jennings
gang robbing banks; it was trains they
were robbing. He has the Bass gang rid-

ing into Round Rock on July 21, but Bass was shot there on July 19. Frank Jackson is incorrectly called Jim, and he says "that Jackson has raised a good family that is a credit to his community." Most authorities claim that Jackson changed his name to Bill Downing and was killed as an outlaw in Arizona.

The author has Billy the Kid a vicious killer who "had only one desire at the end of his short career, and that was to kill another man." He is also wrong in saying that some of the men he killed "were store clerks and barbers who were unarmed" and that he "bushwhacked and shot others in the back." The Kid was far from being that vicious, and he never killed any store clerks or barbers. He is also mistaken in having Henry Starr and Belle Starr holding up a bank together. Belle never held up a bank, and they never worked together, for Henry was a mere boy when Belle was murdered. He misspells Jack Mc-Call's name as McColl, but that could be a typographical error. He also misspells Ogallala as Ogallie.

37. CLARK, NEIL M. (ED.). Camp-fires and cattle trails. Recollections of the early West in the letters of J. H. Harshman, edited by Neil M. Clark. Caldwell, Idaho, Caxton Printers, Ltd., 1970. Stiff wrappers.

This is a collection of letters to the editor with the latter's comments. The letters tell about the writer's various experiences in the West, but some of his memories are evidently hearsay. He says, "Billy [the Kid] had an adobe house where he used to hole up for sleep when not on one of his expeditions." He says that while Billy was away Pat Garrett "got into his house and hid behind his bed and waited for him to come back" and that when the Kid returned Garrett shot him. We know that the Kid was killed by Garrett in Pete Maxwell's bedroom, and the editor corrects this in a footnote.

He says that Doc Holliday was chased out of Dodge City and then Trinidad before he went to Las Vegas, New Mexico. He has Las Vegas bootleggers "slipping *down* into the Indian Territory from Las Vegas to sell liquor to the Indians." If they went to the Indian Territory from Las Vegas they would surely go up, not down, and that would be a long way to go for such a deal. He has Len Woodruff getting into "a fight with three cattle rustlers and killing all three before they shot him." That was the "big fight" at Tascosa, and the men shot were not rustlers but ordinary cowboys.

Like many others, he is also mistaken is having Bat Masterson the sheriff of Dodge City, a county job, and says, "He ruled the town with an iron hand." Masterson was sheriff of Ford County, and he had nothing to do with ruling the town. The letter writer also says that he "heard later that he [Masterson] was Chief of Police in San Francisco," but that is also incorrect.

The editor, in an appendix, has a Mr. Kuykendall stating that John Wesley Hardin's first killing was the shooting of a policeman, and intimating that this happened in New Orleans. His first killing was the shooting of a Negro with whom he had trouble when he was very young. He also says that Hardin was the only man who made Wild Bill Hickok "put up his guns." That has never been proved satisfactorily; it is merely a tale Hardin himself told. Kuykendall also says that Hardin was the inventor of the road agent's spin, but Curly Bill Brocius has been credited with inventing it, and it is commonly called the "Curly Bill spin."

He has Charlie Siringo stating that

Bat Masterson was the owner of a saloon in Dodge City and tended bar himself, but Bat owned no saloon in Dodge. He says that he met Billy the Kid in Dodge City in late 1878, but I am afraid he is in error here too. The editor also has Siringo saying that the man who hired Jim Miller to kill Garrett was a banker with a grudge of many years' standing. He does not name the banker, but he says that Garrett rode in a buggy with him. That would be Carl Adamson, and he was no banker. He also has the killing of Gus Bobbitt (whom he calls Bob Gossett) all wrong. He has Billy the Kid killing twenty-one men and misspells Tom O'Folliard's name as O'Phalliard. Most of the statements by Siringo are wrong, but the editor does not correct them.

38. CLARK, Donald Henderson. The autobiography of Frank Tarbeaux, as told to Donald Henderson Clarke . . . . New York, Vanguard Press, MCMXXX. Cloth.

Tarbeaux claims that he and his father opened the Chisholm Trail in 1863, which is untrue. He says that the herds were divided into "bands" of 5,000 and that with each band were a mess wagon and ten or fifteen cowboys. That would be an unwieldy herd for that number of cowboys. When a cowman speaks of a "band," he means horses; he uses "herd" when referring to cattle. The author speaks rather disparagingly of Buffalo Bill Cody and says, "All his history is pure fiction." He makes the strong statement that "Buffalo Bill never killed an Indian in all his life, and those people who say they saw him do it are suffering from hallucinations." He has Wild Bill Hickok a marshal of Dodge City, a position he never held, and further states that he [Tarbeaux] had just left a poker game in Deadwood when Wild Bill was killed and that Hickok was killed by "one of the McCoys [sic] who was sent to do the job by Johnny Varnes who had it in for Bill." He says the killing took place in Mann and Manning's Saloon, but it was in Saloon Number 10. There are many other unreliable statements; for example, he says that Calamity Jane was first heard of in Deadwood, where she was just an ordinary dance-hall girl, and he calls her a "great pioneer heroine." He also claims to have been a close friend of Wild Bill, the James boys, and many other western outlaws. He claims to have shot Bob Ford through the lungs in a fracas in southern Colorado.

He writes that the vigilantes hanged Joseph Slade because of a murder he had committed, but he was hanged because he had a habit of making a nuisance of himself. Tarbeaux's tale about gambling with the men who robbed the stagecoach Johnny Slaughter was driving when he was killed is one of his own imagination. During the holdup the horses ran away, and the robbers failed to get any money. He claims to have been in the robber band himself, but that is not true. The men who took part in the robbery were Joel Collins, Sam Bass, Jim Berry, Frank Towle, and Reddy McKemmie, the last being the one who killed Slaughter.

39. COE, Wilbur. Ranch on the Ruidoso. The story of a pioneer family in New Mexico, 1871–1968, by Wilbur Coe. New York, Alfred A. Knopf, 1968. Cloth.

The author is the son of Frank Coe, of Lincoln County War fame, and though he writes some history he does not write as a historian. Therefore few dates are given, making it difficult to grasp the chronology of events. He has a man he calls Bob in the party with Tunstall at the time of his killing along with Billy the Kid, Dick Brewer, and John Middleton. He evidently means Robert Widenmann. He is mistaken in having Olinger firing the shot that killed Tunstall, and again when he writes, "Morton and Baker following suit, after which the members of the posse added their bullets," but Tunstall was not shot that many times. He adds: "Morton shot his horse. Then Ollinger [sic] walked to Tunstall's body, kicked it in the head, put a final touch to the ghastly spectable by firing another shot into the victim."

That did not happen. His account of the Lincoln County War is full of errors. In spite of the fact that the Coe ranchhouse was burned by the John Selman gang, he credits the crime to the "Murphy outlaws." He mentions action occurring around the church at San Juan during the killing of Sheriff Brady, but that church was not built until 1887.

He writes as though George Coe lost his trigger finger in a separate shot, but he lost it from a bullet that richocheted off Bowdre's belt buckle. He also says, "Bowdre's bullet had gone through Robert's *chest*," but Roberts was shot in the abdomen. He is also mistaken in having Roberts die just an hour after he had killed Brewer. He did not die until the next day. He has Frank Freeman killing a Negro soldier after the death of Tunstall, but Tunstall was killed in February, 1878, and the Negro had been killed in December, 1876. He says that Tunstall was unarmed when he was killed, but he carried a pistol from which two shots were fired to make it appear that he had fired first.

He has Billy the Kid, with others, "lowering the body [of Tunstall] into the grave," but the Kid was not there; he was being held prisoner by the Murphy crowd at the time. We wonder about the portrait of Frank Coe shown with white hair, a mustache, and a Van Dyke beard, dated 1878. He was still a young man at the time.

Like so many others, the author misspells many proper names, such as Ollinger for Olinger, Hendry Brown for Henry Brown, John Brady for William Brady, and Gilliam for Gylam. In the first part of the book he speaks of the Harroll War though he does correct it later to Horrell. He also has Sheriff Peppin leading posses that were actually led by Sheriff Copeland, and many important incidents that he should have known are omitted. The book would be more useful if it had an index.

40. COLLINGS, Ellsworth, and Alma Miller England. The 101 Ranch, by Ellsworth Collings, in collaboration with Alma Miller England, daughter of the founder of the 101 Ranch. Norman, University of Oklahoma Press, 1937 [2d ed., 1971].

There is some mention of the Dalton gang and Henry Starr, but the authors are mistaken in saying that Emmett Dalton lived in the Cherokee Strip "for many years after his brothers were killed in the Kansas holdup." Emmett was wounded in that raid, after which he was in prison for many years. After his release he went to California to spend the rest of his life, not to return to Oklahoma.

41. COLLINS, A. Lloyd, and Georgia I. Collins. Hero stories from Missouri history, by A. Lloyd Collins and Georgia I. Collins. Kansas City, Missouri, Burton Publishing Company, Publishers, [1956]. Cloth.

This book has chapters on many noted Missouri characters, but those of interest for this work are *Frontier Justice*, and *Was Jesse James a Second Robin Hood?* In the latter chapter the authors repeat the old legend of the widow and the mortgage and are also mistaken in saying that "Bob and Charlie Ford drew their pistols and shot him [Jesse]." Bob was the only one who did any shooting. There are also some misspelled proper names, such as Samuels for Samuel, Dick Liddil for Dick Liddill, and Cell Miller for Clell Miller.

42. CONWAY, JOHN. The Texas Rangers. A concise history of the most colorful law enforcement group in the frontier West, [by] John Conway. . . . Derby, Connecticut, ₁Monarch Books, Inc., 1963₁. Stiff col. pict. wrappers.

Another of those unreliable pocket-book histories in which the author says John Wesley Hardin and his "Wild Bunch" hired as gunmen to the rustlers. Hardin never had any connection with cattle thieves, and he had no "Wild Bunch." The author says that Ranger McNelly arrested King Fisher and nine of his men and recovered eighty head of stolen cattle, but the authorities turned the men loose because they "were in fear of their lives." That is ridiculous.

He states that Sam Bass went up the trail to Deadwood with a beef herd, but the herd was driven to Kansas. He says that after this herd, which did not entirely belong to Collins, was sold Collins spent the money recklessly. Yet he says that Collins was an "honest man" and looked around to see how he could raise money enough to pay off his creditors. He took to holding up stagecoaches, which one would not consider to be the works of an "honest man." He says that

the $60,000 from the Union Pacific robbery was split three ways, but it was split six ways, $10,000 for each of the six robbers. He says, correctly, that Collins and Heffridge were killed in Kansas, but he says that "another pair was never heard of again." The two he had in mind were Jim Berry and Tom Nixon. Berry was killed in Mexico, Missouri, and Nixon was thought to have made it to Canada.

He has Sam Bass dying the day after he was wounded, but he was wounded on the 19th and did not die until the 21st. He is also mistaken in saying that the Rangers under Lieutenant N. O. Reynolds made a forced march from Austin to Round Rock; they rode from Lampasas, much farther away. There are many other errors, as usual in this kind of book.

43. COWLES, GEORGE C. I killed to live, by George C. Cowles, the original "Montana Kid." ₁Chicago₁, Haywood Publishing Company, 1968. Pict. cloth.

The author claims that this is a story of his own life, but it reads more like wild fiction. He performs unbelievable stunts and has his other characters asking many questions that no true westerner would ask. He hits his enemies over the head with the butt of a six-gun which no westerner would do. He "cinches a diamond hitch," but a real westerner would never use this term. He would "throw" it, and although he spends most of his time far from civilization, he never runs out of lump sugar with which to spoil his horses.

He has Bat Masterson with him much of the time, and says Bat had a son-in-law named Bob Wilmony. But Bat never had a daughter, and he was never in that region of the country. He also misspells Justin, the bootmaker, as Judson. The reader might find this book entertaining, though it has no plot, but as history he should take it with a dose of salt.

44. CUSHMAN, DAN. The Great North Trail, by Dan Cushman. New York, McGraw-Hill Book Co., [1966]. Cloth.

It is true that trails have played an essential role in the development of this continent and have witnessed some of the wildest and most thrilling events of western history. Therefore, the record of any trail holds an interest for the lover of the past of his country. But I find the title of this book somewhat confusing. The author names a specific and singular trail, and yet he writes about more than a score of other trails that have no relationship to the Great Northern Trail. Just because some trail led northward is no reason it should be called a "northern trail."

The author goes back many thousands of years to the glacial age when Asiatics crossed Alaska and came south before the ice broke away the land bridge between Siberia and Alaska. This was his North Trail, but he also writes about such trails as buffalo trails, Indian trails, whisky trails, the Klondike Trail, gold trails, Spanish trails, and cattle trails. There is even a chapter on the barbed-wire, or fenced, trail.

With a few exceptions, his chapter on the Henry Plummer gang is fairly accurate. I find the book interesting, and the author writes with vitality. He must have done a great deal of research on his subject—a rather large one. But I wish that he had been more careful to separate legend from fact. I fail to see why the Johnson County and Lincoln County wars have any place here. They had

nothing to do with trails. Evidently his excuse is in his own words: "The Lincoln County cattle war was fought along the southern anchor of the Great North Trail."

He relies too much on legend for his account of this war. He claims that Billy the Kid's real name was William H. Bonney, though contemporary newspapers named him Henry McCarty, and he calls Buckshot Roberts by the name Buckshot Williams. He says that Buckshot, "entrusted with the task of assassinating McSween, was himself run down and killed at a sawmill." Of course, he means Blazer's Mill, but Roberts was not "run down." He went there on his own accord on a bounty hunt for some of Brewer's posse. And this is the first time I have read that he was to kill McSween. McSween had been killed some time before this. The author also misspells Hindman's name as Hindeman and gives the Kid credit for killing Morton and Baker, as well as Beckwith, though others were shooting at them too. He is mistaken in saying that Sheriff Brady was leading the posse that killed John Tunstall, and his statement that the Coe boys "were of desperate fame" is also untrue.

When Brady was killed, he writes, "Billy's and Murphy's forces, behind adobe walls on opposite sides of the street," dared not show themselves. One would think that they were drawn up in battle array. The Kid's gang was the only group behind a wall; the sheriff's group was in the street heading toward the courthouse. He claims that Chisum, after McSween's death, hired Billy the Kid, that the Kid "was unable to collect his wages and threatened the cattle king with violence," and that Chisum offered a reward for the death of the Kid. He calls Pat Garrett "a tall Texan" and says that he was supposed to be a Dolan man, but Garrett took no sides in this war. The author is also wrong in having Garrett "standing near the head of the bed" when he killed the Kid. He was sitting on the bed talking to Pete Maxwell.

In his chapter on Wyoming the author credits the familiar saying, "Thank God the tally books won't freeze," to a ranchman during a severe winter storm when many cattle were dying; but it is well known fact that the expression, "Cheer up boys. Whatever happens, the books won't freeze," is credited to a bartender named Luke Murrin, who worked in a saloon popular with the owners of the larger ranches and coined the saying when a group of them were gathered in the saloon. In those days cattle were largely sold by "book count."

The author has real-estate boomers arriving in Abilene, Kansas, and building pens and loading chutes for the cattle trade, but it was Joseph McCoy who did all that.

He tells a story of Wyatt Earp that I have not read before: "Earp, who in his Arizona years was said to have ridden 87 miles to shoot through the hotel room occupied nuptially by a female relative because he disapproved of the groom."

45. CURRY, Tom, and Wood Cowan. Famous figures of the Old West, by Tom Curry and Wood Cowan. Derby, Connecticut, Monarch Books, Inc., [1965]. Stiff col. pict. wrappers.

This book deals with many of the western outlaws and gunmen, as well as peace officers, Indian chiefs, scouts, and other characters. On one page is a tabloid biography of the character, and on the opposite page is a drawing of that character and an account of some of his activities.

The authors say that Clay Allison emigrated to Texas when he was a small boy, but Allison fought in the Civil War before coming to Texas and so was not a child. They also repeat the legend about his pulling the dentist's teeth, and they have his killing of Chunk Colbert all wrong.

They have Billy the Kid's mother marrying Antrim before they moved to New Mexico, but, as we know, they were married in Santa Fe. They write that the Kid and his gang "were trapped in a store and the building set on fire," but it was the McSween home, not a store. After the Kid was captured, they say, "the rickety Lincoln County jail wouldn't hold such a man so Sheriff Garrett put him in a store with two guards." When the Kid was killed, they have Garrett *"seated in the shadows of Maxwell's porch,"* but we know that the killing took place in Maxwell's bedroom.

Their account of the killing of Fred White by Curly Bill Brocius is all wrong, and they have Calamity Jane born in 1848, but she claimed that she was born in 1852. They also repeat the legend about Egan naming her Calamity. They also claim that the Lincoln County War broke out because of the stealing of Chisum's cattle. They have the killing of Mannen Clements wrong, and they are mistaken in having Virgil Earp going to Arizona to join Wyatt, Morgan, and James. Virgil was the first of the Earp brothers to go there. They are also mistaken in having Wyatt early appointed U.S. marshal at Tombstone. They have the mob scene in Tombstone all wrong and claim that Wyatt stopped the men as they "marched on the jail to lynch the captives." The man they wanted was Johnny-Behind-the-Deuce O'Rourke, and he was not in jail.

Of the capture of the Kid at Stinking Springs, they say the prisoners were taken to Santa Fe "where the Kid was condemned to hang." He was tried in Mesilla, not Santa Fe. They say that Brazel shot Garrett through the head, but it has now been conceded that Jim Miller shot him from ambush. Their account of John Wesley Hardin is very weak, and they say that "he made his debut in the Taylor-Sutton feud," but he had killed many men before that. They also have some of Wild Bill Hickok's killings wrong.

They also have the Northfield bank robbery wrong when they say that the robbers "charged into the main section of town firing their guns and shooting it up to terrify their victims." They are also wrong in having the Ford brothers cousins of the James boys. They have the origin of Masterson's nickname "Bat" wrong, and they have him quite a dude for dress. They have Belle Starr born in 1846, but she was born in 1848. They have Jim Reed killed "by a range detective," but, as we know, he was killed by Deputy John Morris. They are also wrong in having one of Belle's suitors a banker whom she met at the bank and robbed of $30,000. They are wrong in having her killed by Edgar Watson. He was tried for the killing but was found not guilty.

They are also wrong in having Ben Thompson in Sweetwater, Texas, when Sergeant King was killed and Bat Masterson shot. Their account of the killing of Thompson and King Fisher is also unreliable. There are many more errors typical of such attempts at writing history.

46. DAGGETT, Thomas F. Billy LeRoy, the Colorado bandit; or, the king of American highwaymen. New York, Richard K. Fox, [1881]. Pict. wrappers.

This is one of the *Police Gazette* series on criminals, and it is printed on the familiar pink paper of this series. Purporting to be the life of Billy the Kid, it is the fruit of a hack writer's vivid imagination, with just enough half-truths to make it confusing. Though a collector's item, it is a piece of worthless trash historically.

The author lays the scene in Colorado instead of New Mexico, and his hero is an actor impersonating a female character. The author has invented a brother, Sam, to join the Kid (in one place he calls him Arthur). Although the author names no names, he has the killing of Bell and Olinger all wrong and repeats the tale about the Kid shooting cowboys who worked for Chisum. The book ends with a preposterous account of the hanging of Billy and his "brother" in Del Norte, Colorado.

In the early 1880's there really was a noted highwayman named Arthur Pond, who used the alias Billy LeRoy. He operated in the San Juan section of Colorado and in 1881 was sentenced to serve ten years in a Detroit prison. It is possible that the author of this book had heard of this character and took the name for his story; but he leaves the impression that he was attempting to write about Billy the Kid.

47. DALE, Edward Everett. Frontier ways. Sketches of life in the Old West, [by Edward Everett Dale]. Illustrations by Malcolm Thurgood. Austin, University of Texas Press, [1959]. Cloth.

This is an interesting book about pioneer life on the western frontier by an able and well-known author. But in writing of Charlie Russell, the famous cowboy artist, he is mistaken in his statements concerning the artist's famous picture "Waiting for a Chinook." "Charlie Russell, the cowboy artist," he writes, "was in charge of a herd of five thousand head belonging to a group of Eastern capitalists." Russell was only a wrangler out of work and spending the winter as a chuck-line rider at this ranch. It was owned not by eastern capitalists but by Stadler and Kaufman, two cattlemen of Helena, Montana.

"Toward spring," the author continues, "his [Russell's] employers wrote him a letter asking how the cattle were doing. Russell's painting, which he sent as a reply, has become famous. It is a picture of a gaunt and lonely old cow in the midst of great snow drifts, standing with drooping head like a bovine at the gate of Paradise and in the corner Russell had written the title 'The Last of Five Thousand.' "

Actually the owners had written to Jesse Phelps, foreman of the O H Ranch where Russell and a few other cowboys were spending the winter. When Phelps began to answer the letter Russell drew this picture to be included in the letter. After Phelps saw it, he decided to let it tell the story instead of a letter. Also Russell did not title the picture "The Last of the Five Thousand" but entitled it "Waiting for a Chinook." The original shows this title in the lower left-hand corner. Later someone gave it the title "The Last of the Five Thousand."

48. DICK, EVERETT. Tales of the frontier. From Lewis and Clark to the last roundup. Selected and retold by Everett Dick. Lincoln, University of Nebraska Press, [1963]. Cloth.

This book has a tabloid description of the Johnson County War, but the author is wrong in writing that Sheriff Angus arrived with Colonel J. J. Van Horn

"from Fort McKinney with three troops of cavalry." Sheriff Angus was with the attacking party at the TA Ranch, not with the soldiers.

In his account of the robbery of the Union Pacific by Joel Collins and his gang, he is mistaken in saying that Sam Bass "was building a reputation as a cattle rustler." Bass had nothing to do with any cattle stealing; he was robbing stagecoaches. The author is also mistaken in saying that the eastbound express that they robbed passed through Big Springs "around midnight." It was scheduled to arrive at 10:48, and it was on time. He, like others, is also mistaken in including a man named John Underwood in the gang; a Henry Underwood did join Bass after he organized his new gang at Denton, Texas. The author also says that the messenger was savagely beaten because he did not know the combination of the safe, but all he received was a cut lip when Jack Davis shoved his pistol into his mouth.

The author is also mistaken when he writes that the outlaws "turned up $300,000 in gold bullion being shipped East from the California gold fields, but this the bandits left in the car" because it was too heavy to carry. The truth is that they did find $1,200 in silver ingots, which they left behind because of its weight, but the $60,000 in $20 gold coins they divided among themselves. The author is also wrong in his account of the activities of M. P. Leech. He writes: "He soon picked up the trail of Collins and Hefferidge [sic], who had joined a group of drovers conveying some cattle to a Kansas Pacific shipping point." The two train robbers did not join anyone. They were making their way back to Texas with their $20,000 strapped onto a pack horse.

The author is also wrong in having Collins and Heffridge ride into Buffalo

Station on September 26. They arrived on Wednesday the 25th. He says that the two robbers stopped to buy provisions from a store run by the station agent, but the store belonged to Jim Thompson, who ran the section house. He is also mistaken in having the station agent wiring Sheriff Beardsley [sic] of Hays who with "ten cavalry troopers . . . set out in pursuit." The troopers with the sheriff were already on the trail to intercept the robbers.

Again writing of Leech, he says, "By the following summer he was close to the trail of Jim Berry." It was on October 5 that Berry returned to Mexico, Missouri. He writes further, "Unfortunately that day before he [Leech] caught up with him, Berry was killed. . . . He had carelessly deposited large sums of gold in banks in that area and became so restive when questioned about it that the peace officers were compelled to shoot him." This is far from the way things happened. He is also mistaken when he writes, "Sam Bass and Tom Nixon made their getaway safely to Texas." It was Jack Davis who went to Texas with Bass. He also states that "nobody seems to know what became of the sixth bandit, John Underwood." There was no John Underwood. He misspells Sheriff Bardsley's name as Beardsley and Heffridge's name as Hefferidge. In one place he has Tom Nixon's name as Tim, but that is evidently a typographical error.

49. DORSET, PHYLLIS FLANDERS. The New Eldorado. The story of Colorado's gold and silver rushes, [by] Phyllis Flanders Dorset. London, Macmillan Company, Collier-Macmillan, Ltd., [1970]. Cloth.

This author writes that Bob and Charlie Ford "had connived to kill their friend Jesse James and collect the $10,000 offered by Governor Crittenden," but they never collected such an amount. She says that the Ford brothers "tracked" Jesse to St. Joseph, Missouri. They did not have to track him, for they were invited to his home. She is mistaken in stating that Dave Rudabaugh fled to Creede, Colorado, "after killing a sheriff in Las Vegas," where he went to work for Soapy Smith. It was not a sheriff but a jailer whom Rudabaugh killed and it is very doubtful that he ever worked for Soapy Smith. In fact, there is no record of Rudabaugh ever being in Colorado. Like so many others, she writes Ed O. Kelly's name as Ed O'Kelly. I wonder where she got the information that Kelly had married the sister of Cole and Bud Younger. She is another who spells Alfred Packer's name as Alfred. She says that Bob Ford "put together a barn of a building" in Creede for a saloon. His saloon was in a tent.

50. DORSON, RICHARD M. American folklore, by Richard M. Dorson. Chicago, University of Chicago Press, [1959]. Pict. cloth.

In a section on outlaws the author deals with Jesse James, Billy the Kid, Sam Bass, Pat Garrett, Bob Ford, and Jim Murphy. Like so many other writers, this author has Jim Murphy dying by poison "he apparently drank deliberately." Actually Murphy was taking some medicine for his eyes when some of it got down his throat. He is also mistaken in saying that Theodore Roosevelt awarded Pat Garrett with a postmastership." He made Garrett a collector of customs at El Paso, Texas. He is also mistaken in his account of Garrett's death. He writes: "He made the mistake of badgering a young tenant farmer of his, who retorted sharply; stung beyond control, Pat drew, but the younger man drew faster, shot Pat dead and was acquitted in court on the plea of self-defense." As we know, Brazel was no farmer, and Garrett did not draw his gun. It is well known that Pat was shot from ambush by Jim Miller.

He has Frank James in the Liberty Bank robbery and "showing his kid brother, Jesse, his share of the spoils." But the James boys did not take part in this robbery. He also has the James boys killing anyone who resisted during their robberies.

51. DORSON, RICHARD M. America in legend. Folklore from the colonial period to the present time, [by] Richard M. Dorson. New York, Pantheon Books, division of Random House, [1973]. Pict. cloth.

In his chapter on the American cowboy the author has Sam Bass selling his own cattle that he took up the trail. The cattle did not belong to Bass, though the author says, "He had bought them in the country of Southwest Texas to sell in Kansas." It was Joel Collins idea to drive the cattle up the trail, and the herd was made up largely of other ranchers' cattle trusted to Collins' care on credit.

The author also writes that in Bass's "last abortive effort [he] tried to hold up a bank in Round Rock, Texas." He was only planning to hold up the bank and was not as yet trying to rob it. He is also mistaken in placing the Union Pacific train robbery in Big Springs, Texas. It took place in Big Springs, Nebraska. Unlike his other book, he does not claim that Jim Murphy committed suicide, but he is still mistaken in saying he swallowed a poison prescribed for his eyes. Some atropine trickled down his throat accidentally when he was trying to drop the medicine in his eyes.

52. DOUGLAS, CLARENCE BROWN. Territory tales. Oklahoma in the making from the Twin Territories, by a pioneer editor who was there, Col. Clarence B. Douglas. El Reno, Published by El Reno American, 1951. Stiff wrappers.

The author's account of the killing of Bill Dalton is inaccurate, and so are some of his other statements. He writes: "Soon after the battle at Ingalls, Bill Dalton returned to California, there not being room in any bandit gang for both him and Doolin." That is untrue. Dalton was in Doolin's gang, and he never returned to California until he was carried there in a coffin. The author says that Dalton formed a new gang in California and "soon became the most famous outlaw of his time." Yet in the next paragraph he says he was killed "not in the heat of battle with officers of the law that he defied; not in the thick of a daring train robbery or a bank hold-up; not facing the enemy 'with blazing guns—but running half stooped, his back to a posse of U.S. Deputy Marshals looking for a small-time country bootlegger, he went out unexpected, unknown and for 48 hours was unidentified." All of this is wrong. In telling of the hanging of Jim Miller, the author misspells Gus Bobbitt's name as Boggett.

53. DRAGO, HARRY SINCLAIR. The great range wars. Violence on the grasslands, [by] Harry Sinclair Drago. New York, Dodd, Mead Company, [1970]. Cloth.

On page 50 the author writes: "According to the evidence, the Kid killed eighteen men in his brief lifetime," but there is no absolute proof that he killed more than four. On the same page he claims that McSween "was naïve enough to believe he could destroy" the Murphy crowd. He is also mistaken in having Sheriff Brady a deputy U.S. marshal, and I fail to see how he places Pat Coghlan as one of the fighters on the McSween side.

He further states that, because of the people's fear of the Dolan outfit, the Tunstall store and its "groceries and assorted merchandise gathered dust on their shelves." The truth is that Tunstall's business was hurting Dolan's; hence his underhanded actions to get rid of the competition. The author is another who has Billy the Kid at the Tunstall funeral, but at the time he was being detained by the Dolan crowd. He too misspells Henry Brown's name as Hendry and Olinger's name as Ollinger. He has Billy the Kid killing Morton and Baker and says, "Two quick shots and it was all over." Morton alone had nine bullet holes in his back. Somebody else must have been shooting at him too.

The author says that Morton slipped McCloskey's pistol from his holster and shot him, but most accounts have McNab doing this job with his own gun. Drago does not mention McNab being with the party. Immediately after the killing of these two, the author has Brewer leading "his posse to Blazer's Mill and from there sent a Mexican out to bury the dead men." But Brewer rode directly to Lincoln to seek the advice of McSween.

I fail to see where he gets the hour five o'clock as the time of Buckshot Roberts' arrival at Blazer's Mill. According to Maurice Fulton, the most reliable historian of the Lincoln County War, Brewer's posse arrived there at eleven o'clock A.M., and the men were eating a noon meal when Roberts arrived. The author says, "The shadows were beginning to deepen," when Brewer was killed, but all the fighting took place soon after noon. He writes that Brewer's men "lingered at Blazer's Mill three or four days after Dick Brewer had been given a decent burial," but according to Fulton "the loss of their leader threw the others into confusion. They deserted the field without even stopping to take up the body of their leader and retired to George Coe's place on the Ruidoso."

The author says of Billy the Kid: "He was William Antrin before he was William Bonney," but he was Henry Antrim, really Henry McCarty, taking the name Antrim from his stepfather. During the battle when McNab was killed, Al Sanders (whom the author calls Bud Saunders) was wounded, and Frank Coe was captured, the author has McNab "darting into a little canyon" to do battle, but at the first volley he fell from his horse, his body riddled with bullets. The author is also mistaken in saying that when Mrs. McSween called upon Colonel Dudley he "stepped out of his tent to meet her." He was not that courteous.

The father of the Beckwith boys, Henry Beckwith, was not present at the battle at the McSween home as the author says. He says that Chapman, Mrs. McSween's lawyer, was killed at noon, but he was killed in the evening. In his chapter on the Graham-Tewksbury feud, he calls Frank Wattron by the name Watrous.

Of the Johnson County War the author says, "Walcott, making use of the wagon Flagg had left behind, had it wheeled to the rear of the stable where it was filled with pitch pine faggots and what hay could be scraped up." The wagon was already on the Champion place.

54. DRAGO, HARRY SINCLAIR. The legend makers. Tales of the old-time peace officers and desperadoes of the frontier, [by] Harry Sinclair Drago. Illustrated with photographs. New York, Dodd, Mead & Company, [1975]. Cloth.

This book is devoted to many of the better-known gunmen and outlaws of the West. Like most of Drago's other books, it is full of errors. One reviewer wrote: "It will be useful to young people who want some elementary information about the great western peace officers and the desperadoes who appeared there, but to anybody wanting solid historical fare, it will be a major irritation. The publishers call it a 'well documented account.' It is anything but that. Mr. Drago has clipped, pasted, borrowed and paraphrased, ignored almost all his obligations and done serious wrong to the hard working researchers who have done his work for him."

He again has Henry Brown's name as Hendry and insists that it was not Henry, and he has him a city marshal of Tascosa, Texas, and also a deputy sheriff of Oldham County. He was only a city police officer. After Brown became the city marshal of Caldwell, Kansas, he and his assistant, Ben Wheeler, were so well thought of by the citizens that they were beyond suspicion. But the author practically accuses them of robbing two wealthy cattlemen of the money they had received from the sale of their cattle.

When Ed Masterson was shot, he killed Jack Wagner and Al Walker, the men who had shot him. Masterson died soon after. Drago says, "Bat came bounding across the plaza" and "put three slugs into Wagner and two into Walker." Contemporary newspapers did not say that Bat was present but reported that Ed lived long enough to shoot both

of them himself before he went across the street to Hoover's saloon and collapsed. According to the account in the *Dodge City Times*, Drago is wrong in having George Hoy (whom he calls Ed Hoyt) inside the Comique Theater when he did his shooting through the walls. He was outside with companions on horseback and was shot by officers as he crossed the bridge on his way to camp. The author is also wrong when he states that, when he arrived at Tombstone, Wyatt Earp was "wealthy enough to buy an interest in the immensely profitable Oriental Saloon." He was given a small interest to act as a protector of the establishment.

In writing about Billy the Kid, the author says, "We do not know when nor where [Mrs. Antrim, the Kid's mother] became acquainted with Bill Antrim, or how she chanced to be in Santa Fe." If he had done a little more research, he would have found that she met Antrim in Indianapolis, where he was an express driver. Later both moved in Wichita, Kansas, and both owned property there. They had been acquainted for about six years when she went to a doctor and discovered that she had tuberculosis and was advised to go to New Mexico for the dry climate. She died of the disease a little more than a year and a half after her marriage to Antrim.

He calls Dick Brewer Jim in one place. Tom Hill is called a rancher, but he owned no ranch and was just another thug. The author gives the Kid credit for killing Morton and Baker: "The pair made a break for it. The Kid got them in his rifle sights and that was all there was to it." He says that this occurred when the Kid's party "surprised Baker and Morton in the Pecos bottoms," but the two were not killed until after their capture and on their way to Lincoln.

The author is also wrong in saying

that Sheriff Brady was killed "on his way to serve an important attachment on McSween." He was on his way to the courthouse to post a notice of the postponement of a court session. Where did he get the information that Dick Brewer had managed to get the information to Buckshot Roberts that Brewer's posse would be "lying out at Blazer's Mill"? He has Roberts arriving at the mill at 5 o'clock in the afternoon, but he arrived before noon, while Brewer and his men were eating lunch. The author makes some doubtful statements about the battle that now took place at the mill. He says "By accident, a slug shattered Coe's right hand," but only his trigger finger was lost, torn off by a bullet that ricocheted off Bowdre's gun belt. He seems to think that Bowdre was the last to shoot Roberts "from around the corner of a 'dobe," but Bowdre was the first to shoot him, and in the open.

The author has Bowdre, O'Folliard, and three other men escaping from the McSween home as soon as it was set on fire, but that is not true. Then he says that the Dolan gunmen "snapped to attention as McSween walked out, followed by his partisans" and says that McSween was killed "as he took his first step." He also has the Kid coming out with McSween, but that is incorrect too. The author is mistaken in having Pat Garrett a deputy sheriff when he captured the Kid's gang at Stinking Springs. He was the duly elected sheriff.

He is wrong in having Bob Olinger going across the street from the courthouse to eat his supper and bring back the prisoners' supper. He took the prisoners with him. He has Bell removing the handcuffs "from the Kid's right hand," which was followed by a lick over the deputy's head that knocked him unconscious. He then says that the Kid got possession of Bell's gun and killed him. That is not the way it happened, nor did the Kid get a rifle and cartridges with which to kill Olinger. He got Olinger's own shotgun, with which the Kid had been threatened many times.

The author also has the escape of Jim Courtright from the Rangers all wrong. He says that the original name given Tombstone, Arizona, was Watervale. That will be news to historians throughout the West, and he says that Tombstone was more fiitting because of the town's bleak appearance. He must have got this information from John Myers Myers' book *The Last Chance*. The more common account of how Tombstone received its name is that Ed Schieffelin, prospecting for gold in a country filled with hostile Indians, was told that he had better prospect for a tombstone. The word stuck in his memory, and when the town was founded, he named it Tombstone.

The author says that the Mitchell-Truitt feud was one of the most noted in Texas history, but it was nothing compared with the Taylor-Sutton, the Horrell-Higgins and the Jaybird-Woodpecker feuds. He also says that no one knows why Butch Cassidy took that name. Yet it is well-known that Robert LeRoy Parker took this name from the real Cassidy, who had befriended Parker, taught him what he knew of outlawry, and then left the country.

The author is also mistaken in saying that Kid Curry killed Pike Landusky because he called Curry a Negro. Their enmity was deeper than that. He also has Bob Lee's name as Leigh, which is incorrect. He says that Harvey Logan, after his arrest in Knoxville, Tennessee, "bribed a prison guard and escaped," but that is not true. Logan, after many days of planning, escaped on his own with the use of a wire secured from a broom. He also says that this was Logan's "last brush with the law," but that is not true either.

In the note section of his book the author says Ben Wheeler was born Ben Robertson and had just escaped from the Huntsville prison when he joined Henry Brown in Caldwell. In another note he says Luke Short died in 1916 in a Kansas City hospital, but he died in August, 1893, in Geuda Springs, Kansas, where he had gone for his health. He misspells Curly Bill Brocius' name as Broscious.

55. DRAGO, HARRY SINCLAIR. Notorious ladies of the frontier, by Harry Sinclair Drago. New York, Dodd, Mead Co., 1969. Cloth.

In this interesting book the author does much to correct some of the false history written about these notorious females of the West, especially Belle Starr and Calamity Jane. However, he makes some errors that need to be corrected. He is mistaken in saying Bat Masterson was shot by Sergeant King while Bat was in bed with Molly Brennan (which he spells Brenan). Bat was shot while he was dancing with Molly; she was killed and he was wounded in the pelvis. In spite of his wound Bat got off a shot that killed King. The author does not mention Molly being killed.

The author says "beyond doubt" Pearl Starr was sired by Cole Younger, but Younger emphatically denied it. He also says that Calamity Jane married Clinton Burk in Deadwood, but the records show that they were married in El Paso, Texas. Calamity Jane herself said that she married him there in August, 1885, but Drago has her marrying Burk on September 25, 1891. He says that this is on record, and I would like to know where this record can be found. Every account I have read indicates that the marriage took place in El Paso, where Burk was a cab driver.

Drago writes: "Late in August word spread among the Texans that the leaders of their faction were to be deported [from Ellsworth]. Ben Thompson was in Ellsworth. He knew that his name would head the list. He left for Kansas City at once and advised his friends Cal Pierce, Neil Cain and John Good to leave with him." Thompson did not leave town but stayed to face his enemies. The author does not mention that Sheriff Whitney was killed at this time.

56. DRAGO, HARRY SINCLAIR. Outlaws on horseback. The history of the organized bands of bank and train robbers who terrorized the prairie towns of Missouri, Kansas, Indian Territory and Oklahoma for half a century, by Harry Sinclair Drago. Illustrated with photographs and a map. Endpaper drawings by Lorence F. Bjorklund. New York, Dodd, Mead & Company, [1964]. Cloth.

It is good to see more and more writers, this author among them, correcting some of the false legends that have been plaguing historians for many years. But is hard to understand why in the very beginning (page 2), the author says that the James brothers and the Younger brothers were first cousins, though he later denies it. He is also wrong in having Jesse James in the Liberty bank robbery when it has been proved that he was in bed at the time recovering from a lung wound.

The author says that Henry Starr's robbery career began "with the looting of the People's Bank in Bentonville, Arkansas, on June 5th, 1893," but he and some companions robbed the agent of the Missouri Pacific at Nowata, Indian Territory, in July, 1892.

He is mistaken in having Preston Shirley preceding his father, John Shirley, to Sycene, Texas (now a part of Dallas). Preston settled in Collin County, Texas, near McKinney. For John Shirley's excuse for leaving Carthage, the author writes: "The killing of his son [Ed] seems to have filled John Shirley with a burning desire to get out of Missouri as quickly as possible. He sold his inn and livery business, put the family belongings into two covered wagons and started for Texas, driving one wagon himself and Belle and her mother the other." He had no business to sell, for it had been burned when the whole town went up in flames. He simply wanted to go where it was safer for his family and start life anew.

The author seems to rely greatly upon Paul Wellman's *A Dynasty of Western Outlaws*, a most unreliable book. In the robbery of what the author calls "the Huntington National" (though it was the Bank of Huntington), he has "an unidentified member of the [James] gang laying dead in front of the Huntington National. It very likely was Art McCoy." He also claims that this robbery was a failure. McCoy was not there, there were no dead men in front, and the haul was a good one. His account of the Northfield Bank robbery is unreliable, and he accuses Jesse James of killing Heywood, though that has never been proved. He has Frank James wounded in the battle that followed the robbery, but that is untrue. On one page he has Frank wounded at the scene of the robbery when he was mounting his horse, but a few pages further he has him being shot in the knee by the posse and the bullet being embedded in Jesse's thigh. He says they made a doctor in Iowa remove the slug.

The author admits that in *Hands Up!* Sutton indulges in "fantastic fabrications" but claims that "if the material he gathered first hand was only folklore, it was good folklore and deserves to be preserved." That is the trouble with so many historians—they try to make folklore into history. (For an opinion of Sutton's book see *Burs Under the Saddle*).

The author seems to doubt that the Daltons were ever in California, but there is much evidence that they were. He is the only writer I know of who has Frank Canton in the fight at Ingalls. Most accounts of the killing of Jim Reed claim that he was killed for the reward and that his killer, John T. Morris, failed to receive the reward because Belle, his wife, refused to identify Reed as her husband [though that is also a legend]. Drago writes, "Morris got his reward and lived to enjoy it." On page 165 the author says that Henry Starr was the nephew of Belle Starr by marriage, but on page 291 he says that Belle was his cousin by marriage.

On the whole this book holds one's interest, and the author has done much to correct the many legends about Belle Starr, the Ingalls fight, and Rose of Cimarron.

Though Cole Younger denied that he had fathered Belle Starr's first child and Jim Reed apparently accepted her as his own, Drago claims that she was Cole's daughter "beyond a reasonable doubt. It was only hinted at first, but as the years passed, evidence to the effect became so overwhelming as to leave no room for speculation." What evidence?

57. DRAGO, HARRY SINCLAIR. Road agents and train robbers. Half a century of western banditry, [by] Harry Sinclair Drago. Illustrated

with photographs. Endpaper drawings by Lorence F. Bjorklund. New York, Mead & Company, [1973]. Cloth.

This is another of Drago's many books dealing with the well-known outlaws of the West but revealing nothing new. On page 55 lines 20 and 21 are misplaced in the copies I examined.

In his chapter on Deadwood the author gives the name Abe Simmons to the driver of the stagecoach held up by the Collins-Bass gang. The driver, as is well known, was Johnny Slaughter. The author insists that Pearl Younger was Cole's daughter, though Cole always denied it. He is also mistaken in claiming that Jesse James planned the bank robbery at Liberty, though he does not say that James was actually in it.

He is also in error in saying that Preston Shirley, John Shirley's oldest son, owning a farm at Sycene, Texas, near Dallas. He lived near McKinney, in Collin County. He also writes that Belle's father "bought a farm, built a commodious house, and resumed his old occupation of innkeeper at Scyene." Running an inn on a farm would have been a rather peculiar occupation for him. The author is also mistaken when he says that Frank Dalton was killed by Cherokee horsethieves. He was killed by bootleggers. He has Cherokee Bill Goldsby's given name Clarence, but it was Crawford. He makes the statement that Belle was killed by Edgar Watson. Watson was tried for the crime and acquitted. No one seems to know for certain who killed her, but several others have been suspected of the deed, including her own son, Jim July, and John Middleton's brother.

58. DUNLOP, RICHARD. Great trails of the West, [by] Richard Dunlop. Nashville, New York, Abington Press, [1971]. Cloth.

An entertaining book giving a condensed history of the various trails of the West. The author is mistaken in having Billy the Kid escaping from the jail at Mesilla. His escape was from the prison in Lincoln. He writes: "the outlaw Sam Bass and his gang, grown tired of robbing stagecoaches on the trail, tried their hand at bank robbery," but they had mostly been robbing trains and had not as yet tried to rob a bank when Bass was killed. He also has Bass shot on July 18, but it was on the 19th. He is also mistaken in having the Marlow brothers a bunch of rustlers, and he misnames Henry Newton Brown as John Henry Brown. He is also wrong in having McCanles the first man killed by Wild Bill Hickok.

59. DURHAM, PHILIP, and EVERETT L. JONES. The Negro cowboys, by Philip Durham and Everett L. Jones. New York, Dodd, Mead & Co., [1965]. Cloth.

This book is the first devoted to the Negro cowboy, but it is regrettable that the authors omitted one of the most noted Texas Negro broncbuster and cowboy, Bone Hooks, of Amarillo. The authors have Billy the Kid killing both Morton and Baker, but that was never proved because others also shot at them. They misname Buckshot Roberts as Buckshot Rogers and say that they went after Billy the Kid and his gang when he learned there was a $200 reward on each, and he later *found them* at Blazer's Mill. They, too, like several other writers, have the Murphy crowd drinking and dancing "the grewsome hours away" after their victory at the battle at the McSween home, and the authors are also mistaken in having Negroes in the

McSween home during this battle. The McSweens had two Negro servants, but they were not in the house or in the battle. Afterward they helped bury the dead.

The authors say that Governor Wallace offered Billy the Kid "safe conduct" if he would talk with him and that George Washington, a Negro, was sent to find him, but the note the governor sent to the Kid instructed him to come alone and "not tell a living soul where you are coming."

They are also mistaken in saying that Tom Horn was hanged in Laramie, Wyoming; he was hanged in Cheyenne. They say that the Olive brothers "shot up the Mitchell and Ketchum families," but Ketchum had no family, and they did not bother Mitchell's family. They also have "Mitchell first hanged, then shot, and then doused with coal oil and burned. In fact, Mitchell was shot in the back and then hanged with Ketchum, and both bodies were later soaked with whisky and set afire.

The authors have Wyatt Earp and Bat Masterson marshals of Dodge, but Earp was a deputy marshal, and Masterson was the sheriff of the county. In the Lincoln County troubles, they write, Murphy "was sided by two small ranchers, James Dolan and John Riley." Dolan and Riley were partners in the business, not ranchers. The authors also make an error of small consequence when they write that Cherokee Bill "was captured when he was felled by a blow with a poker." He was hit on the head with a stick of stovewood. They are also mistaken in saying of Charlie Russell: "When his boss wrote in the spring of 1887 to ask about his cattle, Russell made a famous answer. On a postcard he drew a poor, gaunt cow standing on shaky legs, and underneath the picture he wrote, 'The Last of Five Thousand.' "

Russell was not working for that ranch; the name he gave the little picture was "Waiting for a Chinook," not "The Last of Five Thousand"; and it was painted on a cardboard boxtop, not a postcard.

60. DYKSTRA, Robert R. The cattle town, [by] Robert R. Dykstra. New York, Alfred A. Knopf, 1968. Cloth.

This author repeats the legend about John Wesley Hardin shooting through a wall of an adjoining room in a hotel and killing a man because he was snoring. That never happened except in the mind of some legend maker.

61. ELMAN, Robert. Badmen of the West. By Robert Elman. Picture research by Marion Geisinger. [Secaucus, New Jersey], a Ridge Press Pound Book, [1974]. Fabricoid.

This beautiful book is another rehash of the lives of the western outlaws and gunmen. Though published in 1974, after the publication of several books that try to set the record straight, this author continues to make the same mistakes that have been perpetuated for so long.

The author has Jesse and Frank James robbing the Liberty bank and "killing a young bystander in a gun battle." The James boys did not take part in that robbery, and there was no gun battle. A young boy on his way to school was wantonly murdered. He also has them killing more people during their robberies than they actually did. Of the incident of the bomb throwing that tore their mother's arm off, he writes: "There have been conflicting reports as to whether the James brothers were actually there. Evidence indicates that Frank and Jesse and at least one henchman came out shooting and the detectives hastily retreated while the outlaws escaped." The James boys were not at home at the time, and there was no shooting.

He is also mistaken in saying Wild Bill Hickok assumed the name Wild Bill while acting in a play by Ned Buntline named *Scouts of the Prairie*. The name Wild Bill was given to him long before that. He is also wrong in having Hickok walking to St. Louis in 1880 to join Lane's Red Legs. He joined the gang during the Civil War. He is also mistaken in having Hickok the manager of Rock Creek Station. He was only a stableboy. He says that Russell, Majors, and Waddell had bought the land the station was on from David McCanles but does not add that they had also bought the station but had never paid for it. He is also wrong in saying that Hickok "shot down two men the day he took office" in Abilene. In telling of the killing of Phil Coe, the author writes, ". . . and on one occasion he killed a deputy by mistake." Hickok killed the deputy at the same time he killed Coe. He has Jack McCall tried the second time in Laramie, Wyoming. McCall was tried in Yankton, South Dakota.

Like others, the author misnames Jules Reni as Jules Bene. He has Bat Masterson a deputy marshal of Dodge City, but he was the sheriff of Ford County. He is also wrong in placing the prizefight between Fitzsimmons and Maher in Lantry, Texas. It was held on an island in the Río Grande, near Lantry, because Texas would not allow prizefights to be held in the state.

I am glad to see that the author does correct that legend about Wyatt Earp arresting Ben Thompson at Ellsworth after Sheriff Whitney was killed by Bill Thompson. He also admits that "it was probably true" that Ben Thompson was in Sweetwater, Texas, when Bat Masterson was shot by Sergeant King, but there is no record of Thompson ever being in that town. He is also wrong in having Ben Thompson dealing cards in Tombstone. He was never in that town either.

He says that Clay Allison was crippled when "he shot himself in the foot, evidently while practicing his draw," but that was not the cause. He is also mistaken in having the Clifton House, where Allison killed Chunk Colbert, in Red River Station, Texas. The Clifton House was in Cimarron, New Mexico, and Red River Station was also in New Mexico. It is untrue that "Colbert supposedly had shot down a friend of a friend of Allison, and Allison supposedly had killed an uncle of Colbert in a knife fight." It was only the jealousy of one gunfighter wanting to outdo another of his kind for the reputation it would bring him.

In telling about the time John Wesley Hardin left Abilene to chase and kill the Mexican outlaw who had killed his friend Bill Coran (or Cohron), this author says the Mexican's name was Pablo Gutiérrez, but his name was Bideno. He corrects some of the errors about Billy the Kid but makes a few himself, such as saying that Joe McCarty was the Kid's younger brother. Joe was two years older than the Kid. He also says that two posses were after Tunstall when he was killed, but there was only one. He says that Frank McNab was hired as a detective by the Stockman's Association, something I have not seen before, and he misnames Billy Morton as Buck. When Sheriff Brady and his deputy, Hindman, were killed, this author says, all the killers rode away except the Kid, who went to Brady's body to get his guns. That did not happen. He is also mistaken in writing that the Kid "made his position still worse by raiding the Mescalero Reservation for horses and killing Morris Bernstein, a Government clerk." He made no raid on the reservation, nor did he kill Bernstein.

Of the capture of the Kid and his companions at Stinking Springs the author is also completely wrong in saying that they "withstood the siege for three days without food." There was no siege, and the Kid surrendered after holding out one night and the early hours of the next day. He spells Olinger's name wrong and has the killing of J. W. Bell entirely wrong. He has Olinger across the street at La Rue's Bar, but he had taken some prisoners to the Wortley Hotel dining room for a meal. Bell did not unlock the Kid's handcuffs "so the prisoner could eat supper." He says that the Kid, swinging the "dangling handcuffs, felled the guard, snatched his revolver and killed him." He says that Pete Maxwell "ran an adobe roadhouse for ranch hands," but he merely had a residence there. The author has the Kid entering Maxwell's room with a pistol "in his hand," but the Kid carried no gun, and none was found on him. He also misspells Wayne Brazel's name as Brazil.

He is also wrong in having a Dr. Henri Stewart, of Indian Territory, riding with Sam Bass. No such person was ever in the Bass gang. He tells of the robbery at Coffeyville by the Dalton gang, but he does not say why Bill Doolin was not with them. He has Rose Dunn married to Bitter Creek Newcomb, but that is not true, and he repeats the old legend about her (as Rose of Cimarron) carrying ammunition to Newcomb during the battle at Ingalls. He is in error in having the Dunns telling Heck Thomas the whereabouts of Doolin's hiding place and having the marshal surrounding the house with nine or ten possemen. Doolin was killed by Heck Thomas outside as he was moving his family, and the author does not seem to be sure that Thomas killed the outlaw.

He has Belle Starr's father operating a livery stable and blacksmith shop in Carthage, Missouri, but he operated an inn. Again he has the James boys and the Youngers robbing a bank at Liberty, which is not true. He also has Calamity Jane born "about 1848," but Jane herself said that she was born in 1852. He also says that the hanging of Cattle Kate and Jim Averill eventually grew into the Johnson County War. He says that the man who killed Johnny Slaughter during a stage holdup by the Collins gang was "an unidentified bandit." If the author had done a little more research, he would have learned that the killing was done by Little Reddy McKemmie, and the other gang members banished him from the gang because of it. He says that the Union Pacific train robbed by this gang had stopped for water, but it had been flagged down by the station agent under duress.

He has the Bass gang riding into Round Rock and says, "Each wore a belt holster, with the butt and hammer of a six-gun in plain view, ready for fast drawing." That is untrue. The outlaws knew that there was a city ordinance against wearing guns, and they tried to keep them hidden beneath their coats, but in spite of their efforts the suspicious bulges were noticed by a couple of law officers. And it was their inquiry about the guns that started the battle in which the two lawmen were shot—one fatally—Barnes was killed, and Bass was fatally wounded, to die two days later.

The author misnames Henry Newton Brown as George Hendry [sic] Brown. He does not include Brown among those hanged by the mob for the Medicine Lodge Bank robbery. It is true that he was shot and killed first, but he was also hanged, dead, with the others. He is also mistaken in having Black Jack Ketchum born and living most of his life in New Mexico. He was born in West Texas. He is also mistaken in having the Ketchum gang holding up the Colorado and Southern at the same place four different times. It was held up three times, twice by the whole gang except for Black Jack and the third time by Black Jack alone. The author's accounts of these train robberies are wrong; he has Black Jack in the robbery just before the battle with the officers at Turkey Canyon. Black Jack did not take part in that robbery because the others were angry with him and had virtually kicked him out of the gang.

The author then writes that Black Jack was shot in the shoulder and was captured a few days later. Then in August the author has Sam Ketchum holding up the train for the *fifth* time and says that conductor Frank Harrington shattered Sam's arm "with a shotgun blast." It was Black Jack who was attempting this last (and the third) hold-up. He then says that Sam was "captured at a nearby ranch," but it was Black Jack who was captured, picked up the next morning as he sat propped up by a tree on the railroad right of way. The author says that a doctor amputated Sam's arm, but that blood poisoning had set in and, "unaware he was dying, he boasted of his brother's [Black Jack's] banditry."

This author then says that Black Jack Ketchum was tried for the murder of Sheriff Farr and was convicted, but Black Jack was nowhere near the fight that took Farr's life. He was convicted and given a death sentence for train robbery, because New Mexico had just passed a law making train robbery an

offense punishable by death. He is also mistaken in having Howard Benson trying to rob the Southern Pacific train with Ben Kilpatrick near Sanderson, Texas. The outlaw's name was Ole Beck, and he was a former cellmate of Kilpatrick's. On page 51 is a full-page picture of four men; the author claims they are the James and Younger brothers, but there is no resemblance to the real outlaws. The picture has been published several times before, and proved not to be the James and Younger boys; one of the men in the picture made a positive identification of the others.

62. ELMAN, ROBERT. Fired in anger. The personal handguns of American heroes and villains, by Robert Elman. Introduction by Harold L. Peterson. Garden City, New York, Doubleday & Company, Inc., 1968. Cloth.

The author is mistaken in having Belle Starr and Emma Jones burn down a store in an Arkansas village and a stockman named Patterson getting Belle released from jail. He writes that "Belle paid him back by 'entertaining' for a while; he was the only one of her many lovers who wasn't an outlaw." According to the *Police Gazette* this happened in Dallas, but in truth it never happened at all and is only another of the many legends about Belle. The author repeats that old legend about Blue Duck losing Belle's $2,000 in a poker game at Dodge City and Belle holding up the house to get her money back. That never happened either; in fact, Belle was never in Dodge City. He has Blue Duck "a white renegade," but he was an Indian. He writes that Jim Reed was killed by John T. Morris in a gun battle, but there was no battle. He is also mistaken in having Harry Young the bartender at the saloon in which Wild Bill Hickok was killed.

The author has Dave McCanles a horsethief, which he was not, and Hickok a guard of the Overland band of horses, but he was only a stable boy. He is mistaken in having Wild Bill a deputy U.S. marshal at Fort Riley, Kansas, and in claiming that he was both sheriff and city marshal of Fort Hays. He was city marshal at Hays City.

After his fight with some soldiers, the author says, Hickok hid in a friend's house for a month, but that is another legend. The author seems to believe that because Hickok knocked down John Wesley Hardin (which he never did) the Abilene city fathers fired him.

He writes, "Wild Bill's career in Abilene was bloody, beginning with two killings on the day he became marshal and marked by continued gunplay until the local authorities dismissed him a year later for resorting to violence more often than seemed necessary." Wild Bill did not last a year as marshal, and he did not kill anyone on the day he took office. The only two men he killed during his entire stay in Abilene were Phil Coe and his own deputy and friend, Mike Williams, whom he killed by mistake. The author has Captain William R. Massey, a poker player named Frank in the game with Wild Bill when he was killed. He says that when Wild Bill's body was taken to the undertaker "several guns were found tucked in his clothing."

He is also mistaken in saying that Hickok "spent most of 1872 as marshal of Hays again [sic], where he had somehow made his peace with the officers of the army post." Hickok never went back to Hays after his residence there. The author says that Jack McCall, after killing Wild Bill, "tried to shoot bartender Harry Young but the Colt misfired." Harry Young was not the bartender at

Saloon Number Ten, where the killing took place.

In his section on Heck Thomas the author has Heck's brother Jim's train robbed of $2,000 by the Bass gang on February 22, 1876. The robbery took place on that date in 1878, and the loot was only $1,280. After the robbery, the author says, "they pulled four more robberies," but the Bass gang robbed only four trains altogether. He has Heck shot through the cheek during the Hutchins robbery, but that is untrue. He has both Thomases chasing Bass over Texas and says that when they were joined by a "small detachment of Texas Rangers" they killed several of the gang and captured several more. The only one they killed was Arkansas Johnson in a battle at Salt Creek, and the only ones they captured were Jim Murphy and his father, who were not in the Bass gang at the time. He repeats that legend about Heck Thomas fooling the Bass bang by cutting up newspapers in the shape of money and giving it to the robbers, thus saving the company $22,000.

The author makes perhaps his biggest mistake when he writes: "On that date [July 19], the streets of Austin [sic] became a battle ground as the gang decided to make a stand right in the middle of town." The battle took place in Round Rock, some miles north of Austin. "It was not Heck," he writes, "but one of the Rangers who fired the shot that killed Bass." Heck Thomas was not in Round Rock at the time.

"No one kept track of whose bullets felled at least three other badmen," the writer continues. But only two outlaws were killed, Bass and Barnes. Only two others were in the gang, Jackson and Murphy, but the author writes: "The gang numbered about a dozen at this time. Several threw down their arms and surrendered; a few got away, but they were finished as a train-robbing outfit."

In his section on Bat Masterson he says that Bat, the Earps, and Bill Tilghman "killed or captured so many rustlers, horse thieves, murderers, train and bank robbers that no authority has been able to estimate the total." A great piece of exaggeration. He is also mistaken in having Masterson and Wyatt Earp running Clay Allison out of Dodge.

He is another who has Ben Thompson in Sweetwater, Texas, protecting Bat Masterson after Bat was shot by Sergeant King. Thompson was never in Sweetwater. Again the author writes: "It was said that Masterson literally batted Sweetwater into a law-abiding town, and the name Bat was his from then on." But Bat never served as a bouncer in Sweetwater, as this author also claims.

He is also mistaken in having Wyatt Earp the city marshal of Dodge and Bat Masterson a deputy in Tombstone. During his stay in that city Bat was a gambler. The author writes as though Benjamin Simms, Mrs. Zerelda James's second husband, died leaving her a widow, but they had separated before he died. He writes: "Only one of the Dalton boys, Bill, seemed to be staying out of trouble." Bill was an outlaw; several other Dalton brothers were honest farmers. He also says that Cherokee Bill's mother was a Cherokee and his father a half-blood Sioux, but his father was a mixture of Mexican, white, and Sioux, and his mother was one-fourth Cherokee, one-half Negro, and one-fourth white. He also says that former deputy Isaac Rogers was acquainted with Cherokee Bill's sweetheart, Maggie Glass. He should have been, for she was his cousin. The author's account of how Cherokee Bill got his nickname is one I have never seen before and a doubtful one.

Altogether, however, in spite of the errors about the gunfighters, there is much in this book to interest and enlighten gun buffs.

63. ELMAN, Robert. "Wild Bill" Hickok. By Robert Elman. . . . [Hartford, Conn., 1969]. Stiff pict. wrappers.

This is Number 3 of the Lawman Series published by the Colts Firearms Company. It is a pamphlet reprint of the author's section on Wild Bill in *Fired in Anger* (entry 62 above) and so contains the same errors. The author has Wild Bill killing twenty-one men. He has Dave McCanles stealing horses, and he seems to believe that Wild Bill fought ten "rustlers," including Dave McCanles, though he says that at the trial only three were mentioned. He also has Hickok performing some miraculous shooting stunts.

He is also mistaken in having Hickok city marshal of Fort Hays. He was marshal of Hays City. He is also mistaken in having Hickok go to Abilene, Texas, and serve as city marshal there. Of course, it was Abilene, Kansas. In one place he quotes Harry S. Young, a most unreliable writer. Of the killing of a buffalo hunter by Hickok at Abilene, the author writes: "Unfortunately, and apparently through no fault of Hickok's, the buffalo hunter was only one of a succession of Abilene hellions—including the notorious Phil Coe—who died in gunfights with the marshal." Hickok did not kill a buffalo hunter while he was in Abilene; Phil Coe and Hickok's own deputy were the only men he killed there.

The author says that the deputy was accidentally killed when he got in the line of Hickok's fire, but Hickok, not knowing who he was, killed his deputy deliberately as he came from behind a building to aid Hickok. He has Hickok knocking down John Wesley Hardin, but I have never seen this claim anywhere else (except, of course, in *Fired in Anger*). Hardin in his autobiography does not mention such an act. The author is also wrong in having Hickok going back to Hays and serving as marshal again. That was one place he avoided. He also has Hickok pursuing Mrs. Lake all over the country trying to persuade her to marry him, but it was she who wanted to marry Hickok.

He is mistaken in giving the first name Frank to William Massey, one of the poker players with Wild Bill when he was killed.

64. EMRICH, DUNCAN. Folklore on the American land, by Duncan Emrich. Boston-Toronto, Little Brown and Company, [1972]. Cloth.

This bulky book contains short chapters on Jesse James and Sam Bass with a mention of other gunmen. The author is mistaken in having Jesse James killed on April 4, 1882. He was killed on April 3 of that year. He is also mistaken in saying that Jesse was hanging a picture when he was killed. He was merely straightening it. He is also wrong in saying that Jesse took off his guns and placed them on a chair and "stood on a bed" to fix the picture. It was the other way around. He placed the guns on the bed and stood on a chair, which would be much more sensible.

He is mistaken in saying that Bass went to "the Dakotas with a trail herd from the Collins ranch," where the herd was sold. But the herd was sold in Kansas, at that time the cattle market, and

Collins owned no ranch but was a bartender. He also says that the Bass gang "planned a bank holdup on Friday, July 19, 1878," but they planned the robbery for Saturday, July 20, and had ridden into town on the 19th to have a final look at the bank. He also says that the money from the robbery of the Union Pacific train was "10,000, or more"; it was $60,000. In parentheses he states that one Ranger was killed in the battle at Round Rock, but the only lawman killed was Grimes, a deputy sheriff, who had, however, been a Ranger at one time.

65. FALLWELL, GENE. The Texas Rangers. A factual illustrated account of the nation's oldest and most famous law enforcement officers since 1823 ..., [by Gene Fallwell]. Connell Printing Co., 1959. Wrappers.

In a little section about Sam Bass the author leaves the impression that he was killed on July 19, 1878, when he writes, "thus ending the ten-month outlaw career of Bass on his twenty-seventh birthday." He was shot on the 19th all right, but did not die until the 21st, his birthday. He also leaves the impression that Bass was killed instantly.

66. FARRELL, CLIFF. The mighty land, by Cliff Farrell. Garden City, New York, Doubleday & Company, Inc., 1975. Cloth and boards.

Even at this late date writers continue to make inexcusable errors and repeat as history legends that have long been discredited. This author repeats the tall tale that Billy the Kid killed twenty-one men, one for each year of his life— but he does say, "It has been said. . . ." Many of his errors are preceded by such phrases as, "It was said," and, "The fight [at Rock Creek] was said to have been over the favors of a woman." He is mistaken in placing Rock Creek Station in Kansas. It was in Nebraska. He is also mistaken in saying that this fight "was the first of many Hickok six-shooter episodes."

He says that Ben Thompson ran a saloon and dealt crooked cards "and killed victims who objected," but Thompson killed no one while in Abilene. He writes that Hickok "added to his edge over Thompson by killing Thompson's partner, Phil Coe—without retaliation by Thompson." When Coe was killed, Thompson was not in Abilene, but was laid up with a broken leg. He is also wrong in saying that this killing "was the climax of the smouldering feud with Thompson and there seems little doubt the basic cause was a dispute over brothel and saloon graft." The enmity between Coe and Hickok was over a woman.

He says some things about Hickok that no other writer seems to have known, such as, "After Hickok had worn the badge in a frontier town, that place was no longer rated as really tough." He also has Hickok walking the line "each night, nattily dressed, sometimes in evening clothes complete with top hat and cape lined with scarlet silk." This I would like to have seen, back in those wild days. In telling of the murder of Wild Bill, the author says that he sat with his back to a door "rather than trouble a friend to change places," but he did argue and plead with others to let him change seats with them, and they only teased him for his superstition.

The author spells Reni's name as Bene and says, "Ben Ficklin . . . had Jules [Reni] strung up by the neck," a statement I have not seen elsewhere. He adds that Reni "was tough" and that he

was still alive when he was cut down. Nor have I seen elsewhere his statement that Slade was taken to Chicago for treatment of wounds suffered in his fight with Reni. (When I say, "I have not seen . . .," I mean that I have read practically every book that has been written about western outlaws, yes, thousands of them.)

The author misspells some names, writes others incorrectly, such as Haywood for Heywood and John Henry Brown for Henry Newton Brown. He has Frank Hulfish in the robbery of the Union Pacific by the Collins gang. I suppose he means Bill Heffridge, for he was the one killed with Collins. He is also wrong in saying that Tom Nixon was the only one who "escaped the hand of the law," but Jack Davis (whom he does not mention) also evaded the law. He says Collins and Hulfish [sic] "were killed by officers near Ellsworth, Kansas," but they were killed at Buffalo Station. He is also mistaken in having Henry Underwood in this robbery and spending "years in an Indiana prison."

Again he is mistaken in having Bill Dalton failing to make it to Coffeyville with the Dalton gang "because of a disabled horse." It was Bill Doolin who failed to make it for that reason; Bill Dalton did not join the gang until it was Bill Doolin's gang.

In his account of the robbery of the bank at Medicine Lodge, Kansas, he is mistaken in saying that the robbers "left their leader dead on the bank steps." He writes that "the outlaw who was killed on the bank steps turned out to be John Henry Brown [sic]." We know this to be untrue, for Brown was killed by the mob that night after he had been captured and jailed.

The author has the killing of Pike Landsuky by Kid Curry all wrong, saying that they had a fist fight, with Curry "taking a terrible beating" and later securing a gun and killing an unarmed Landusky. They were both armed during their fight, and when Curry had Landusky on the floor, the latter was trying to get his gun from beneath his overcoat when Curry shot him.

He also calls the Oriental Saloon in Tombstone the Orient. He is also wrong in having twenty men in the gang that hanged Cattle Kate Watson and Jim Averill. There were only six, and this hanging was not "the spark that touched off the Johnson County War." There are other doubtful statements and unreliable "history."

67. FAULK, ODIE B. Arizona. A short history, by Odie B. Faulk. Norman, University of Oklahoma Press, [1970]. Cloth.

This author says that Ike and Billy Clanton "moved their operations from Mexico to Tombstone, where they hoped to get rich from the big payrolls of the miners and the rich shipments of bullion." They were not payroll robbers, nor did they work in Mexico. They were cattle rustlers. It was Old Man Clanton who robbed Mexican smugglers at Skeleton Canyon. He writes that the O K Corral fight lasted fifteen seconds. It was a short fight, but other historians allow them thirty seconds. He is also mistaken in saying that the fight actually took place in a nearby alley. Fremont Street could hardly be called an alley.

He is also wrong in saying that "the public sympathized with the Clantons, and several shots were fired from ambush at the Earps and their followers." He is also mistaken in saying that the Earps fled the territory before they could be brought to trial. They were brought to trial before Judge Wells Spicer, and

after hearing the evidence, the judge discharged them. His account of the robbery at Bisbee is also unreliable and meager.

68. FAULK, ODIE B. Tombstone. Myth and reality, [by] Odie B. Faulk. New York, Oxford University Press, 1972. Pict. cloth.

This book on a much-written subject is full of errors and misspelled proper names. On page 78 the author has John Carr elected mayor of Tombstone "following Randall's resignation," but John Clum was elected mayor in January, 1881, and John Carr in January, 1882. On page 90 he titles the photo the "Tombstone Courthouse," but though it is in Tombstone, it is the Cochise County Courthouse. On page 92 he has two banks in Tombstone, but Cochise County Bank came much later.

He has Russian Bill coming to Tombstone after applying for a leave from the Imperial White Hussars of Russia, and there "he dressed like an outlaw." How did an outlaw dress differently from the other citizens? He has Sandy King "a local thief" and says that Sandy and Russian Bill were caught and hanged for horse stealing. No doubt Russian Bill was hanged as a horsethief, but Sandy King had shot the finger off a store clerk's hand and was hanged because he was a general nuisance.

The author has the date of the incorporation of Tombstone wrong. It was incorporated in November, 1879, not in December of that year. He is also wrong in having the city council in the summer of 1881 passing an ordinance against carrying concealed weapons. It was passed in the spring of 1880. He misspells the name McLaury as McLowery (also spelled McLoury, he says) throughout, and his statements about Johnny Ringo are incorrect.

He is also mistaken in saying that Wyatt Earp left San Bernardino, California, and went to Lamar, Missouri, in 1869. On page 139 he has the wrong date for Wyatt's arrest in Wichita, and Doc Holliday was not as tall as the author claims. He leaves the impression that Doc went to Texas and directly to Fort Griffin, but he went first to Dallas to practice dentistry. There he killed a man and escaped to Fort Griffin. The author is also wrong in saying that Doc Holliday, "after several arrests at Fort Griffin," went to Denver. He escaped, with the help of his girlfriend, Big-Nose Kate, to Dodge City.

Virgil Earp did not go to Tombstone to assist L. F. Blackburn. And Wyatt was not dismissed as a deputy sheriff; he resigned. He did not work as a shotgun messenger for Wells Fargo after his resignation as deputy sheriff, but before he became deputy. Wyatt did not deputize Virgil Earp to arrest Curly Bill Brocius, and the city council did not appoint Virgil as the city marshal; he was only acting city marshal. The author is also mistaken in calling the Earps a gang. He says that Buckskin Frank Leslie was a member of this gang, but he was not. Nor did Wyatt run against Sippy on January 4, 1881.

In spite of the common legend, Bob Paul did not change seats with Bud Philpot just before the stage holdup near Drew's ranch. The author also seems to think that the woman called Sadie (page 148) is different from Josephine Sarah Marcus, but they were one and the same person. Most of the author's statements on page 149 are ridiculous.

His street map on page 150 is entirely wrong. The location of the Episcopal Church is incorrect; the site of the Bird Cage Theater is wrong; and the spot where Curly Bill shot Fred White is wrong, and the date was not 1881 but October, 1880. The location of the O K Corral fight is wrong, as is the site of the ambush of Virgil Earp. On the following page (151) he has the entire fight in the wrong location and quotes an unreliable statement from an eyewitness who claims that "Frank McLowery [sic] was sitting on his horse and at the first fire fell mortally wounded, but game to the last he returned the fire wounding Virgil in the arm, leaving that member useless for any further gunplay in the life of Virgil Earp." It was later, on December 28, that Virgil was shot from ambush and wounded in the arm.

He misspells Zwing Hunt's name as Zweig. I thought this to be a typographical error, but the spelling is repeated in the index. The author is also mistaken in having Wyatt going from Arizona to San Francisco. He first went to Colorado with Doc Holliday. He also has him meeting Josephine Marcus in San Francisco, but that is incorrect. He is also wrong on the date of Wyatt's death; he died on January 13, not January 3, and his funeral was not held in Colman. There are many other mistakes, too many to list without tiring the reader. And the author is a teacher of history.

69. FAULKENBERY, JESSIE D., SR. Gathering the past, by Jessie D. Faulkenbery, Sr. Snyder, Texas, Raun's Publishing Company, [n.d.]. Stiff pict. wrappers.

This privately printed little book depicts some memories of an early settler and tells about some of the post–Civil War western outlaws, but the author seems to be afraid of naming names. He tells about his father meeting four outlaws, and from what he says they must have been Sam Bass's gang. He writes: "While riding the range one day, he [his father] encountered four men on horseback who asked him the way to Round Rock. . . . They turned out to be four Texas outlaws who were going to Round Rock to rob a bank. All got killed, for the people there had been warned that the gang was coming (I have seen the leader's grave and it wouldn't do to tell to [sic] much for there are books written on that subject already)" We know that not all the gang members were killed: Frank Jackson made his escape, and Jim Murphy did not take part in the fight. There are some misspelled words, and one wonders about the spelling of Jessie. There is some mention of train robberies and cattle rustling.

70. FENLEY, FLORENCE. Heart full of horses, by Florence Fenley. Final compilation by Belle Fenley Edwards. San Antonio, Texas, Naylor Company, Book Publishers of the Southwest, [1975]. Pict. fabricoid.

This book of horse stories was published after the author's death; many of them were taken from the writings of years past. Her book is included in this work. It contains a story entitled "Don (the Horse That Took Billy the Kid to Safety on a Hundred Mile Ride)" by my late old friend Jack Potter, who knew Billy the Kid while he was managing the New England Cattle Company at Fort Sumner. Potter has the wrong date for the capture of the Kid at Stinking Springs by Garrett's posse. He gives it as December 22, 1880. It was a day later, the 23d. He has the killing of Bell all wrong and misspells Olinger's name as Ollenger and Godfrey Gauss's name as

Goss. Otherwise it is an interesting horse story.

71. FIELDER, MILDRED. Wild Bill and Deadwood, by Mildred Fielder. Seattle, Superior Publishing Co., [1965]. Cloth.

This is largely a book of interesting early pictures. In her text the author tells nothing new but does make some errors, such as misnaming Rock Creek as Rock Springs. She says that Texas Jack Omohundro was killed in 1876, but he died of pneumonia on June 28, 1880. She is also mistaken in having Con Stapleton a member of the poker game in which Hickok was killed. It was Charlie Rich.

She lists the true and false incidents in Wild Bill's life and says: "take them or leave them, nobody seems to be sure of any facts." It is the duty of one who is writing history to learn the facts and correct the falsehoods. She occasionally quotes J. Frank Dalton (the old man who claimed to be the original Jesse James). She quotes one account that says that Wild Bill was playing seven-up when he was killed. He was playing poker, his favorite game. There is no evaluation of the many quotations, the author leaving it to her readers to decide which are true and which are false. She says that Wild Bill, while marshal of Hays City, killed "several soldiers," but he wounded only two, one of whom died. She also repeats the legendary story about a Wild Bill show in Niagara Falls, during June, 1870. As an afterthought she correctly states that the show took place in 1872. She is mistaken in stating that Wild Bill received $1,000 a month for his services as marshal of Abilene. She has Hickok in Evanston, Wyoming, in 1873, where, she says, he was "convicted of riot and assault on the sheriff and fined fifty dollars and costs." There is no evidence that Hickok was in Evanston. There were several other Wild Bills in the West at that time, and this one was probably Wild Bill Kress. There are also errors in the captions of some of the pictures.

"The Phil Coe incident," she writes, "occurred while he (Wild Bill) was marshal of Junction City, across the Republican River, and about three miles west of Fort Riley; Phil Coe's cousin was Jack McCall who later murdered Wild Bill at Deadwood." Such a statement is ridiculous. The killing of Coe took place in Abilene, and McCall was no kin to Coe. Except for its pictures this book is of little historical value.

72. FIERMAN, Dr. FLOYD S., and Dr. JOHN O. WEST (EDS.). Billy the Kid, the cowboy outlaw; an incident as recalled by Flora Spiegelberg, edited by Dr. Floyd S. Fierman and Dr. John O. West. [Philadelphia], Press of Morris Jacobs. Reprinted from the American Jewish Historical Quarterly, Vol. LV, No. 1 (September, 1965). Wrappers.

The tale Flora Spiegelberg tells is the substance of which legends are created. She has Billy the Kid robbing stagecoaches and doing other things that never happened. "Trying to escape, he was shot and killed by the sheriff," she writes, but we know that that is untrue.

"In 1878," she recalls, "Billy the Kid still continued his bold holdups in parts of Southern New Mexico. He spread such fear that business men hesitated to travel alone or even in stagecoaches." Whatever else could be said of the Kid, he was not a robber of stagecoaches. The editors of this little pamphlet know,

however, that this account of Billy the Kid by Flora Spiegelberg is merely a folk tale.

73. FLETCHER, BAYLIS JOHN. Up the trail in '79, by Baylis John Fletcher. Edited with an introduction by Wayne Gard. Norman, University of Oklahoma Press, [1968]. Boards.

This little book contains a chapter devoted to the Big Springs robbery of the Union Pacific by Joel Collins and his gang. The author makes the mistake of calling M. F. Leech by the name Billy Lynch. He also tells a story about Leech following the robbers that is different from those told by historians. He says that his group joined a Texas outfit that was "also delivering cattle to an agency" and that they later learned that the Texas outfit was really Sam Bass and his gang, who, on their way home, robbed the Union Pacific. It was not Bass's gang, and they were not driving cattle just before the robbery. The author also says they "buried the loot, fled to Ogallala and separated."

The author has a cowboy arriving at the station while the robbers were waiting for the train they were to rob and says that the man escaped during the holdup and went to Julesburg. He then returned east to Omaha, sought the general superintendent, and told him who had held up the train. The author is also mistaken when he says that the gang got $1,000 from a small safe.

He gives Bill Heffridge the name Henry, and he gives the names Charley, Shorty, and Dutchy to three of the robbers. That will be news to historians. He gives Jim Thompson the name Thomas, and he puts the killing of Collins and Heffridge in the wrong place. According to him the wife of Heffridge identified him as her husband just before he was buried, crying, "That's Henry, my husband!" That never happened either. He is also wrong in saying that Jim Berry was killed "while resisting arrest"; he was shot by Sheriff Glasscock while he was running away. The author is also wrong in having Joel Collins offering to join a posse to hunt the bandits. In fact, he has Collins leading a "brave band of cowboys" who "scoured the plains for many miles around Big Springs." He has the robber gang dividing the spoils long after they actually did so.

He has Frank Jackson wanting to kill Jim Murphy because he was reported to be a traitor, but it was Jackson who defended Murphy from the other members of the gang, and he is wrong in having Bass his protector. He is also wrong in having Murphy mailing a warning to Sheriff Everheart, of Grayson County, from Belton that the Round Rock bank was to be robbed. He sent the warning letter to Major Jones of the Texas Rangers. He has Dick Ware fatally shooting Bass in Round Rock, but no one knows for certain who shot Bass.

It is disappointing that the editor, who is an authority on Sam Bass and has written the best biography of this character, did not call attention to the author's many errors. Perhaps he disliked criticizing another's work, but he could at least have added his corrections in footnotes.

74. FLOREN, LEE. John Wesley Hardin, Texas gunfighter, by Lee Floren. [New York, Macfadden-Bartlett Corporation, 1962]. Stiff col. pict. wrappers.

Typical of the pocketbook accounts of western outlaws, this one is full of errors and unreliable statements. The author says that Phil Coe was one of Wild Bill's deputies in Abilene, but he was Hickok's enemy and one of the two men Hickok killed while in Abilene. He also spells Mannen Clement's given name as Manning throughout.

When Hardin was arrested in Florida, the author says his captor was a former Texas Ranger, but Armstrong was still a Ranger. He calls Jeff Milton by the name Jim. He claims that Bass Outlaw was an outlaw, but that is untrue. He has the killing of Dallas Stoudenmire wrong, as well as the killing of McRose. Most of his material on John Selman and Jim Miller is unreliable and he seems to think that Gonzales County is in East Texas.

75. FLORIN, LAMBERT. Ghost town album, by Lambert Florin. Seattle, Wash., Superior Publishing Co., 1962. Cloth.

This book deals with some ghost towns of the western states and has material on such gunmen as Alferd Packer (whose name he spells Alfred), Bob Ford, Ed O. Kelly (whose name he spells Ed O'Kelly), Soapy Smith, Dave Rudabaugh, Billy the Kid, Joaquin Murieta, and Black Bart. He repeats many of the legends about Murieta and writes that Russian Bill was hanged in Socorro because the population was "fed up" with his pranks, the climax being that he had shot a finger off a gambler trying to show off his marksmanship. That is not the reason Russian Bill was hanged. He was a horsethief, and it was Sandy King (hanged with him) who had shot off a finger of a store clerk. Both were hanged in Shakespeare, New Mexico, not in Socorro.

The author has Bob Ford building a saloon in Creede, Colorado, that "enjoyed a phenomenal business due to his popularity with the sporting crowd."

Ford's saloon was in a tent, and he was not very popular because of the cowardly way he killed Jesse James. The author has the fight at the O K Corral on October 27, 1881, but it happened on the 26th. (Too many writers are careless with their dates.) He says that only Doc Holliday "escaped unscathed." Doc was shot; Wyatt Earp was the only one who was not wounded.

76. FLORIN, LAMBERT. New Mexico and Texas ghost towns, by Lambert Florin. Drawings by David C. Mason, M.D. . . . [Seattle, Wash.], Superior Publishing Company, [1971]. Pict. stiff wrappers.

Of Socorro the author writes: "The town, during the old, wild days, was the current hangout of Russian Bill. Not actually a killer, Bill only liked to pose as one. He suffered from a compulsion to stay in the public eye and the only way he knew how to do it was to keep up a constant stream of practical jokes. The town's patience grew thin, and one Christmas Eve, reached the breaking point. The main hotel boasted of a card room, as well as a dining hall, and it was there Bill played his last game of poker. He got drunk and bragged about his marksmanship, proving how good he was by expertly shooting one finger from the hand of one of the players. The rest of the gamblers grabbed him by the scruff of the neck, read a charge against him of 'being a damned nuisance,' and hanged him right then and there in the hotel dining room."

That is entirely wrong. Russian Bill was hanged in Shakespeare, New Mexico, with Sandy King. He did not shoot the finger off another gambler. It was Sandy King who shot a finger off a store clerk. Russian Bill was not gambling, and he was hanged as a horsethief.

In his chapter on Shakespeare the author states that Russian Bill was a fugitive from Russia, which is untrue; but he does correct his earlier statement that Russian Bill and Sandy King were hanged in Shakespeare, not Socorro.

77. FLORIN, LAMBERT. Tales the western tombstones tell. By Lambert Florin. . . . Seattle, [Wash.], Superior Publishing Company, [1967]. Cloth.

This book deals with the tombstones of various western states and has some material on several outlaws and gunmen. There is some information on Calamity Jane, Pearl Hart, Joe Boot, Jack Galleher, George Ives, Boone Helm, Club-Foot George Lane, and Haze Lyons and on the hanging of the Plummer outlaws at Virginia City by the vigilantes. There is also some information on Wild Bill Hickok. The author is wrong in saying that Jack McCall bragged of killing Hickok in Cheyenne. It was Laramie where he bragged of this deed. He has Calamity Jane born "about 1848," but she claimed that she was born in 1852. Some of his other statements about Jane are also doubtful.

There is some material on Tom Horn and his murders and hanging. There is also some material on the hanging of Russian Bill and Sandy King at Shakespeare, New Mexico, and the neglect of their graves until Mrs. Emma M. Muir, Shakespeare's historian, placed a handsome stone at their grave.

78. GALBRAITH, DEN. Turbulent Taos, by Den Galbraith. [Santa Fe, N.Mex., Press of the Territorian, 1970]. Cloth. Also pub. in wrappers.

This book contains a section on Clay Allison, in which the author says that

Clay and an enemy dug a grave together and then stood at opposite ends and shot it out. All the accounts I have seen claim that the men fought with knives. The whole thing is likely a tall tale.

"With all his escapades," writes the author, "Clay Allison died a rather ignominious death. No sheriff, no rope, no young gunman beating him to the draw, no lurking desperado pumping him full of lead. In 1884, he was jarred from a freight wagon and a wheel ran over his head." That is not exactly correct either, for when he fell he hit his head on a front wagon wheel and received a concussion of the skull from which he died.

79. GAY, FELIX M. History of Nowata County, by Felix M. Gay. Stillwater, Oklahoma, Redland Press, 1957. Stiff wrappers.

This book has a small section on the Dalton boys, but the author is careless with his proper names. He says, correctly, that the Dalton boys' father was named Louis but spells the name Lewis. He also says that an older brother named Fred was a U.S. marshal; he was, but his name was Frank.

80. GILL, ROBERT T. The Southwestern Historical Wax Museum. . . . Biographical sketches and souvenir guide book, by Robert T. Gill. ₁Dallas, Texas₁ Southwestern Historical Wax Museum Corporation, ₁1964₁. Stiff wrappers.

This little pamphlet has sketches of characters from Jean Laffite to Texas Governor John Connally with some gunmen in between. It was published when the museum was in the State Fairgrounds of Dallas, but the museum has since been moved to Arlington, Texas, halfway between Dallas and Fort Worth.

Some wax figures have been added, such as those of Belle Starr and Sam Bass. During the unveiling of these two figures Wayne Gard and I were invited to make some comments about the history of these two characters.

There are short sketches on Frank and Jesse James. The author is mistaken in saying that they were living in California when their father died there. The author has Frank speaking several languages, which is not true, and he is also mistaken in saying that Frank left California when Jesse was killed and surrendered to Governor Crittenden. He also has Cole Younger saying that Frank was not at Northfield during the bank robbery there.

There are sketches of Cole Younger, Clay Allison, King Fisher, Bill Tilghman, Chris Madsen, Pat Garrett, Billy the Kid, and Bob Olinger. The sketch of Bill Longley is full of errors. In his sketch of John Wesley Hardin he is mistaken in saying that Hardin first got into trouble when he stabbed a schoolmate. Then he has him killing a Negro bully in self-defense, but he did not kill the Negro until the day after they had had their trouble. In his sketch of Ben Thompson the author is mistaken in saying that Thompson and King Fisher were killed "by unknown assassins," but these killers were well known.

In his sketch of Wyatt Earp the author is again mistaken in having Earp a deputy marshal at Wichita. He was a city policeman. In his sketch of Doc Holliday, the author has Doc going under the aliases Tom McCay and John Posers, something I have not seen elsewhere. In his sketch of Bat Masterson the author is mistaken in saying that when his brother Ed was killed Bat retaliated by killing "one of the attackers and mortally wounding the other." Bat took no part in that fight; Ed had killed them before he died. There are also sketches on the O K Corral fight and the hanging of Jim Miller with three others in a barn at Ada, Oklahoma.

81. GRANT, Blanche C. Carlsbad Caverns, by Blanche C. Grant. [N.p.], Privately printed, [n.d]. Stiff wrappers.

In one chapter the author mentions the "cattle war" of Lincoln County and misspells John Chisum's name as Chisholm and McSween's name as McSwain. He claims McSween was "another cattle king," but he was a lawyer, not a cattleman. In mentioning Black Jack Ketchum, the author says that he held up a train in Colorado and was shot in the arm. He was shot while trying to hold up a train in New Mexico.

82. GREEVER, William S. The bonanza West, by William S. Greever. Norman, University of Oklahoma Press, [1963]. Cloth.

The author says that Calamity Jane was born "about 1851," but she was born in 1852. He says that she "entered Deadwood for the first time in early August, 1876," but she had been there several weeks before Hickok was killed on August 2 of that year. I think that he is also in error when he says that Jack McCall lost a sack of gold dust in a poker game with Wild Bill the morning before Hickok was killed that afternoon. Where would a saloon bum get a sack of gold dust? He also says that McCall bragged of his killing of Hickok in Cheyenne, but most historians claim that this happened in Laramie.

The author says that most writers describe Calamity Jane as beautiful, but she was likely far from that. His account of Soapy Smith is unreliable.

83. GREGORY, Lester. True wild West stories, [by] Lester Gregory. London, Andrew Dakers, Ltd., [n.d]. Cloth.

Although the author has "true" in his title, there is very little truth in his text. Like so many others, he has the James boys and the Youngers first cousins, and he repeats this statement many times, but they were no kin. He says that Jesse was older than his brother Frank; Frank was born January 10, 1843, and Jesse was born September 5, 1847. He repeats the old story about Jesse giving the widow money to pay off her mortgage and has him using modern slang. He has the James gang riding into Northfield, going into a restaurant and ordering a meal. They did not stop to eat but went directly to the job they came for—robbing the bank. His entire account of the robbery is wrong. He also says that Jesse moved his family to St. Joseph in April. He was killed on April 3 and had been living in St. Joseph for some time. He is also wrong in having Frank James "twice tried in court and found not guilty." Frank surrendered and was pardoned.

He is also wrong in saying that Joseph Slade was hired by the merchants of Julesburg to clean up the town, and he has the killing of Jules Reni all wrong.

He says that Wyatt Earp's reputation began in Wichita, Kansas, where he was marshal, hired especially to get Mannen Clements, whose first name he misspells Manning. Earp was never marshal of Wichita, but a city policeman who did not have much standing among the other law officers. He has Earp stopping Clements from crossing a bridge entrance to Dodge, but that never happened. He also has Earp a U.S. marshal when he went to Tombstone and has the Clantons sending word to the Earps from the O K Corral that they were waiting there for a showdown. He has Wyatt with only three brothers, Virgil, Morgan, and Warren, forgetting the two others, James and Newton. He is also mistaken in saying that Billy Claiborne was also in the corral fight and was doing quite a bit of shooting. Billy had made tracks when he saw the Earps coming. The author calls Claiborne a brave man "who never shunned a fight." Billy did not show his bravery that day. The author even says that Doc Holliday "downed Claiborne with a couple of shots."

He is also wrong in saying that Ike Clanton was armed and spent many days in jail for this affair and that he begged to be placed in jail to "save him from a mob of angry citizens." That statement is indeed ridiculous.

He has the McCanles gang notorious outlaws who had been holding up stages and terrifying inhabitants and says that they were all "wanted men and known killers." According to him they were waiting at Rock Creek Station to rob the stage, and Hickok "was a green kid" driving the stage. He is also wrong in having Hickok a deputy marshal at Fort Riley. He then has him going to Abilene, "where his guns were kept busy." He also repeats some of the legends about Hickok's marvelous shooting stunts. He has Wild Bill walking down the street "with spur chains chunking, but he wore no spurs because he rode no horse. Though he says that Hickok's gun was kept busy in Abilene, he only killed two men there, Phil Coe and his own deputy, by mistake. He has Calamity Jane saving Hickok's life several times, and says, "When he refused to take her advice he lost his life." She had nothing to do with his killing. The author is wrong in calling Jack McCall "a notorious gun-slinger."

The author is also mistaken in having John Wesley Hardin "just a boy when he killed a Northern soldier who had molested his sister." Nothing like that happened. He seems to think that this was the first man Hardin killed, but the first man he killed was a Negro named Mage. He confuses the Chisholm Trail with the Chisum Trail. He states that the trail-driving cowboys began carrying guns because of the Jayhawkers and that the cowboys' efficiency as gunmen blasted a clear trail through to the Kansas railhead." Cowboys had always carried guns, and their guns had no effect on the opening of the trail.

He evidently thinks that Billy the Kid was much older than he was when he left New York with his parents, for he says that Billy had to fight and show his pugilistic ability to hold his own there. He refers to the Kid as the boy "who had fought with bare knuckles in the dark alleys and back streets and found fresh excitement in the West, where men wore guns lashed to their thighs." Billy was only three years old when his parents left New York. He has the Kid's family "shiftless and never amounting to much," but his mother worked hard running a boardinghouse. He writes, "It is conceivable that young Billy Bonney more than once saw Wild Bill walking down the street's board walk," but Billy was never in any Kansas town where Hickok held forth. He also says that the Kid "was christened in a local church as William H. Bonney," but he was born a McCarty. The author joins the large list of writers in claiming that the Kid had killed twenty-one men by the time he was twenty-one years old. When he writes that the Kid learned to "bulldoze a steer," he evidently meant "bulldog," though the Kid was not that much of a cowboy.

He misnames John Tunstall as Mr. Turnbull, and has the killing of Tunstall entirely wrong. He says that Sheriff Brady and Deputy Hindman were killed in a fierce battle, but all the shooting was on one side. He also says that when Garrett captured the Kid he had twenty-one notches on his gun and that he was placed in jail at Mesilla. He was jailed in Lincoln after his trial in Mesilla, and he did not cut notches on his gun. The author leaves the impression that Garrett captured the Kid singlehanded. He also has the Kid killing his jailers "by a ruse, luring them one at a time into his cell." One can see how ridiculous this statement is. He does not mention the killing of Morton and Baker or the fight at Blazer's Mill or even the battle at Lincoln. He is also mistaken when he says that the Kid was killed on July 15; it was the 14th. He further says that the Kid was killed "before the sun set," but it was near midnight when he was killed. Of this killing he writes: "He came by night to a house in Fort Sumner where Garrett had previously forced him to surrender," but the only time the Kid surrendered was at Stinking Springs. He has the Kid sitting at a table pouring over a list of his enemies just before he went to the place of his death. That never happened either. The book is filled with ridiculous conversations and other errors too numerous to enumerate here. Why do authors write about subjects of which they know so little?

84. GRISHAM, NOEL. Tame the restless wind. The life and legends of Sam Bass, by Noel Grisham. Illustrations by Col. Gene Fallwell. Austin, San Felipe Press, 1968. Pict. cloth.

"Why add to the voluminous amount of literature on Sam Bass"? writes the author in his introduction. "Only to update, composite, inject a few details unrelated by other accounts, and to reinterpret the man and the legend." He injects some new details all right, but the trouble is that they are mostly untrue.

Though the author says that this book "contains new details," there is not much new except a lot of conversation that no one recorded at the time. The author is wrong when he says that Joel Collins had made four trips up the trail with cattle. He is also wrong in saying that they "met on Joel Collin's ranch." Collins owned no ranch. He was a bartender.

He tells us that one experienced drover was hired and that the others were inexperienced and apprehensive, but he had already said that Collins had made four trips up the trail and so should have known what it was all about. He writes that at Doan's Store near Red River one could "get all the ingredients necessary for that trail delicacy 'son-of-a-gun stew." One did not buy the ingredients for this dish at a store but got them from a freshly killed calf. Neither was it a trail delicacy. There was no time to prepare such a dish when one was on the trail. The author talks about tumbleweeds blowing about Doan's Store, but I am afraid that he would find no such vegetation at this point.

He has Joel Collins selling the herd of cattle in Deadwood, but they were sold in Kansas. He writes that "other Deadwood contemporaries with Bass and Collins were Kitty LeRoy and Mary Jane Canary [sic]," but that is incorrect. Calamity Jane did not arrive in Deadwood until just before Wild Bill Hickok was killed on August 2, 1876, and her name was not Mary. At that time Bass and Collins were just gathering a herd of cattle to take north.

The author is mistaken in having Joel Collins becoming well acquainted with the station agent at Big Springs. Collins never saw the station agent until the night of the robbery of the Union Pacific. I think that the author is mistaken in saying that "Collins and Heffridge [after the robbery] rode toward Texas by way of Leadville, Denver and Albuquerque." Going to Texas by way of these cities, especially the last, would certainly have been far out of the way. On page 42 the author says, "It was on September 26 that Collins and his two companions had gone into Buffalo Station." The date was September 25, and Collins had only one companion, Heffridge. The author writes that "Collins, Heffridge and Berry were overtaken and killed within a few days; . . . $40,000 had been recovered since Berry was carrying Nixon's $10,000 in addition to his own."

In another place this author has Berry and Nixon "starting for Missouri." He is also wrong in saying that Collins and Heffridge did not fire a shot, but there was a battle. He has Bass and Davis traveling toward Texas with a group of soldiers searching for the Union Pacific robbers, but they only had supper with them one night.

Another near miss occurs when the author says that Tom Spottswood "had joined the gang by February 23rd, 1878." He was in the robbery at Allen, Texas, on February 22 of that year. The author has Frank Jackson a student of medicine, but he was an apprentice tinner. He also has Jackson a cousin of Jim Murphy, but they were no kin. He says that Collins owned a saloon in San Antonio, but he was just a bartender. He also says that Collins owned a ranch near the city, but that, too, is incorrect.

He is mistaken in saying that Sam Bass became acquainted with Henry Underwood soon after starting to work for Mr. Carruth. Underwood did not arrive in Texas for about a year after Sam's arrival. He says that Julius Alvord, the conductor of the train robbed at Mesquite, shot Jackson in the shoulder and that Alvord was shot in the left arm but kept fighting until his ammunition ran out. The author says that Alvord went into the sleeping car and fell unconscious, but he went back into the train to get his six-shooter (he had been using a derringer). Neither Jackson nor Alvord was wounded.

The author has the Bass gang stopping at Salado on their way to Round Rock and has one of the gang going to a house to learn the news and, according to the author, learning that "a young Illinois cattle dealer Joseph G. McCoy, had just built, during the previous summer, a fine cattle market with loading pens and a hotel in Abilene, Kansas, at the end of the Chisholm Trail." He had already had Bass and Collins going up the Western Trail, and this was a long time after the Chisholm Trail was established. He is writing of Bass going to Round Rock in 1878, but the Chisholm Trail was established in 1868, ten years earlier.

He is also wrong in having Sheriff Everheart in Round Rock while the Bass gang was on its way there. He has Grimes a sheriff, though he was only a deputy. He has Bass saying that he had never killed a man and hoped he never would, but, according to the author, the moment Grimes asked him if he was carrying a gun, Bass shot him. He is also mistaken in having Bill Longley a sheriff. He misspells Henry Koppel's name as Kopperal. He has Jim Murphy, while the gang is on the way to Round Rock, dropping off at Old Town, as he told Bass, to look out for lawmen, but his excuse was to buy some horse feed. There are other mistakes.

85. GUTIÉRREZ, Juan José. The La Lutz I remember, by Juan J. Gutiérez. [N.p., n.d.]. Stiff pict. wrappers.

This little book contains a short account of Albert Jennings Fountain and Billy the Kid. The author has Billy's father dying "soon after the family moved to Coffeyville." He also writes "Mrs. Bonney found it difficult to support herself and her small son during those hard days. Eventually she married again, not knowing that her husband would die at the hands of her own son, Billy." She had not one but two sons to support, and Billy did not kill his stepfather. The author also has the Kid escaping from Pat Garrett by climbing up a chimney. The author must have had in mind the time Billy while he was just a schoolboy escaped from Sheriff Harvey Whitehall after he got in trouble for stealing some clothes from a Chinese while just a schoolboy.

86. HADLOCK, Adah. My life in the Southwest. The memoirs of Adah Hadlock, early day El Pasoan, amateur artist, champion golfer, avid wildcatter and gold seeker. Introduced and annotated by Kenneth A. Goldblatt. El Paso, Texas Western Press, the University of Texas at El Paso, 1969. Pict. cloth.

This has some material on the Apache Kid and a mention of Billy the Kid. The author says that Billy and Pat Garrett were good friends. "In fact," she writes, "they were pals and Pat had helped him many times to escape jail or from some gunman who was out to get him." In this she is very much mistaken. True, Garrett and the Kid played cards together, and it is claimed that they even stole cattle together, but Garrett never helped the Kid escape from any jail or protected him from any other gunman.

87. HALSELL, H. H. Cowboys and cattleland, by H. H. Halsell. Nashville, Tenn., Printed for the author by the Parthenon Press, [n.d.]. Pict. cloth.

This is the author's story of his life in early West Texas. He tells of the Marlow brothers and their fight with the mob. He misspells Siringo as Seringo, John Chisum as Chisholm, and Jesse Chisholm as Chisum. "John Chisum [sic]," he writes, "a half breed Indian, no kin to John Chisholm drove a herd, or rather piloted about the first herd, 600 steers, from Texas frontier, going north by old Fort Cobb, and it is presumed this is the origin of the Chisholm Trail." There is no truth in this. He is also mistaken in saying that "one of the first trail drives north from Texas was made by Oliver Loving, Sr." Loving never drove any cattle over the northern trail, except north to Denver from the Pecos.

He has Billy the Kid born on July 9, 1859, and follows the legend of his killing his first man at the age of twelve. Most writers about the Kid have him killing a man for each year of his life. This author has him killing his twenty-second man at the age of twenty-two. Of the killing of Carlyle at the Greathouse home, he writes: "The Kid offered to surrender on terms to Sutten [sic] and Jimmy Carlyle. Garrett agreed and sent these two men to the house. "When all efforts to arrive at terms failed, the two men returned to Garrett, but before they reached him a hail of bullets reached them and Carlyle, Sheriff Brady and George Hinderman [sic] were killed." The author evidently got his information from Fred Sutton's ridiculous account, which he wrote for

The Trail Drivers of Texas. We know that Brady and Hindman were killed in Lincoln at a different time and that Garrett was not present at the Greathouse fracas.

The author continues, "Later Garrett located the Kid in Fort Sumner, found where he was to sleep, slipped into his room, and when the Kid, during the night, came in, Garrett killed him." That is not true.

Of the herd Joel Collins and Sam Bass drove up the trail the author writes: "Collins started a herd from San Antonio to the Black Hills. On arrival there he got drunk and gambled off the proceeds. The herd belonged to his father and brother." That too is not true.

88. HAMMONDS, DOROTHY, and GEORGE HENDRICKS. The Dodge City story, by Dorothy Hammonds and George Hendricks. Illustrations by Dorothy Hammonds. Indianapolis, Kansas City, New York, Bobbs-Merrill Co., Inc., [1964]. Fabricoid.

This book contains an abbreviated story of Dodge City, Kansas, in its heyday, with material on Wyatt Earp, Doc Holliday, and Bat Masterson. The authors are mistaken in saying that Earp served Dodge City as marshal three different times and that he was the "most outstanding marshal the old West has ever known." He was never more than an assistant marshal, and his exaggerated reputation was due to his able press agent, Stuart Lake, not to his ability. Like so many others, these authors have Bat Masterson sheriff of Dodge City. He was sheriff of Ford County. They spell Bill Tilghman's name Tillman and make many other mistakes.

89. HANAUER, ELSIE V. The Old West: People and places, by Elsie

V. Hanauer. New York, A. S. Barnes and Co., [1969]. Cloth.

This unusual book is made up of drawings of various western characters made by the artist-author with a sketch of each character on the preceding page. Her information about most of the outlaws is full of errors. In her sketch of Murieta she states positively that there was such a man and says that he was captured by Harry Love and his Texas Rangers. What were Texas Rangers doing in California? She says that John Beidler was "the evil leader of the Montana Vigilantes," delighted in seeing men hanged, and "became known as the Red Butcher because of his psychotic brutality. This evil leader and his cutthroat followers rode roughshod over the country committing countless atrocities." He was no such character, though he was a terror to lawbreakers. She says that he "left a trail of an estimated 300 dead." She then says that Beidler fled the country and was never heard of again after settlers began to move in. This, too, is ridiculous.

Like so many others, this author has the Youngers related to the Jameses, which is untrue, and she says that Bob Ford received a $10,000 reward for killing Jesse James. He did not receive that amount. She says that Jesse rode with Quantrill in his early years, but it was Bloody Anderson with whom he rode. She seems to think that Jesse and Frank did not get along well and says that on one occasion Jesse turned on Frank with a gun. She also says that Ed Kelly was related to the Youngers. Her sketch of Calamity Jane is full of errors. She has Jane born and reared in Fort Laramie, Wyoming, and says that Jane met Wild Bill Hickok in 1867 and that "the two became very close." She is also mistaken in having Jane die on August 3. She died on August 1.

She is mistaken in having Wild Bill "sheriff of Hays City." This was a county job. She is another who has Clay Allison meeting his death when a wagon ran over his neck. He fell off the wagon and his head struck a wheel, causing a concussion. This author has Billy the Kid running away from home at the age of twelve after killing his first man, and she adds that "the half-witted hoodlum left a trail of blood across Arizona and New Mexico." She follows that old legend of the Kid killing twenty-one men, one for each year of his life.

In her sketch about King Fisher she says that he had a hundred men under his command and controlled a territory three hundred miles wide. She does not mention his death. She has Sam Bass going into the cattle business, but he only helped drive a herd up the trail for the first time. She says, "On July 18, 1878, Sam rode into Round Rock and was shot down by the waiting lawmen." This leaves the impression that he was shot immediately after he rode into town, but he was in a store buying tobacco when he was shot on the 19th, and he did not die until the 21st.

She does not have a good word for Wyatt Earp and says that "in his entire career [he] was marshal only in Dodge City." But he was not marshal in Dodge, only deputy marshal. She also says, "Gambling and prostitution were his main interests which paid a million dollars after a few years." He never made any such money in anything. She is also mistaken in saying that he killed Pete Stillwell in Tombstone. That happened in Tucson. She also says that Earp left Colorado, where he had escaped from Tombstone, "worth close to a half-million dollars," bought a ranch in California, "and married a girl from San Francisco." She is determined to make him a rich man, but he never was.

She is also wrong in having Buckskin Frank Leslie killing ten men in one day, starting with Billy Claiborne while he was tending bar at the Oriental Saloon. The woman for whose killing he was sent to prison was not his wife but a woman living with him. She says that Pat Garrett was assassinated by an unknown assailant, but it is pretty well assumed now that he was ambushed by Jim Miller, a hired killer.

Of Bat Masterson she writes: "The closest the ex-buffalo hunter ever came to being a marshal was a brief hitch as a policeman in Dodge. Convinced that he was not tempermentally suited to be a lawman, Bat left Dodge and wandered about the West as a gambler." After Bat's "short hitch" he was elected sheriff of Ford County and was a good one, effecting many arrests. She has the O K Corral fight in 1885 instead of 1881, and also says that Kate Fisher "felt nothing but scorn for any man until Doc Holliday crossed her path in Dodge City." Kate met Doc long before either of them went to Dodge. They met in Fort Griffin and went to Dodge together.

This author is also mistaken in having Henry Starr a nephew of Belle Starr. She misspells Harry Longabaugh as Longbaugh and is wrong when she says that Black Jack Ketchum "as a child . . . had a favorite game of hiding in the brush and shooting herdsmen." There are sketches of most of the western outlaws, and most of them of little value historically.

90. HARRIS, PHIL. This is Three Fork's country, by Phil Harris. [Muskogee, Okla., Hoffman Printing Co., 1965]. Stiff wrappers.

In a chapter on Belle Starr the author is in error when he says that Belle's husband, Sam Starr, was the son of "Old Sam Starr." He was the son of Tom Starr. He also has Cole Younger her "former husband." He intimates that the Youngers were in prison in Minnesota when Belle acquired her home at Younger's Bend, but the Youngers and the Jameses visited her there before they went to Minnesota. He is also wrong in saying that "the Youngers and Starrs had known each other for years."

91. HARRISON, FRED. Hell holes and hangings, by Fred Harrison. Clarendon, Texas, Clarendon Press, 1968. Cloth.

In his chapter on New Mexico the author states that Sheriff Brady led the posse that killed Tunstall, but that is not true. He writes that Governor Axtell asked for a ninety-day leave of absence "and swiftly left the Territory," and he is wrong in saying that Governor Sheldon replaced Axtell. He was removed for inefficiency and replaced by Lew Wallace. He gives Billy the Kid credit for killing Sheriff Brady, and he is also mistaken in saying that McSween "gathered forty-one gunmen and barricaded them within his home near the edge of the village." McSween's "gunfighters" were scattered through several houses in Lincoln, and his home was not on the edge of the village but right in the center of it. He has the battle at the McSween home lasting three days, but it was five.

He mispells Billy Claiborne's name as Clayborn and Bill Doolin's as Dolan. In his chapter on Indian Territory he says that Belle Starr "was never convicted" of a crime, but Belle and her husband, Sam, were in the Detroit House of Correction for nine months. He also says

that Jim Reed was "shot from ambush and killed," and he intimates that this happened immediately after he had returned from California.

In his chapter on Arizona he has Buckskin Frank Leslie installing "a pretty young housekeeper" at a ranch he was managing, and he says that Frank got drunk one day and forced his attention on her and "she slapped his face —hard." But she was a dance-hall girl with whom he had been living for some time. When Leslie killed her in a drunken quarrel, he was sent to the penitentiary at Yuma.

92. HART, WILLIAM SURREY. William S. Hart in Wild Bill Hickok. Los Angeles, Will A. Kistler, Printers, 1923. Pict. wrappers.

This book is evidently based on the movie Hart made about Hickok, and, like most movies, it is anything but history. He has the McCanles "fight" at what he calls Point of Rocks instead of Rock Creek. He repeats that fable about eight men fighting Hickok and has them all killed, unlike most other writers, who let two escape. He says that Hickok had to spend a year in the hospital in Kansas City and that he was a flute player. I have never seen that before. He has him killing twelve men at Hays City, twenty-five in Abilene, and nine in Ellsworth. Quite a killer.

He claims that when a young girl from Boston got off the train at Dodge City, Wild Bill fell in love with her and that she was the only love of his life. Hart has Hickok killing seven soldiers, after which he promised General Custer that he would never carry a gun again. Hart has Hickok sending McCanles' son Monroe (whom he misnames Lawrence) money every month after he killed his father. He has both Calamity

Jane and Jack McCall in Dodge and Wild Bill a gambler there. None of these characters was in Dodge City. He says that Calamity Jane was an illegitimate child and that Hickok was deeply in love with her—this after saying that the girl on the train was the only love of his life. The book is poorly written fiction that tries to appear to be history.

93. HASSRICK, ROYAL B. Cowboys. The real story of cowboys and cattlemen. [By] Royal B. Hassrick. [London, Octopus Books, Ltd., 1974]. Pict. cloth.

This author refers to Billy the Kid as William Bonny [sic] and makes a statement I have not seen before: that McSween transferred his property to John Tunstall when he was charged with embezzlement of the Fritz insurance policy. The author also repeats the legend of the Kid killing twenty-one men by the time he was twenty-one years old. He is also mistaken in saying that the chuck-wagon cook "might serve up a concoction of kidney stew affectionately referred to as son-of-a-gun stew." Kidney was not an important ingredient, and it was not thought of as kidney stew.

94. HAWGOOD, JOHN A. America's western frontier. The exploration and settlement of the Trans-Mississippi West, [by] John A. Hawgood. New York, Alfred A. Knopf, 1967. Cloth.

The author says that Wild Bill Hickok "was shot in the back, as every school boy knows, in a tavern brawl." There was no brawl, and Wild Bill was shot in the back of the head, not in the back. There is some mention of Calamity Jane, whose last name, Cannary, the author misspells as Cormody. He also misspells Stuart Lake's first name as Stewart.

95. HICKS, EDWIN P. Belle Starr and her Pearl, by Edwin P. Hicks. Little Rock, [Pioneer Press], 1963. Cloth.

The author intimates that Cole Younger was the leader of the gang that robbed the bank at Liberty, Missouri, but he was not. All through the book he has Cole constantly reading his Bible. I do not think he was that religious. He also says that Preston Shirley, Belle's older brother, had moved to Scyene, Texas, before the Civil War, but he went to McKinney, Texas, in Collin County. He has Belle running off with Cole and becoming pregnant by him.

He says that Belle's brothers were shot down, which is true, but the killings happened far apart in time. The author has the James boys and the Youngers robbing stagecoaches in California, but I do not believe this to be true. He also says that Belle dashed through the streets of Dallas filling the air with lead without the local law attempting to stop her. I find no record of that. He repeats the legend about Belle setting fire to a store, and a man named Patterson giving her $2,000 to get her out of trouble. Unlike most writers, he has this event take place "in a small prairie village."

This author has Cole Younger the father of Belle's daughter and has Belle sending Cole all the money she could raise for his defense after the Northfield bank robbery. The author repeats the legend about Blue Duck losing $2,000 that he had borrowed from her and says that when she learned of it she went to the gambling hall in Dodge City and held it up to get her money back. The author says that Sam Starr and John

West were cousins, but they were enemies and eventually killed each other.

He is mistaken when he has John
Middleton, lover of Belle, the same John
Middleton who rode with Billy the Kid.
When the latter Middleton left the Kid
at Tascosa, Texas, he was nearing middle age, and the John Middleton of Indian Territory was still a young man—
twenty-five years old, says the author.
He also says that Billy the Kid shot both
Morton and Baker and that Buckshot
Roberts shot Middleton at the battle of
Blazer's Mill, and "he had been at
death's door for weeks," but that is untrue. He has Roberts named Bill, but his
name was Andrew.

He is also wrong in saying that "other
companions of Middleton when he was
with Billy the Kid included the notorious Jim French, who later was one of
Belle's favorites, and Charlie Bowdre
and Tom O'Folliard. The John Middleton of Billy the Kid fame went to Kansas, where he lived at various places for
quite a few years. The author is also
mistaken in saying that Middleton left
the Kid's gang in 1880. He left the Kid
at the same time Henry Brown and Fred
Wayt left, and that was in the fall of
1878.

He has Middleton joining Belle Starr's
gang and falling in love with her. That
is not true. When John Middleton of
the Kid's gang left New Mexico, he went
to Sun City, Barber County, Kansas,
where he had a small grocery store.
After that he went to many little towns,
all in Kansas. The author has a Samuel
Wells with the James boys in the Northfield bank robbery, but there is no record
of anyone by that name in the robbery.

The author has evidently done some
first-hand research on his subject,
though in his list of sources he refers to
many books that are very unreliable,
such as Harman's *Hell on the Border*,
which he says "was most valuable" but
which I have found most unreliable. He
says that Belle was murdered by Jim
Middleton, John's brother, who believ-
ing that Belle had murdered John for
the money he carried in his saddlebags.
Most accounts have her murdered by
her neighbor, Edgar Watson, or by her
own son, Ed. Of late most of the evidence seems to point to her "husband,"
Jim July, as her murderer.

96. HILDRETH, Samuel C., and
    James R. Crowell. The spell of the
    turf. The story of American racing,
    by Samuel C. Hildreth and James
    R. Crowell. With 32 illustrations.
    Philadelphia and London, J. B.
    Lippincott Company, 1926. Pict.
    cloth.

Several pages are devoted to Frank
James as a betting commissioner at the
race tracks, the authors telling of his
honesty and of his earlier surrender to
Governor Crittenden. The authors are
mistaken, however, in saying: "One of
his family, I believe it was his mother,
had been shot and terribly wounded by
one of those cutthroats who fought for
neither side and preyed on unprotected
families of both. When this happened
he and Jesse pledged themselves to get
even with the world." Of course, we
know that Mrs. James's arm was blown
off by a bomb thrown by Pinkerton detectives and that the James boys had become outlaws before that happened. The
authors also mention the capture of John
Wesley Hardin and Bill Langley [*sic*],
the former given a life sentence and the
latter hanged. Their information concerning these two is all wrong.

97. HILLERMAN, Tony. The great
    Taos Bank robbery, and other In-
    dian country affairs, [by] Tony

Hillerman. Albuquerque, University of New Mexico Press, [1973]. Cloth.

There is a short chapter about Black Jack Ketchum and his robberies of the Colorado and Southern trains at exactly the same spot. The author states that the railroad company "put on some guards and they wounded Ketchum and caught him," but it was conductor Harrington who shot Black Jack. He is also mistaken in saying that "the rest of the gang got away." Black Jack attempted to rob the train alone. The author is also mistaken in saying that the gang "drifted over into San Miguel and Santa Fe County and got elected to the legislature."

98. HILTON, Tom. Nevermore Cimarron nevermore, by Tom Hilton. Fort Worth, Texas, Published by Western Heritage Press, [1970]. Cloth.

In this brief account of Cimarron, New Mexico, the author has some of his history confused. He claims that Clay Allison was crippled when he fought a duel in an open grave and received a terrible stab wound in the thigh. He was crippled when he accidentally shot himself in the foot while he was guarding a band of mules. The author has Allison shooting himself in the foot during a "bedlam of gun-made thunder and from a pitching deck of saddle" during a gunfight. He also has the killing of Chunk Colbert wrong and is certainly exaggerating the truth when he writes that when, Allison went to Dodge City, Wyatt Earp "hid out in the attic of a vacant building for two or three days until Allison left town."

He has Allison killed when he fell from a wagon and a wheel "crushed his neck," but the most reliable accounts have him falling on a wheel and fracturing his skull. He is also mistaken in saying that Elfego Baca held off "a hundred Texas cowboys for two or three days" who were "trying to take a prisoner from him." Baca had no prisoner with him during the fight. Like so many other authors he spells Ed O. Kelly's name as O'Kelly.

He seems to be very prejudiced against the Earps. He calls them "those great procurers of women, whose operators of gambling dens and saloons, those lawmen who used the law as protection while they murdered and stole, those fine men of the West, the brothers Earp." He is wrong when he claims that they came through Cimarron with "their crooked gambling equipment from Dodge City and that they were in search of a new location." They were on their way to Tombstone to seek some mining interests. He is also mistaken in saying that they had a group of dance-hall girls with them and that "as they were leaving Cimarron they first came in contact with the mad little dentist, Doc Holliday." They 'had known Holliday for some time and had been with him during their stay in Dodge City.

In his chapter on Tom Ketchum the author, who misspells his name as Ketchem, says that he "was probably a greater outlaw in his brief career than the James brothers." He is also mistaken when he says that conductor Harrington shot Ketchum "as he was forcing the opening of the strongbox in the express car." He had not gained entry to the express car. Like a few others, he is also wrong in saying that Tom's oldest brother, Berry, had started his brothers on the trail of outlawry. Berry was a respected rancher, but this author has Black Jack telling Governor Otero that his brother had started him on the life of crime. Aside from these few unreliable statements, this little book gives an interesting history of Cimarron.

The author seems to think that Black Jack wanted to die and that that was why he attempted to rob the Colorado and Southern alone. "He wanted to die," he writes, "sought the welcome release of death. Conscience ridden and alone, he wooed death, courted it with the passion of a lover and in the damning end, he wedded the old whore death. Took the stinking old bitch for his lawful wedded wife. How else does one explain his insane attempt to rob the same train for the third time, at the same place, and this time alone." The truth is that Black Jack had had a falling out with his brother Sam and the others who had robbed the train the second time and wanted to show them he could go it alone. Certainly he did not try it because he wanted to die. He exaggerates the amount of money the Ketchum gang got in the second robbery. He later says, "Most of the $10,000 lies in a shallow grave somewhere."

99. HOLLON, W. EUGENE. Frontier violence; another look, [by] W. Eugene Hollon. New York, Oxford University Press, 1974. Pict. cloth.

This author takes his readers all the way back to the landing of the Pilgrims and works his way west to show the violence in America. He writes: "It was during that war [the Lincoln County War] that Billy the Kid alone killed somewhere between a dozen or more than twenty-one men." If he was not sure, it was up to him, as a historian, to research the Kid's record. He also claims that Butch Cassidy was killed in Bolivia, South America, but it has now been proved that Butch visited his family in Circleville, Utah, in 1929. In fact, his sister has recently written a book telling about his return home. It is said that he died in the Northwest in 1936. [Publisher's note: See also *In Search of Butch Cassidy*, by Larry Pointer (Norman, University of Oklahoma Press, 1977.)]

Of Black Jack Ketchum the author writes: "He was finally captured in New Mexico in 1899, convicted of several local murders and robberies, was sentenced to be hanged." The New Mexico legislators had passed a law making train robbery a death penalty, and that is why Ketchum was condemned to be hanged. The author has him being moved from the Folsom jail to Clayton because they feared a rescue, but he was in the Santa Fe prison and was moved to Clayton for the trial.

The author writes that Wyatt Earp and Doc Holliday "stayed around Tombstone until the middle of 1883. By that time local citizens had had enough of them and 'requested' that they leave the territory." That too is untrue, as is his statement that Alexander McSween accumulated a "vast empire in Eastern New Mexico."

In telling of the murder of Tunstall, the author writes: "The sheriff's posse sent out to serve legal papers against the Englishman met him and five or six of his cowboys on the road en route to town. In a senseless act of violence, the deputies immediately opened fire and killed Tunstall." There were only four others with Tunstall, John Middleton, Dick Brewer, Robert Widenmann, and Billy the Kid. The author writes as though the whole posse opened up on Tunstall. He is wrong in writing that when Frank Baker and William Morton were captured by Brewer's posse they "murdered them on the spot"; they were murdered sometime later while on their way to Lincoln. He also has the battle at the McSween home lasting three days, instead of five.

On page 188 the author writes: "And before Sheriff Pat Garrett's pistol ended his [Billy the Kid's] career in May, 1881, he established a reputation of killing twenty-one men." Later the author corrected the date to July, 1881. He also has Black Jack Ketchum starting his outlaw career in Wyoming, but he started it in his home state, Texas. He misnames Joel Fowler as Jim, and he has Frank Dalton and Kit Dalton brothers, but they were no kin.

100. HOPE, Welborn. Four men hanging; the end of the Old West, by Welborn Hope. Oklahoma City, Century Press, [1974]. Cloth.

This little book gives a good history of Ada, Oklahoma, from its founding days. The author's father was the first banker of the town and an influential citizen. A dramatic photograph in the book shows the author as a small boy looking through an opening in the stable where Jim Miller, Joe Allen, Berry Burrell, and Jesse West were being hanged for the murder of Gus Bobbitt. There is mention of Billy the Kid, Pat Garrett, Wayne Brazel, and Russian Bill.

Of Russian Bill the author writes: "There is the case of the Russian Cossack officer in the 80s who had been reading about them [Tombstone outlaws], and who came over here to try his hand at being a desperado. On his first bid for fame he shot up the town of Shakespeare, New Mexico, . . . and for his pains he was promptly hanged from the ceiling of the dining room in the local hotel. The affair almost touched off an international explosion." We know that this tale is untrue. When the author writes about early life in Ada, his book is a valuable addition to his-

tory. But when he attempts to write about the outlaws of other states, I find him unreliable.

101. HUBBARD, Earle R. Sparks from many camp fires, [by] Earle R. Hubbard, [N.p., n.d., (ca. 1959)]. Stiff pict. wrappers.

This book contains some material on the Montana vigilantes, Henry Plummer, Jack Galleher, Buck Stinson, Ned Ray, Haze Lyons, and their hanging by the vigilantes. The author writes: "Upon Plummer's arrest, one of his gang forked a horse and rode the twelve miles to his ranch on the Madison River, to tell his wife. She at once grabbed a horse and got to town about a half hour after the hanging was over. She was grief stricken but being a fine lady, she did not bawl anyone out." The author evidently confused Plummer with Joseph Slade, for it was the latter's wife who rode into town to try to prevent the hanging of her husband. Plummer's wife had left him before he was hanged; she had gone to the East when she learned that he was a criminal. Slade's wife did not take his hanging so calmly.

102. HUGHES, Delbert Littrell, and Lenore Harris Hughes. Give me room! by Delbert Littrell Hughes as told to Lenore Harris Hughes. El Paso, Hughes Publishing Co., 1971. Pict. cloth.

This privately printed book is purported to be a biography of Marion Littrell, a sheriff of New Mexico, as told by his nephew to his wife, but little is said about Littrell until the latter part of the book. There is much general history about the state that has nothing to do with the subject. Several chapters are devoted to Clay Allison. In telling of the meeting between Allison and Wyatt

Earp at Dodge City, the authors depend upon the unreliable book about Earp written by Stuart Lake. They tell quite a bit about the Maxwell land grant and the troubles relating to it, including the murder of the minister, Tolbert.

They tell about the murder of John Tunstall and say that Billy the Kid was "a lone wolf who was always dodging the law, gambling, killing those who crossed his path and riding on." These statements are not quite true; the Kid was not quite such a callous killer. The authors make the mistake of saying that Dave Rudabaugh was wanted by the Las Vegas mob for robbing a train and stagecoach. They wanted him for killing a Las Vegas jailer. They also have Bat Masterson a "former marshal of Dodge," but he was the sheriff of Ford County.

They report a conversation concerning Black Jack Ketchum wherein a character claims that "Black Jack's correct name was Black Jack Kellison." Of course, that is incorrect. The same character claims that Black Jack was named for Black Jack Mountain in Arizona and that this mountain contained a cave in which Ketchum holed up. They tell about his robbing the Colorado and Southern train and his hanging, but both accounts are unreliable.

They say of Wild Bill Hickok: "Before becoming U.S. Deputy Marshal, he had killed many thieves and outlaws and was reputed to have numbered on the handle of his gun forty-three men in ten years." This statement is very unreliable—and a gunman did not call the stock of his pistol a "handle."

In telling of the fight between Sheriff Farr's posse and the Ketchum gang, the authors fail to mention who the outlaws were, but Black Jack did not take part in this fight. It was the fight at Turkey Canyon in which Sam Ketchum was fatally wounded.

103. HUGHES, JOHN R. The killing of Bass Outlaw. Austin, Texas, Brick Row Book Shop, 1963. Stiff wrappers.

This is a facsimile of a letter and telegram sent by Captain Hughes to General W. H. Mabry of the Texas Rangers, telling him of the killing of Ranger Joe McKittrict by Bass Outlaw, and of the killing of Outlaw by John Selman. The editor makes some mistakes in his foreword, such as having Selman killed by John Scarborough; Scarborough's first name was George. He also has Scarborough killed by Kid Curry on April 6, but he was fatally wounded by parties unknown and died on April 5. He says that Outlaw died on April 6, but the letter from Hughes was dated the 5th.

104. HUTCHENS, JOHN K. One man's Montana. An informal portrait of a state, by John K. Hutchens. Philadelphia and New York, J. B. Lippincott Company, [1964]. Cloth.

There are chapters on the Plummer gang and the hanging of Joseph Slade. There is also a chapter on Calamity Jane, but the author is mistaken when he writes: "Maybe it really was true that she [Jane] cornered his [Wild Bill's] cowardly murderer, Jack McCall, with a butcher knife." The author also says that he met Emmett Dalton after his prison term, but he is mistaken when he says that during the Coffeyville raid Emmett "was saved from lynching only by a quick-thinking coroner who told the townfolk that Emmett, too, had died."

105. JAMESON, HENRY B. Miracle of the Chisholm Trail, by Henry B. Jameson. [N.p.], Published by the Tri-State Chisholm Trail Centen-

nial Commission, [ca. 1967]. Stiff wrappers.

This book contains chapters on Tom Smith and Wild Bill Hickok. When the author writes that Hickok's father was a Harvard graduate, he makes a statement that I have never seen before. In his chapter on Hickok he writes, "Many of the stories about his escapades in Abilene and elsewhere are grossly exaggerated or were pure fabrications in the first place." Yet he follows old legends in saying that Hickok "wiped out the McCanles gang of robbers at Rock Creek, Nebraska, stage coach station in 1861." This author also has Hickok making a "deal with the famous Jesse James to lay off the rich Abilene payrolls and cattle receipts in turn for 'protection' from the law at intervals when the James gang needing hiding, rest and supplies."

He also repeats the legend that Hickok, after he shot Phil Coe, sent for a preacher to pray for Coe, and also the one about Coe's mother offering $10,000 to anyone who would bring Hickok's head back to her. He intimates that Wild Bill married Mrs. Lake in Kansas City, but they were married in Cheyenne. He says that Hickok later showed up in Deadwood, South Dakota, with his "old girl friend" Calamity Jane and is mistaken in having Hickok killed in the Bell [sic] Union Saloon. He was killed in Number Ten Saloon. He is also wrong in saying Jack McCall was a desperado from Texas (writers who are careless with their history tend to credit Texas with all the outlaws). He writes: "McCall was tried, convicted and hanged" as though that happened immediately after Hickok's murder, but he was first tried in Deadwood and released. His conviction and hanging came later in Yankton, at a second trial

after McCall had bragged about his deed. His statement that "if they hadn't blazed the Chisholm Trail a hundred years ago you might not have been eating hamburger and steaks today" is a rather foolish one. There are also some misspelled proper names.

106. JEFFREY, JOHN MASON. Adobe and iron. The story of the Arizona Territorial Prison, by John Mason Jeffrey. La Jolla, California, Prospect Avenue Press, 1969. Cloth.

To date this is the best and most nearly complete history of the Territorial Prison at Yuma, Arizona. There is some material on Johnny Behan, the former sheriff of Cochise County; Pearl Hart, the female stage robber, as a prisoner there; and Buckskin Frank Leslie during his term in prison. The author, however, is mistaken in calling May Killeen by the name Mary Galeen, and he is wrong about the details of Leslie's killing of Killeen.

107. JENKINSON, MICHAEL. Ghost towns of New Mexico. Playthings of the wind, by Michael Jenkinson. With photographs by Karl Kernberger. Albuquerque, University of New Mexico Press, 1967. Cloth.

Some of these ghost towns were the hangouts of the southwestern outlaws, such as Black Jack Ketchum, the Apache Kid, Sandy King, Russian Bill, Zwing Hunt, and Billy the Kid. The author makes a statement about Black Jack that I have not seen before: "His last request was for banjo and fiddle music at the hanging, and that he should be buried face down."

Much has been written correcting the legend that Billy the Kid killed twenty-one men by the time he was twenty-one years of age, yet at this late date (1967) this author repeats the legend. It seems hard to convince some writers that the legend is untrue. This author has the Kid conferring with Governor Wallace at a hotel in White Oaks, but it is well known that he met the governor at the home of Justice of the Peace John B. Wilson in Lincoln. He is also mistaken in saying that "during the range war he [the Kid] had been hired as a gunman by John Chisum."

The author is also mistaken in saying that the Kid's gang was stealing cattle from the Mescalero Apache Reservation and that, "when the Indian agent objected, the Kid shot him." Other legends (also untrue) have it that it was horses they were after, and Bernstein was not shot by the Kid but by a Mexican member of the party. The author is also mistaken in saying that the Kid and his gang were captured at Stinking Springs on Christmas Eve, 1880. They were captured on December 23. He also says that the capture came "after a prolonged battle in which two rustlers were shot," but there was no battle, and only one (Bowdre) was shot. He was shot when he stepped out of the door that morning to feed the horses. Some time later the others surrendered. Finally, on the night of the Kid's murder the author says, Garrett shot three times—"perhaps the most celebrated shots in the annals of western history"; but the records show that Garrett only shot twice, his last shot missing entirely, and these "most celebrated shots" did much to brand Garrett for taking a cowardly advantage.

The author has one old man saying that the Kid killed his stepfather, which is untrue. Of the fight at the Wildey Well Ranch, when Pat Garrett and his posse tried to arrest Oliver Lee and William McNue, the author says that they were on an adjoining roof, but only Lee and McNue were on a roof. Garrett and his men were on the ground.

108. JOHNSON, DOROTHY M. Famous lawmen of the Old West, by Dorothy M. Johnson. New York, Dodd, Mead & Co., 1963. Cloth.

In her chapter on Commodore Perry Owens the author says that Andy Cooper was expecting him when Owens went to arrest him and that Andy's brother had spotted the sheriff and had taken Andy's horse when Owens approached the house. But Andy and the rest of the Blevins were in the house, and Owens shot him through the door. After Andy was shot the first time, the author has him moving about and being shot by Owens again, but the first shot finished him.

She has McDonald, Tom Smith's deputy, a sheriff going with Smith to arrest Andrew McConnel. The sheriff at that time was Joseph Cramer, and after Smith was killed McDonald ran like a scared rabbit.

She has Hickok killing only one man at Rock Creek—McCanles—and says that the other two were killed by Wellman and Brink. It was Mrs. Wellman who used the hoe to kill Woods. The author has Wild Bill sheriff of Hays City, but he was town marshal. She is also wrong in saying that McCanles was the first man Wild Bill killed, and she says that he got the name Wild Bill because of his courage. She says that Hickok left Hays City the day after his term expired at the instance of his friends because he had killed three soldiers and had stirred up the fierce anger of General Phil Sheridan. She says that Dave Tutt won Wild Bill's watch in a poker game, but he just picked it up off the table when he quit "and then embarrassed him by wearing it in public."

She repeats the legend about Wild Bill killing a man in a restaurant who was trying to shoot him in the back. She is the only one I recall saying that Wild Bill was wounded by Phil Coe when the latter was killed in Abilene, and she says that Wild Bill shot him twice. He only shot Coe once; the second shot killed his friend and deputy, Mike Williams. She is also mistaken in having Jack McCall going to Cheyenne after he killed Hickok and there boasting of his deed. That happened in Laramie.

The author repeats the tale about Wyatt Earp arresting Ben Thompson in Ellsworth, Kansas, but she does add, "That's the way Wyatt told the story." She says, "Wyatt refused the Mayor's offer of a permanent job as marshal of Ellsworth and moved on to Wichita where he worked as a deputy marshal." He was not in Ellsworth and was not offered a job as peace officer there, and he was only a city policeman in Wichita, and one of little consequence. She writes that after the cattle season was over in Dodge, Wyatt, as a deputy U.S. marshal, spent the winter chasing outlaws over half of Texas. That is untrue, and he had no federal commission at that time. She says that Wyatt moved to Tombstone in the fall of 1879, but it was December 1 when he rode into town. She says that his brothers and Doc Holliday soon followed him there, but James and Virgil went with him, Virgil joining him in Prescott. She repeats that Stuart Lake tale about Wyatt not caring to run for sheriff when Cochise County was cut out of Pima County, but he wanted that office very badly.

She has the Clantons sending word to the Earps from the O K Corral, "If you don't come downtown to fight it out, we'll pick you off in the street when you try to go home." It has been proved that the Clantons were trying to leave town and were not looking for a fight. She says that Ike Clanton and Billy Claiborne ran to hide but a group of businessmen took them to jail and put a guard around Earp's home as protection from outlaws. Nothing could be further from the truth.

She states that Doc Holliday and Wyatt Earp became friends in Dodge, but they had met earlier in Fort Griffin, Texas. She says that the Earps and Doc left Arizona because "too many people wanted to kill them." They left because there was a warrant for murder against them.

She states that soon after Bat Masterson was shot by Sergeant King, and while he was still walking with a cane, Wyatt Earp hired him as a deputy marshal of Dodge. Wyatt himself was only a deputy marshal and had no authority to hire anyone. She is mistaken in saying that Doc Holliday was arrested in Denver for the murder of Frank Stillwell. She also says that Deputy Stillwell was waiting in Tucson "to finish off Virgil," but he was killed himself.

She has Pat Garrett killing Tom O'Folliard "in a quick gun battle" with Garrett and his posse "hot on their trail." There was no battle, and Garrett and his posse did not go after the outlaws until the next day. She says that Billy the Kid's real name was Bonney, but most authorities claim that his name was McCarty. She has the killing of Bell all wrong when she writes: "While Olinger was out for supper, the Kid distracted Bell's attention, shoved the gunroom door open, grabbed a loaded six-shooter, and shot Bell." That is far from the way it happened. After the Kid's escape the author has him dancing around the upstairs balcony for almost an hour and says, "The people of the town were so terrified that they were paralyzed," but most of them were in sympathy with the Kid. She is also mistaken in having the Kid carrying a pistol the night he was killed. She says that some believed that Garrett was killed by Jim Miller but that "other men believed that Miller paid Brazil [*sic*] a large sum of money to kill Garrett." Miller was a "hired killer" himself and certainly would not have hired another to do his killing, especially such a man as Brazel. On the death of Garrett she writes, "There is still a mystery about who shot him, and why."

109. JOHNSON, DOROTHY M. Western badmen, [by] Dorothy M. Johnson. Illustrated with photographs. New York, Dodd, Mead & Company, [1970]. Cloth.

This little book has chapters on the Harpes, Joaquin Murieta, Black Bart, Henry Plummer and his gang, Joseph Slade, Rattlesnake Jake, the Renos, Sam Bass, the James and Younger boys, Belle Starr, the Daltons, Bill Doolin, Billy the Kid, Ben Thompson, John Wesley Hardin, Doc Holliday, Augustin Chacon, Tom Horn, the Wild Bunch, Bill Miner, Henry Starr, and Al Jennings. We find nothing new, just a rehash of the many accounts that have been written about these characters.

The author mentions only one stage robbery in South Dakota by the Collins gang and has that wrong. She has a wounded passenger on the Union Pacific train identifying Joel Collins, but that never happened either. She has one stagecoach that the Collins gang did not rob carrying $350,000. I have never seen this statement before.

The author is mistaken in having Joel Collins and Bill Heffridge killed "when they stopped at a small store in Texas to buy supplies." They were killed at Buffalo Station, in Kansas, on their way to Texas. She also says that "two of the robbers succeeded in reaching Mexico, Missouri, but Jim Berry was the only one who got off the train from Jefferson City when it reached Mexico. She says that Leech crept into the gang's camp while they were asleep and "found the $60,000 in gold sewed in a blanket so that it could be loaded on a mule," and "he did his best to drag the burden out of camp, but that much gold is very heavy." Then she has him trying to open the blanket to carry part of the gold away, "but one of the robbers woke up." That never happened either. She is also mistaken in having Jack Davis leaving Bass for New Orleans before they reached Texas. Davis did not leave Bass until they had reached Fort Worth.

She is mistaken, too, in saying that the Bass gang on their first Texas train robbery, at Allen, got $2,000. They only got $1,280, and that was the largest amount Bass got from any of his Texas robberies. She has the wrong date for Bass's death. She has Jim Murphy leaving the gang when he rode in "to watch for Rangers," but his excuse was "to buy corn for the horses," and she says that he "went into a store where he could look out the window," but he stopped in Old Town, and the others went on to New Town, some distance away.

She intimates that Bob Ford killed Jesse James because he was afraid Jesse might learn that he [Bob] had killed Jesse's cousin, Wood Hite, and he knew that if this happened he had little chance of living.

In her chapter on Belle Starr the author writes that Belle's parents moved to Texas "to get away from guerrilla warfare in Missouri," but they left because the whole town had been burned. In telling of the Grayson robbery, she states that the Graysons gave up the money [$30,000] when they kept pulling the rope and choking him [Grayson], but it was not until they began giving his wife the same treatment that he gave in.

She tells of the killing of Jim Reed by John T. Morris, but she does not tell how it was done, only saying that "Morris stopped him cold by shooting him in the head." She does say, however, that "this man Morris seems to have been a trusted member of Jim Reed's own gang until he turned against them." He was not a former member of Reed's gang but a deputy sheriff who was after Reed for the reward. She repeats that legend about Belle and a companion burning down a store and says that when Belle was jailed for stealing horses "she escaped by grabbing the jailer's gun and threatening him with it." Others say that she used her feminine wiles on him.

In her chapter on Billy the Kid the author says that John Middleton was killed in the battle at Blazer's Mill, but he was only wounded in the chest. She says that George Coe lost a thumb and forefinger of his gun hand, but he only lost a forefinger. She writes: "Just why they went after Buckshot Roberts is not known," but he had been seen in the mob that killed Tunstall, and that marked him. "One story," she continues, "says that Murphy had offered a hundred dollars per scalp for McSween's men and Roberts had been trying to collect it." Murphy had nothing to do with offering a reward, but the county had offered $200 a head for the killers of Sheriff Brady and deputy Hindman, and Roberts was a bounty hunter. She has Bowdre's bullet going through Roberts' chest, but he was shot in the abdomen. As Hindman lay wounded, she says, a man brought him water from the river in his hat. Actually Ike Stockton, a Lincoln saloonkeeper, brought him a drink. She leaves the impression that Sheriff Brady was killed after the Blazer's Mill fight, but he was killed April 1, and the fight took place on April 4.

She writes: "Now a peculiar thing happened. An army officer moved into the scene with a company of artillery and a couple of cannons." She is speaking of Colonel Nathan Dudley's interference in the Lincoln battle, but there was nothing peculiar about it, for Dudley was under obligation to the Murphy outfit. This is the first I have read that "some of the Kid's party [went] up onto the roof and [were] crouching in the protection of the parapet" firing at the enemy. Another detail, apparently original with her, is that while the McSween home is already burning, someone with a can of coal oil saturates the furniture and sets it on fire. She says, "Now the house was burning inside, too." It had been burning inside all the time; the adobe on the outside would not burn.

She has the Kid killing Beckwith, but Maurice Fulton, the most reliable historian of this war, says that, when McSween offered to surrender to Beckwith, John Jones advanced toward him and that when Jones tried to shoot McSween "Beckwith, realizing that John Jones was about to shoot down a man in the act of surrendering, and not wishing to countenance so atrocious a deed, threw up his hands to grasp the rifle and deflect the aim. Beckwith, however, was luckless enough to contribute to his own death. When Jones pulled the trigger, the bullet went through Beckwith's wrist and on into his head." That should settle the argument about who killed Beckwith. The author says that McSween "stubbornly refused either to surrender or to run," but he did offer to surrender.

She says that the circumstances of the

killing of Bernstein are not really known, but George Coe, in his book *Frontier Fighter*, tells what took place here (this book is not in her bibliography). She writes: "Maybe Billy the Kid shot him down in cold blood when Bernstein tried to stop the gang from stealing some horses." But they were not trying to steal any horses at the time, and Billy the Kid did not try to kill Bernstein.

She is in error in saying that "Murphy died just before the final battle of the Lincoln County War." This battle was in July, 1878, and Murphy died on October 19 of that year. She gives Dave Rudabaugh the first name Dick, and she is the only writer I have found who has Bowdre, after he was shot at Stinking Springs, saying more than "I wish— I wish—." She has him saying, "I'm dying."

In her chapter on Ben Thompson she is mistaken in saying that the buggy accident in which Ben's leg was broken and his wife's arm crushed occurred in Abilene, Kansas. It happened in Kansas City, Missouri, where Ben had gone to meet his wife who had come from Texas to visit him. The author has Thompson going to San Antonio to look for an outlaw when he killed Jack Harris, but that is untrue. She says that, just before Thompson and King Fisher were killed, Thompson hit Joe Foster in the mouth with his pistol. That will be news to historians. She has the entire event confused.

She is another who has the Clantons and the McLaurys (which she spells McLowerys) sending word to the Earps to come to the O K Corral and fight it out, but that did not happen. The Clantons and the McLaurys were preparing to leave town. She misspells Longabaugh's name as Longbaugh and is mistaken in saying that Henry Starr's father was a brother of Sam Starr. He was a brother of Tom Starr, Sam's father. And, of course, she is wrong in saying that Tom Starr was Henry's grandfather. She also says that Emilio Kosterlitsky was from Poland. Though he lived for a time in Poland, he was born in Moscow, Russia, November 16, 1853, attended military school in Russia, and later became a sailor in the Russian navy.

110. JONES, LLOYD. Life and adventures of Harry Tracy. "The modern Dick Turpin," by Lloyd Jones. Chicago, Jewett & Lindrooth, Publishers, 1902. Col. stiff wrappers. Also publ. in cloth.

The author says that Bat Masterson was "a celebrated gambler, confidence man and crook." There is quite a bit of false information about Soapy Smith with whom he claims Harry Tracy spent a lot of time, even to going to Alaska with him. He writes that Smith "was in every way a quiet, religious man" who "always prayed for success just before he was after the other fellow's wealth."

He has Soapy killing ten men in one fight, a tale I have never read elsewhere. He has Soapy killed in a fight that took place in a saloon and says that sixty-six men were killed and eighteen wounded. None of this is true; Soapy was killed by Frank Reid, and no other men were directly involved. He mentions Pat Crowe and says that Tracy had him kidnap Cudahy's child, but he does not mention that the father was the Cudahay of the Cudahay Packing Company. He was just a man who was trying to make love to Tracy's wife. The author says that Tracy's wife was named Florence, but most historians have her Dave Merrill's sister Rose. He has Harry Longabaugh and Butch Cassidy with Tracy in Oregon, which I greatly doubt, and he also has the killing of Merrill by Tracy all wrong.

He does not mention any of Tracy's activities in the Hole-in-the-Wall country. He writes as a newspaper reporter, as a close friend of Tracy, one whom Tracy trusted and often went to for secret interviews. But much of his narrative is a product of his imagination.

111. JONES, MATT ENNIS. Fiddle-footed, by Matt Ennis Jones, with the Assistance of Morice E. Jones. Denver, Sage Books, [1966]. Cloth.

This author misspells Bill Doolin's name as Doolan. He has Bill Cook a member of Doolin's gang, but Cook was never with that gang.

112. JONES, RALPH F. Longhorns north of the Arkansas, [by] Ralph F. Jones. San Antonio, Texas, the Naylor Company . . ., [1969]. Cloth.

This author is mistaken when he repeats the claim that the XIT Ranch brand represents "Ten in Texas." He is also mistaken in saying that the two brothers Ab and John Blocker were with the XIT and drove their cattle north for two decades. John Blocker was a rancher on his own account and did not work for the XIT. However, Ab Blocker did name the XIT brand when he delivered some cattle to them at the beginning.

He tells of the killing of Johnny Slaughter during the holdup of a stagecoach by the Collins gang, but he does not say who the gang members were or who killed Slaughter. He tells of the hanging of Cattle Kate Watson and Jim Averill, but his account is unreliable, as is his account of the crimes of Tom Horn and his hanging.

113. KEATING, BERN. An illustrated history of the Texas Rangers, by Bern Keating. Chicago, New York, San Francisco, Rand, McNally & Company, [1975]. Cloth.

This author made an honest effort to record the history of the Texas Rangers, but he made many errors. One of his first is having Ranger Jim Gillett a captain. He was only a sergeant. He has Samuel Walker a captain, but he was a lieutenant colonel.

He has Captain Gillespie killed during a battle, but he did not die until the next day. He claims that during the Reconstruction years after the Civil War "the Texas Rangers remained very active indeed." He writes, "Even so painstaking a historian as Walter Prescott Webb says flatly, 'For nine years after the Civil War the Texas Rangers were nonexistent.'" Webb was correct. When Governor Davis took office, he disbanded the Texas Rangers.

The author tells about Fort Jackson in 1874, but the fort's name had been changed to Fort Richardson in 1867. On page 115 there is a photograph with the caption "The Winchester people used this picture of a company of Texas Rangers to advertise their rifle." This picture is of a company of Arizona Rangers taken in 1903 after the Morenci riot. He gives Fisher's name as "King (John) Fisher," but it was John King Fisher. He has Ben Thompson a "brutal outlaw," but he was no outlaw, though he was a notorious gunman.

On page 158 there is a picture of Captain John Sanders mounted on a horse with the caption: "Like those of most Rangers his gun belt carries spares for the rifle rather than the pistol." That is not true. One of the more glaring errors the author makes is his statement that the so-called Santa Claus bank robbery of Cisco, Texas, occurred in Marshall. Marshall is in East Texas, and this robbery occurred at the First National Bank of Cisco in West Texas. In the group photograph on page 174 the author identifies the man on the far right as Frank Hamer, but it is Tom L. Heard. He is also mistaken in having Ted Hinton a Dallas County sheriff. He was at the time only a deputy. Many of the comments in the illustration captions seem to be an attempt to be facetious, but to readers they may smack of sarcasm.

The author accuses John Wesley Hardin of "sometimes killing as a hired assassin, but more often he killed for frivolous and non-profitable reasons." That is not true. Hardin killed to protect his own life, and such legends as his shooting a man in an adjoining hotel room for snoring is merely that—a legend. He has the Collins-Bass gang robbing the Union Pacific train on September 19, 1877, but the robbery was on the 18th. He says that Bass, after his return to Texas, "more or less invented or at least perfected the art of robbing trains." That is ridiculous; Bass's Texas train robberies were never successful moneywise.

He states that Major Jones of the Texas Rangers "had infiltrated the Sam Bass gang with a small-time crook named James Murphy," but Murphy was a friend of Bass and agreed to turn on Bass only to save himself and his father from prison. This author, like so many others, persists in the claim that Murphy committed suicide, which is not true. He is also wrong in having Bat Masterson the sheriff of Dodge City. He was sheriff of Ford County. There are some typographical errors such as *sagest* for *safest*, *Salada* for *Salado*, and a small *c* in *Colts*. There are other mistakes.

114. KEMP, BEN W., with J. C. DYKES. Cowdust and saddle leather, by Ben W. Kemp, with J. C. Dykes. Norman, University of Oklahoma Press, [1968]. Cloth.

This biography of the author's father is interesting but contains many errors. In the foreword the coauthor writes that "it would be a miracle if some minor errors in dates and in the spelling of the names and places and some of the characters who appear briefly in the story did not appear. Benny and your editor have done the best we could to eliminate such errors, but we know we didn't find them all." Yet they should have discovered such glaring errors as the one on page 58 where they state that Dick Ware, the Texas Ranger, "was in the fight at Round Rock on July 20, 1889, when Sam Bass was killed." The year was 1878, and the fight occurred on Friday, the 19th. Bass was severely wounded, but he did not die until Sunday, the 21st.

They have Bill Johnson and Dallas Stoudenmire in a fight, but it was no fight. Drunken Johnson shot at Stoudenmire with a shotgun but missed, and Stoudenmire did not. They also have the killing of Stoudenmire entirely wrong.

They are also wrong in having Sergeant Gillett bringing in Elfego Baca from Old Mexico for the murder of A. N. Conklin, the Socorro newspaper man. The Bacas who murdered Conklin were Antonio Baca and his cousins Abreau and Onefrio Baca, and it was the latter two brought back by Gillett.

In their chapter on Black Jack Ketchum there are many errors. The author states that "Black Jack and two of his gang tried to rob a Santa Fe train near Clayton, New Mexico. Just as they were about to succeed, a porter on the train eased open a door at Black Jack's back and shot him through the arm, shattering the bone." Black Jack was alone at this attempted robbery, and he nowhere near succeeded. It was a Colorado and Southern train, not the Santa Fe. Also, it was conductor Harrington, not a porter, who shot Black Jack with a shotgun and shattered his arm.

The authors say that Ketchum tried to reach "an isolated ranch" but "was so weak from the loss of blood that he fainted and fell off his horse a number of yards short of the house." They write, "When he regained consciousness, he crawled into the shade of a nearby tree and called to the people at the house to bring him a drink of water, but they had heard about the attempted train robbery and were afraid to go near him." News must have traveled fast. Black Jack did not mount any horse after his arm had been shattered but made his way to a tree on the edge of the railway right of way. The authors have a posse following Ketchum to this isolated ranch. The posse "saw him sitting with his back against a tree," but he willingly gave himself up to the crew of a freight train passing by. They write: "The men [the authors do not say who] knowing they were facing a dangerous and desperate criminal were afraid to ride across the three hundred yards of open ground that separated them." The authors say that he was rushed to Clayton, where a surgeon had to amputate his arm to save his life. Most other accounts have the amputation performed in Trinidad, Colorado.

They have Ketchum one of the two bandits robbing the bank at Hillsboro, but that happened after Ketchum was hanged. They also assert that Ed Kilpatrick and Ben Kilpatrick were the same men going by different names, but they were brothers.

Many varying accounts have been written about the death of the Apache Kid, but these authors relate an entirely different one. They have him killed in the latter part of 1907 after he and a companion stole a band of horses. Earle R. Forrest, in *Arizona's Dark and Bloody Ground*, has the Kid killed by Walapai Clark "about 1893 or 1894." Later, in *Lone War Trail of Apache Kid*, in which he collaborated with Edwin B. Hill, Forrest admitted his mistake and acknowledged that the Kid was wounded and vanished. Joe Chisholm, in *Brewery Gulch*, has the Kid killed in Mexico by Sheriff John Slaughter and Captain Benton "sometime in 1897 or 1898." William Sparks, in *The Apache Kid, a Bear Fight and Other True Stories of the Old West*, claims that the Kid died in Old Mexico of consumption. Jesse G. Hayes, in *Apache Vengeance*, says that the circumstances of the death of the Apache Kid are unknown. None of these versions has been officially accepted.

This book has the first account I have seen claiming that George Scarborough served a term in the penitentiary. If Tom Tucker did kill seven of Curly Bill Brocius' gang with one blast of a sawed-off shotgun, it is strange that the story has not appeared in any other account. Tom could not have killed so many with only one blast unless he was very close to them and they were in a compact group.

They have one character telling of the "alleged killing" of Billy the Kid and saying that "he helped bury the corpse of the man Garrett killed and it was not Billy the Kid."

The greater part of the book is concerned with Ben Kemp, the coauthor's father, and is no doubt correct, but their attempt to deal with the historical events of others is poorly done, though very interesting.

115. KETCHUM, PHILIP. Wyatt Earp, by Philip Ketchum. Illustrated by Robert Boremus. Racine, Wisconsin, Whitman Publishing Company, [1956]. Col. pict. boards.

On the copyright page is this note: "The publisher and the author acknowledge their indebtedness to 'Wyatt Earp, Frontier Marshal,' published by Houghton Mifflin Company of Boston and New York, copyright 1931 by Stuart Lake, and express their thanks to the publishers and the author of said work for their permission to base certain portions of this book upon it."

And so this author makes some of the mistakes Lake made, especially having Earp in Ellsworth when Bill Thompson killed Sheriff Whitney, and having him appointed city marshal by the mayor of the town to arrest Ben Thompson. In spite of Lake, that never happened. Nor was Wyatt ever marshal of Wichita, as this author and Stuart Lake have him. He was only a city policeman, and one not well thought of at that.

This author's account of Wyatt Earp stopping Mannen Clements' crowd from crossing the bridge and forcing their way into Wichita is just a piece of fiction. No records have been found indicating that the Clements brothers ever made an attempt to hurrah Wichita. If that had happened, there surely would have been headlines in the newspapers or court records of arrests.

The author is also mistaken in saying that Bat Masterson was at one time the marshal of Abilene. He follows the Lake account of Wyatt running Clay Allison out of Dodge, but that never happened either. The author has Earp a deputy U.S. marshal "since his days in Wichi-

ta," and has him riding south to break up a band of outlaws in Texas. He has Wyatt appointing Ed Masterson marshal of Dodge during his absence. He had no legal right to appoint anyone to an office. During this time, the author says, Ed Masterson was killed, and the lawless element of Dodge took over the town and began wearing their guns again. He seems to forget that Bat Masterson and other officers were still in town, and the law was still working. He has Bat killing the men who killed his brother, but Ed shot them himself before he collapsed. Soon afterward Doc Holliday came to town in time to save Wyatt Earp from a mob, and after that Dodge was tamed and Wyatt was soon on his way to Tombstone, Arizona.

This author has Wyatt going to Tombstone as a U.S. marshal, which is untrue. Like Lake, he has Wyatt receiving an officer's badge in Tucson from Sheriff Sibell. He has a crowd of twenty-five Clanton outlaws attacking them near Tombstone and of course Wyatt whipping the whole crowd, but no such battle occurred. He also has Crawly Dake appointing Wyatt a U.S. marshal soon after his arrival in Tombstone, but that happened much later, and besides, the author had already had him a marshal.

This author also has Wyatt going to the aid of City Marshal Fred White, but it was Virgil Earp who did so. Also, like Lake, he says that when Johnny-Behind-the-Deuce O'Rourke committed a murder in Charleston and a mob chased him to Tombstone, Wyatt saved him from the mob. That is not true either. The book ends with the famous gunfight at the O K Corral. Like Lake, the author has Wyatt Earp a man without fear or faults. There is much conversation that no one recorded, and the book reads like fiction written for juveniles. Throughout the book the author misspells the McLaury brothers' name as McLowery.

116. KING, DICK. Ghost towns of Texas, by Dick King. San Antonio, Texas, Naylor Co., [1953]. Cloth.

This author tells about Sam Bass using a cave near Salado, Texas, as a refuge just before he went to Round Rock and says that the citizens earlier made a truce with Jesse and Frank James saying that they would not make depredations upon them while the gang used Salado as a refuge. He also says that the Younger brothers were frequent visitors at Salado, but that has not been recorded, and so are doubtful statements. He is also wrong in saying that the killing of Jack Helm by John Wesley Hardin started the Sutton-Taylor feud. The feud had been going on for some time before the killing.

117. KLASNER, LILY. My girlhood among outlaws, by Lily Klasner. Edited by Eve Ball. Tucson, Arizona, University of Arizona Press, [1972]. Pub. in both cloth and wrappers.

This most interesting book of memoirs gives us some heretofore unpublished history of the frontier days of Texas and New Mexico, especially the Lincoln County War and John Chisum, whom the author knew intimately.

Yet I was surprised to learn the author has Sam Bass a refugee in New Mexico, married and running a farm. I thought she must be referring to another Sam Bass until I read her comment, "I believe the robbery of the U.P. train was his first exploit as a bandit." The Texas Sam Bass was never in New Mexico, nor was he ever married, and the Union Pacific robbery was not his first exploit as a bandit. She quotes a letter from a

Mr. McCabe in which he says that the Brewer party "attacked a man by the name of Roberts at Blazer's Mill." This, of course was a reference to the shooting of a bounty hunter named Roberts at Blazer's Mill, where he had gone seeking the Brewer party. The author is also in error in having McNab "elected as captain of the McSween party after Brewer was killed." Billy the Kid appears to have assumed leadership at this time.

She is also wrong in having the attack on the McSween home a three-day battle. It lasted five days. She defends the characters of Sheriff Brady, Frank Baker, and especially Bob Olinger, with whom she was in love. She lays the blame for Olinger's bad reputation on Walter Noble Burns, but his own mother admitted that he was a murderer at heart. When Frank Coe was captured and taken to Lincoln, the author says, Bob Olinger was his guard, but the guard was Wallace Olinger, who was not so bloodthirsty. When some shooting started, Wallace handed Coe his guns and told him to take care of himself. I do not believe that Bob Olinger would have been that generous.

118. LAKE, CAROLYN (ED.). Under cover for Wells Fargo. The unvarnished recollections of Fred Dodge, edited by Carolyn Lake. Boston, Houghton Mifflin Co., 1969. Cloth.

This book is in the form of a diary kept by Fred Dodge and edited by Stuart Lake's daughter from the papers Dodge left after his death. There are many misspelled words and many irritating capitalizations (probably Dodge's own style). The author has Wyatt Earp the marshal of Dodge City, and says that after Wyatt had tamed the town he turned his badge to Mayor Dog Kelly and told him "he was through with the marshal business." He also has Wyatt a U.S. marshal of Tombstone when Johnny-Behind-the-Deuce O'Rourke was about to be lynched, but that was long before he was appointed to that office.

In parentheses the editor says that the *Tombstone Nugget* was owned by Johnny Behan and the rustlers, but that is not true. Of the O K Corral fight the author says, "On arriving in town Ike Clanton had made it known that his gang had come after the Earps," but the Clantons were not hunting trouble. He is also mistaken in having the Clantons opening fire when Virgil Earp told them they were under arrest.

He says that Virgil went to Arizona first and was half owner of a mine near Prescott, but nothing was said of that when Wyatt dictated his book to Stuart Lake. The author makes the statement that Stillwell was Morgan Earp's murderer and that Wyatt ran him down in Tucson and shot him as he resisted arrest in the railroad yard, but that is not the way most historians tell it. He says that Doc Holliday was in the stagecoach robbery when Philpot was killed and that one of the robbers told him so. He also misspells Kosterlitsky's name as Kosterliski.

He has Charlie Bryant arrested by Ed Short at a friend's house in El Reno, Oklahoma, but he was arrested in his home, sick in bed, at a commercial hotel. He also says that Billy Thompson, the brother of Ben Thompson, was a friend "whom I had known in Tombstone days," but I have not seen any record that Billy Thompson was ever in Tombstone. There are other errors.

119. LAMAR, Howard Roberts. The far Southwest, 1846–1912, by Howard Robert Lamar. New Haven, Yale University Press, 1966. Cloth.

The author, writing of the Lincoln County War, says that Charlie Bowdre, Doc Skurlock, and the Coe boys "rode about terrorizing the region," which is not true. He has Billy the Kid "a bucktoothed, left-handed youth," but he perhaps assumed this from the only known picture of the Kid, in which he appears to be left-handed because the negative was printed backwards. He has a company of soldiers from Fort Stanton surrounding McSween's house during the battle at Lincoln and has them fighting with the Murphy posse. Though they did help the Murphy crowd win the battle through their restrictions, they did no fighting.

The author is mistaken in saying that Charlie Bowdre was "caught between two fires" and "killed by outlaws with whom he was fighting." We know that he was killed at Stinking Springs by Pat Garrett's posse and not by outlaws. He writes of the Kid after the Lincoln battle: "To vent their feelings, his frustrated men robbed a nearby Indian agency," but that is untrue. I suppose he has in mind the trouble at the Mescalero Agency, but they did no robbing. He is also wrong in saying, "The turning point finally came when a new sheriff, George Peppin, and a posse aided by Colonel Dudley with soldiers from Fort Stanton surrounded McSween's home and after a seven hour battle, forced him and his men into the open by successfully firing the house." A most inaccurate statement.

He writes of the Kid's death, "Cornering him in a dark room at old Fort Sumner, now the home of Peter Maxwell [it was then his home], Garrett killed the Kid as Billy excitedly asked his unknown assailant 'Quien es? Quien es?' "

The author is also mistaken when he says that Sheriff Johnny Behan "was allied to various cowboy outfits that had drifted into town." Behan was a good and honest sheriff. He also says that the feud between the sheriff and the Earp brothers led to the battle at the O K Corral, but this feud was between the Earps and the Clantons and their friends. He is also mistaken in having the fight take place "behind the O K Corral."

He is mistaken in saying of the killing of John Tunstall that "the incident became a feud when the Deputy U.S. Marshal at Lincoln, Robert A. Widermann [sic] chose to side with McSween, refused to let Sheriff Brady attach Tunstall's property, and organized a band of 'regulators' to resist Brady's posse." That never happened, and as for the "regulators," they were organized by Dick Brewer. He is also wrong in writing that Widenman "had been confined at Fort Stanton for complicity in the murder of Sheriff Brady."

He calls Wyatt Earp "cantankerous" and his brothers "sullen," but except for these and a few other errors, this book gives some real history of the Southwest.

120. LEE, HECTOR. Tales of California from the history and folklore of the Far West, [by] Hector Lee. Illustrated by Sam Sirdofsky. Cover design by Pat Gallacher. ₁Logan, Utah, Utah State University Press, 1974₁. Stiff pict. wrappers.

This is a collection of tales originally told on television and radio under the titles "There is a Telling" and "Tales of the Redwood Empire." There is a chapter on train robbers Sontag and Evans, one on Joaquin Murieta, and one on Black Bart, the stagecoach robber. In a later chapter on feuding the author mentions the O K Corral fight, but is mistaken in saying that the Earp crowd "shot up Ike and Billy Clanton and the

McLowery [sic] boys to a fare-thee-well." Ike Clanton did not fire a shot, and he was not shot. He was too busy running.

121. LEEDY, CARL H. Golden days in the Black Hills, by "the old-timer" Carl H. Leedy. ₁N.p., n.d.₁. Wrappers.

This book has some material on Calamity Jane, but the author is mistaken in saying that Belle Starr was Jane's sister and that she married William Hickok, a cousin of Wild Bill Hickok. He probably got this from some other would-be historian's writings.

122. LEMMON, GEORGE E. Developing the West, by G. E. Lemmon . . . , well-known early day cattle man. Taken from Belle Fourche Bee, Belle Fourche, S.Dak., ₁n.d.₁.

This appears to be bound galley sheets of various articles that have appeared in the *Belle Fourche Bee*. There are only a few copies in existence, and those are bound in various ways by hand, my personal copy being bound in leather with five buckskin ties. Though it is primarily about cattle and the experiences of the author, it does contain some outlaw material with mentions of Bat Masterson, Joseph Slade, and Wild Bill Hickok and an account of the killing of Johnny Slaughter by the Collins-Bass gang.

The author is mistaken in saying that Slaughter was killed by Bill Heffridge; he was killed by Reddy McKemmie. He also says that Collins "came near killing Heffridge for this inhuman and unnecessary act for it caused them to lose the hope for loot." It was McKemmie who was driven from the gang for this killing. He is also wrong in having Heffridge a "spotter" for the James gang. There are also some accounts of

Frank and Jesse James, as well as of Boone May.

The author tells of the arrest of Dave Molasky, Luke Short and Bat Masterson, but says Texas had nothing on Bat Masterson "for he had been a peace officer in Texas cowtowns." Bat was never a peace officer in Texas. The author writes, "[Bat] killed two cut-throat confidence men who had killed his brother for taking exceptions to swindling him. On learning of it from a neighboring town, he went at once and met them on a street of Dodge City, and in a wide open street fight killed them both and was exonorated." Nothing like that happened.

He has the Shorts in a feud in Texas and the governor of the state sending a troup of twenty Negro soldiers to break it up. He says, "The Shorts and their henchmen ambushed and captured them and took them to the Capital, Austin, and delivered them to the Governor, saying to him: 'If you again send Negroes after us we will return them to you in coffins.'" That never happened either.

123. LEVENSON, DOROTHY. Women of the West, by Dorothy Levenson. Illustrated with photographs and contemporary prints. New York, Franklin Watts, Inc., 1973. Pict. cloth.

In this little book the author deals with many women, white, black, and Indian, but she omits some of the first women to go West, the prostitutes. In Chapter 13 she gives some information about Calamity Jane and Belle Starr, but she is mistaken in saying that "until she went into the show business Jane earned a living handling cattle." The only cattle she handled were a few of the freighters' bull teams. The author leaves the impression that she was a cowgirl.

She is also mistaken in saying that Belle Starr "learned to kill during the Civil War riding with the guerrillas of the border states." Belle never killed anyone. She repeats the legend about Belle refusing to identify the body of her husband, Jim Reed, to prevent the killer from getting the reward. She has Belle moving to Indian Territory after her marriage to Sam Starr, but she was already living in the Territory.

124. LEWIS, RICHARD W. Early day history of Home City, Kansas, by Richard W. Lewis. Marysville, Kansas, published by the Marysville Advocate, 1949. Stiff wrappers.

This has some material on the James boys and the incident in which their mother's arm was blown off. The author says that Bob Ford shot Jesse in the back, but it was in the head. He is also wrong in saying Frank was "tried in the courts and was never convicted." He was pardoned by Governor Crittenden without a trial.

125. LIGGETT, WILLIAM (BILL) SR. My seventy-five years along the Mexican border, [by] Wm. (Bill) Liggett, Sr. New York, Exposition Press, [1964]. Cloth.

Of the battle between Commodore Perry Owens and Andy Cooper, (the author does not mention Cooper's name), he says that when Owens killed the young Blevins boy he was so remorseful that he resigned his office of sheriff, "and as a first gesture of self-abatement, he cut off his long hair." Owens had no regrets about shooting the boy; the boy was shooting at him, and it was kill or be killed.

The author names Wyatt Earp's "achievements" as the "cleaning up of the Clements gang in Wichita, Kansas, his protection of Johnny-Behind-the-Deuce, notorious gambler from a Tombstone mob, the battle of the O K Corral, his sawed-off shotgun fight with Curly Bill Brocius, his conquering of the Clanton outlaw, cow thief and murderer." Few of these events actually took place. He is also wrong in having John Clum a sheriff in Arizona. Clum was first an Indian agent and later a newspaper man and mayor of Tombstone. The author also says that Bat Masterson "was sheriff of Cochise County at a later date," but Masterson never held a peace officer's job in Arizona. He is also wrong in having the Apache Kid a rival of Geronimo and is mistaken in saying that Pearl Hart's sister wrote a book about her.

He says that the Pleasant Valley War was "intensified by the fact that the sheepmen were Mexicans and the cattlemen were Texans," but this is not true. He speaks of the Greer family being wiped out, but it was the Graham family. "At first," he writes, "Commodore Owens acted as a free agent in the war, leading cowboy gangs against the sheepmen and killing many." This too is untrue.

126. LINDSAY, F. W. The outlaws, by F. W. Lindsay. [Quesnal, B.C., Canada, 1963]. Pict. col. wrappers.

This author is mistaken in saying that Quantrill was killed in British Columbia where he went under the name Sharp.

127. LOCKE, RAYMOND FRIDAY. The American West. Compiled, edited and with an introduction by Raymond Friday Locke. New York, Hawthorn Books, Inc., [1971]. Cloth. Also pub. in wrappers.

This anthology (a collection of stories that appeared in magazines for men) has two chapters on outlaws and another mentioning the Apache Kid. One chapter deals with the James boys and the Youngers. The author of the chapter is mistaken in having Jesse in the robbery of the Liberty bank in 1866. He admits that there has been some doubt about Jesse's participation, "but," he writes, "it has all the features of his *modus operandi.*"

In a chapter on various outlaws of the West the author has Billy the Kid named William H. Bonney and has his mother marrying a miner and then moving to New Mexico, but she was married in Santa Fe after moving there. He has the Kid killing Sheriff Brady and his deputy, but how does anyone know that? Others were shooting at the same time. He says that Pat Garrett was a friend of the Kid and "had turned traitor and obtained himself a badge, hoping to gain fame by hunting down the Kid." But Garrett was the duly elected sheriff, and it was his duty to arrest the Kid. All he has to say concerning the Kid's killing of Bell and Olinger was that Billy "snatched a gun and killed the guards." There was more to it than that. He also has the Kid killed by Garrett on Pete Maxwell's front porch. He was killed in Pete's bedroom.

There is some information about Johnny Ringo, Calamity Jane, Butch Cassidy, and the Sundance Kid. This author is another who has Cole Younger the father of Belle Starr's daughter, Pearl. Cole denied it. He says that Belle "stayed with Reed for a few years, but left him long before he was killed." That is not true. He has Belle serving a year in prison, but she was sentenced to only nine months. He also repeats the tale about Belle robbing a banker while he was making love to her.

He gives some information about Doc Holliday and Wyatt Earp, having Earp serve as deputy federal marshal of Tombstone which he was not. He also repeats the tale about the time Clay Allison pulled the dentist's teeth because the dentist had pulled the wrong one of Allison's. That never happened. The author makes the tale even taller, having Allison pulling "half a dozen from the screaming dentist's mouth."

He has the Daltons cousins of the James boys and the Youngers, but they were no kin to the Jameses. In another chapter, on Charlie Russell, the famous cowboy artist, the author refers several times to Utica as Utah Station.

128. LOONEY, RALPH. Haunted highways. The ghost towns of New Mexico, by Ralph Looney. New York, Hastings House, 1958. Cloth.

This interesting book has a chapter on the Lincoln County War and Billy the Kid. The author gives a fairly accurate account of these troubles, though when he writes of the battle at McSween's home, he hints that Mrs. McSween played her piano during the fight, prefacing his statement with, "It was reported that. . . ." Elsewhere, in a chapter on White Oaks, however, he writes: "Among those resting here [the White Oaks Cemetery] is Susan McSween, who played the piano during that bloody siege during the Lincoln County War."

I do not understand why the author says that "Billy Bonney was a single participant in the Lincoln County War of 1878." We know that there were many others in this so-called war. The author intimates that most of the outlaws of New Mexico were from Texas. He is mistaken in saying that McSween was hired by Murphy to collect Fritz's

life insurance when he died. That was done by Fritz's heirs, Charles Fritz and Emile Scholand.

The author has five men in the crowd accompanying Sheriff Brady when he was killed, and his whole account of this incident is unreliable. He is mistaken when he says that Hindman, after being shot, was guided by another deputy toward Stockton's saloon. He is wrong in saying that Waite was shot by Matthews while he was trying to get Brady's Winchester. He is also mistaken in stating that Middleton, Brown, and Billy the Kid served warrants for killing Brady. The Kid was the only one to be tried. He is also wrong in having Sheriff Peppin set the McSween home on fire, and he has the killing of Beckwith wrong. He has this battle lasting three days instead of five.

He says that Mrs. McSween "survived the fight and was close by her husband soon after the end." Mrs. McSween had left the house earlier and was not present when her husband was killed. After the Kid had killed J. W. Bell, the author says (after Olinger had taken some prisoners across the street for a meal), "someone called Olinger who left his prisoners at the Wortley [Hotel] and ran to the courthouse." No one called Olinger; he heard the shot that killed Bell and thought Bell had killed the Kid. The author also says that the Kid, after he had killed Bell and Olinger, shook hands with all the onlookers and then rode leisurely off. In telling of the Kid's death he is also mistaken when he says that "two bullets from Garrett's Colt cut him down in a darkened room at Fort Sumner." It is true that Garrett shot twice, but only the first shot found its mark.

There has been much controversy over whether Wyatt Earp really killed Curly Bill Brocius, as he claimed. Some of

Curly Bill's friends claimed that they talked with him after the event at Iron Springs. This author says that "he was brought back to Shakespeare (New Mexico) and died in the general store. He may be buried in the basement." It is doubtful that he lived long enough to be carried to Shakespeare if, as Lake claims, "eighteen buckshot, a double load from Wyatt's Wells Fargo gun as the marshal pressed both triggers, had struck Curly Bill squarely in the abdomen, just beneath the chest wall, well-nigh cutting his body in two."

129. LYON, PETER. The wild, wild West. A chilling illustrated history presenting the facts about a passel of low-down mischievous personages including Joaquin Murieta, Wild Bill Hickok, Jesse James, Bat Masterson, Wyatt Earp & Billy the Kid.... New York City, Funk and Wagnalls, [1969]. Two-tone cloth.

This is a much enlarged account of the author's original, which appeared in the August, 1960, issue of *American Heritage*. The beginning is different, and the main text is much fuller. The author makes an attempt to place the western outlaw-gunman where he belongs—not as the hero of the fiction writer but as the villain he was in reality. He does much to correct the false history that has been written about these characters, but he makes some mistakes of his own that he should have avoided since he seems to have been well versed upon the subject.

He has Wild Bill Hickok already settled in Abilene gambling for a living when he was hired as a city marshal, but he was not yet a citizen of that town. He also writes: "Assuming that she [Calamity Jane] was born in 1845...." But why should he assume? If Calamity Jane knew her own age—and she should —she claimed to have been born in 1852.

The author is also mistaken in having the James boys robbing the bank at Liberty, Missouri. It was proved that Jesse was in bed with a lung wound at that time. He also says that Pearl Younger was the illegitimate daughter of Belle Starr and Cole Younger, but Cole denied it. He is also mistaken in saying that Blue Duck was white. One only has to look at a picture of him to see that he is of Indian blood.

In telling about Jesse James seeking refuge at Belle's Younger's Bend home in 1881, he writes: "Belle, having by now given the boot to such sometime outlaws as Jack Spaniard, Jim French, Jim July, John Middleton, and the white man who incomprehensibly chose to be called Blue Duck, had actually gotten married to a Cherokee named Sam Starr." She married Sam Starr before she took up with the others, and Sam had been killed before she took Jim July for her bedfellow.

This author is another who thinks that Belle Starr was "probably slain by her son, Ed Reed, with whom she had had incestuous relations," but her murderer was never established, though of late it seems evident that she was killed by Jim July (though some still say it was John Middleton's brother).

He continues to misspell McLaury as McLowery, and he is also in error in having Billy the Kid's family moving from New York to Coffeyville, Kansas, in 1863. That was before the town was founded. He also says that the Kid "probably killed a man named Grant, after a brawl in a saloon." There is no doubt about who killed Grant, though it was no brawl. Of the Lincoln County War he writes, "Several persons were killed in the course of this 'war,' and the Kid may have killed one or more of them." Though he did not kill the twenty-one men most historians give him credit for, he certainly killed more than one of them. The author also continues to spell Henry Brown's first name as Hendry, and he says that when Brown left the Kid he rode to Kansas, where a sheriff's badge was pinned on him. But the author fails to say that he stopped first in Tascosa, Texas, to serve for a short while as a peace officer and that, after reaching Caldwell, Kansas, he was appointed city marshal, not elected sheriff.

He has Billy the Kid killed at "a ranch near Fort Sumner, New Mexico," but Billy was killed in the home of Pete Maxwell *in* Fort Sumner. He says that Belle Starr's place, Younger's Bend, was in Oklahoma, but in those days it was in Indian Territory.

The author is also mistaken in saying that Tom Smith, the first marshal of Abilene, was killed when he undertook to arrest a nester "on some unimportant charge." It was a charge of murder and therefore an important one. When Bat Masterson's brother, Ed, was killed, the author says that Bat shot both of his brother's slayers, but Ed himself shot them before he went into Hoover's saloon and collapsed. He is also wrong in saying that Wyatt Earp followed his brother, Virgil, to Tombstone. They met in Prescott and went to Tombstone together with their wives.

In writing of the stage holdup in which Bud Philpot was killed, he says, "Wyatt went to one of his friends, Ike Clanton," to persuade Clanton to forget about Doc Holliday's part in the robbery, but Clanton was no friend of Earp's. He was a bitter enemy.

Before this book went to press, the author called me from New York and asked me to read the manuscript and correct any errors I could find. Later his editor also called me to ask this favor. When I read it and corrected a number of errors and returned it to him, he must have doubted my corrections, for, as we see, it is still full of errors.

130. McCALLUM, HENRY D., and FRANCES T. McCALLUM. The wire that fenced the West, by Henry D. McCallum and Frances T. McCallum. Norman, University of Oklahoma Press, 1965. Cloth.

It seems strange that these authors should bring Billy the Kid into the picture. He had nothing to do with barbed-wire fencing. Of the Lincoln County War they say, "It was the issue of free range versus land enclosure which caused this fighting," and they further state that "basically it was the fight of the farm settlers and small ranchers struggling against the expanding mesh of wire fencing that put John Chisum and his fellow cattlemen . . . into the Lincoln County War." Nothing could be farther from the truth.

They call Billy the Kid by the name William H. Bonney II, and describe him as a professional outlaw. They say that he went to see Governor Wallace "with a Winchester in his right hand and a revolver in his left," but they get this information from Horan and Sann's most unreliable book, *A Pictorial History of the Wild West* (item 193 in *Burs Under the Saddle*).

131. McCARTY, JOHN L. Maverick town, the story of Old Tascosa, by John L. McCarty. . . . Norman, University of Oklahoma Press, 1946. Cloth.

This is the first and best histories of this wild cowtown, but the author continues with the old legends of Billy the Kid, "who carved twenty-one notches on his six-shooter," and was born William H. Bonney, and killed the man who insulted his mother. He has the Kid in the pay of John Chisum while killing to avenge the death of John Tunstall. He had not been in Chisum's employ for a long time, but he was in Tunstall's employ at the time of his murder. "With the good pay of the Chisum job cut off," he writes, "following the removal of Chisum to Texas, Billy had to look to other fields for profit." He has the Kid following Chisum to Texas, but he went there of his own volition with a few followers to steal cattle and sell stolen horses. Some authors have Tom O'Folliard killed from beneath a porch at Fort Sumner, but this writer has him killed from behind a fence, and he is mistaken in having the Kid carrying a gun the night he was killed by Garrett.

132. McCRACKEN, Harold. The American cowboy, [by] Harold McCracken. Garden City, New York, Doubleday & Company, Inc., 1973. Cloth. Also pub. in de luxe limited edition of 300.

This book covers the evolution of the cowboy from the early days to modern times. The author is mistaken in saying that the cowboy's word *chaps* was derived from the Spanish *chaparajos*. It came from the word *chapareras*. He is also mistaken in saying that, even after the hemp rope was introduced, most old-timers preferred the rawhide reata. The latter was strictly a dry-weather rope and no good in wet weather. It was also no good for tying fast.

"The cowboy boot, as we know it today," the author writes, "was developed during the period of the early cattle drives from Texas. . . . Why the sharply pointed toes and the often uncomfort-able tight fitting and extraordinarily high, narrow heels are difficult to understand. The best explanation that has been given that the boot was designed to discourage all cowboys from learning to walk on the ground."

The pointed toe and high heel were designed for a purpose. The pointed toe was for picking up the stirrup easily; the high heel was made to keep the rider's feet from slipping through the stirrup and hanging, and it let him dig in when he was roping on foot. The tightness was not uncomfortable, because the vamp was soft and of light, good leather. That high heel was also a tradition, a mark of distinction and a sign that the man wearing it was a riding man.

The author is mistaken in having Charlie Russell working with Jesse Phelps on the Kaufman and Statler Ranch. He was only riding the chuck line there. He did not draw his famous picture "Waiting for a Chinook" on a piece of paper, but on the top of a cardboard box.

133. McDOWELL, Bart. The American cowboy in life and legend, by Bart McDowell. . . . Foreword by Joe B. Frantz. . . . Washington, D.C. National Geographic Society . . . , [1972]. Pict. cloth.

This book has a mention of Johnny Behan, Billy Brooks, Nate Champion, Ike Clanton, Billy Clanton, Wyatt Earp, Wild Bill Hickok, Doc Holliday, the Johnson County War, Frank McLaury and his brother Tom, Bat Masterson, the O K Corral fight, Nick Ray, and Tom Smith. The author is mistaken when he writes that when Hickok took over as marshal of Abilene he made the cowboys hand over their guns, and that "one man balked, and Bill killed him." Hickok killed only two men at Abilene, one his enemy Phil Coe and the other his friend and deputy, Mike Williams, by mistake.

134. McGIFFIN, LEE. Ten tall Texans, by Lee McGiffin. New York, Lothrop, Lee and Shepard Co., 1956. Cloth.

This little book, which seems to be slanted toward juvenile readers, contains chapters on ten famous Texas Rangers from Noah Smithwick to "Lone Wolf" Gonzuallas, my personal friend of long standing. The author repeats the legend about John Wesley Hardin shooting a man in the next room of a hotel because he snored. She writes of Hardin: "To sharpen his marksmanship, he picked off an innocent store-keeper sitting quietly in the sun near Hardin's favorite saloon." Hardin was not quite that callous. She says of him: "His very name spelled terror in every town and county. He could shoot with his left or his right hand. With a six-shooter in each hand he could put twelve bullets in a playing card at twenty yards." She gives him credit for some marvelous shooting of which I doubt he was capable. Her account of his capture is also unreliable.

"Many a man," she continues, "had seen him twirl a six-shooter by the trigger guard so rapid it looked like a wheel, and then hit his target at the word 'fire.' That was the 'road agent spin' which made even other outlaws give him a wide berth." She has Hardin being arrested by five soldiers and says that while they were taking him to jail "he managed to get his hands untied, stunned one guard and killed the other four." She is also wrong in saying that Hardin "dropped completely from sight for three years" during his heyday as a gunman.

She is mistaken in saying that King Fisher was killed by a police officer, and much of her information on Sam Bass is incorrect. She says that Bass held up seven stagecoaches in Nebraska, but he did not hold up any stages in that state. He held them up in South Dakota. She leaves the impression that he alone robbed the Union Pacific and carried the entire $60,000 back to Texas. She says that he brought his loot back to Texas in a wagon, but he had traded his horses for a well-worn buggy and aged horses to avoid suspicion. She is also mistaken when she writes that he "fanned out over Texas robbing and raiding. Holding up trains became so routine he had a special crew to take over a train while he went down the aisles and fleeced the passengers." In none of Bass's Texas train robberies were the passengers robbed. She also says that Bass's reputation brought all those Pinkerton detectives from the North hot footing it down here."

She says that Bass, Barnes, and Jackson went into Koppel's store in Round Rock to buy some candy, but they were after tobacco. She says that Grimes and Moore recognized Bass and followed him into Koppel's store and that they knew of the reward of $10,000, but neither knew Bass by sight. They saw that he carried a pistol under his coat and made an attempt to arrest him for infringement of the local firearms law. Grimes was killed inside Koppel's store, but she has him falling on his face in front of the store. She is also wrong in having Bass dying on his twenty-eighth birthday, but he was only twenty-seven.

She is wrong in having Ranger Hughes chasing a bunch of horsethieves who she says were members of Butch Cassidy's gang, but Cassidy was no horsethief, only a bank and train robber. Of course, he might steal a horse now and then for his own use, but not a whole band of horses. She also has the capture of Kid Lewis and Foster Crawford, the bank robbers of the Wichita Falls bank, wrong, and says that Captain McDonald prevented a mob from lynching them. They were lynched by the citizens after McDonald and his Rangers had left for other duties.

135. McKENNON, C. H. Iron men. A saga of the deputy United States marshals who rode the Indian Territory, by C. H. McKennon. Garden City, New York, Doubleday & Co., 1967. Cloth.

This author is mistaken in saying that Al Jennings had a courthouse altercation with Temple Houston and that Houston killed Ed Jennings, Al's brother, there. That happened in a saloon after the courtroom ruckus. He is also mistaken in saying that Heck Thomas chased Sam Bass all over Texas—"so doggedly," he writes, "that the railroad company had presented him with a gold watch." Other than the time when Thomas was an express messenger during one of Bass's train robberies, Thomas had nothing to do with Bass. Despite the subtitle, the author does not mention E. D. Nix or Chris Madsen and barely mentions Bill Tilghman. The author is also mistaken in writing of a battle with the Jennings gang at the Spike S Ranch. There was no battle, for the outlaws gave up without a fight, yet the author says that three of the outlaws were wounded. He is also mistaken in saying, "The James outfit made elaborate plans to loot two banks simultaneously in 1876." He is speaking of the First National Bank robbery at Northfield, and at the time that was the only bank in Northfield. Though it is a minor error, he has Ike Rogers hitting Cherokee Bill Goldsby over the head with a

poker when he was captured; he used a stick of stovewood.

136. McLOUGHLIN, DENIS. Wild and Woolly. An encyclopedia of the Old West, by Denis McLoughlin. New York, Garden City, Doubleday & Company, 1976. Cloth and boards.

This colossal work takes up in alphabetical order many western terms and place names and gives short biographical sketches of most of the better-known outlaws and lawmen. Like so many other writers of western history, this author makes many mistakes in his facts, dates, and the spelling of proper names, such as misspelling Jules Reni as Jules Beni; Louis Dalton as Lewis Dalton, Chris Madson as Chris Madsen, and Mrs. Samuels as Mrs. Samuel. He misspells Longabaugh as Longbaugh and James McIntire as McIntyre. He spells Henry Brown's first name as Hendry and Ferd Packer's first name as Fred (a published copy of his signature shows that he spelled it Ferd). He misspells John Larn's name as Laren and spells Bob Olinger's name as Ollinger but admits that there is some controversy about the spelling.

He has a few dates wrong too. He says that Sebe Barnes was shot by the Rangers at Round Rock on July 21, 1878; he was shot on the 19th. He has the date of the first Texas train robbery by the Bass gang at Allen on February 24, but it was on the 22d. He is also wrong in having Bass and his gang arriving at Round Rock on the 21st. He has Tom O'Folliard killed by the Garrett posse on Christmas Eve; he was killed the night of December 19. In one place he has the date of the capture of the Kid's gang at Stinking Springs as December 27, but it was December 23. He repeats the wrong date in a section about Dave Rudabaugh. He also has Garrett killing Billy the Kid on July 13, but it was the 14th (and he has a double-action Colt "dangling from his right hand," but the Kid was unarmed).

In writing about Clay Allison, the author follows many of the legends: that he received a wound that crippled him for life in a duel to the death at a previously dug grave and that he pulled a dentist's teeth after the dentist had pulled the wrong one for Allison.

He is also wrong about Allison's death. He did not fall from a buckboard and die when the rear wheel ran over him and broke his neck. He fell from a loaded freight wagon headfirst on a front wheel and fractured his skull. This author also has the details about Allison killing Chunk Colbert wrong, writing that they sat opposite each other at a breakfast table for *two hours* before shooting at each other.

He is mistaken in saying that Blue Duck was white. Photographs show clearly that he was of Indian blood. He has Billy the Kid killing Morton and Baker as though he alone shot at them. He has Calamity Jane marrying Wild Bill Hickok "in the vicinity of Abilene, Kansas." But that marriage never took place; it was one of Calamity's tales. He is wrong in describing John Chisum's "long rail and jinglebob" as cattle brands; the latter was his earmark. He describes the long rail as "a double knife brand consisting of a gash running from shoulder to flank." The brand was burned with a hot iron, not knife-gashed.

His account of the killing of Billy Claiborne by Frank Leslie is misleading, and he is the only writer I know of who says that Jack Davis of the Collins gang was killed in Nevada after a stage hold-up. Most authors have Davis going to South America after leaving Sam Bass in Texas.

He seems to think that Lottie Deno might be the missing Kate Bender, but such an idea is ridiculous. When Lottie left Fort Griffin, she went, as he says, "no one knew where." If he had read J. Marvin Hunter's *The Story of Lottie Deno*, he would have learned that she became the wife of Frank Thurmond, of Deming, New Mexico. He is also mistaken in having James J. Dolan operating a separate store from L. G. Murphy in Lincoln. They operated the store together, and Dolan took it over after Murphy became too ill to continue running it.

One wonders where he got his information concerning the killing of Bill Doolin by Heck Thomas. He says that Doolin was already dead from consumption when Thomas entered the house, and so, in order to collect the reward for Mrs. Doolin, he emptied both barrels of his shotgun into Doolin's body. Doolin was very much alive and was trying to move his family when Heck arrived.

He criticizes modern writers who know Wyatt Earp for what he was, saying that Earp was "a man who has now been reduced to television corn and who has become the butt of any hack who wishes to reduce such an outstanding figure to the writer's own sorry level." To him Earp seems to be a great hero. He gives Curly Bill Brocius credit for robbing the Tombstone–Bisbee stage, taking part in the shooting of Virgil Earp, and planning the murder of Morgan Earp. He also gives Wyatt credit for killing Curly Bill. He says that Mike Williams was killed by Wild Bill Hickok when Williams got into the line of fire "by a mere fluke," but Hickok shot Williams as he came around the corner of a building, thinking that Williams was another Texan coming to join the fight against him.

The author is another who has the Jameses and the Youngers robbing the bank at Liberty, Missouri, and he is also wrong in having the Jennings gang committing only one robbery. He is mistaken in saying that Tom and Sam Ketchum had a falling out after "a trio of train robberies"; they fell out after the first one. Sam formed a new gang and committed the second robbery, and Tom was trying the third alone when he was shot. The author has Sam's gang committing the fourth robbery and Tom the fifth. There were only two robberies of this train and a third attempt. The author is also mistaken in having Tom tried in Santa Fe. He was tried in Clayton and hanged there.

He has the attempted train robbery by Ben Kilpatrick and Ole Beck taking place at Dryden, Texas, but it happened near Sanderson. He says that, after Tunstall's murder Billy the Kid "speedily switched sombreros, rounded up a few of his buddies and went to searching for targets," but the Kid was on Tunstall's side long before his murder. He also has the battle at the McSween home lasting three days instead of five. He is mistaken in having Bat Masterson killing Jack Wagner and Alf Walker after they shot his brother Ed.

He is also mistaken in saying that, when Dave McCanles went to Rock Creek Station to try to collect some money owed him, he "buckled on his precision-made killing tools and headed for the stage depot." McCanles and his companions were unarmed. He has a man named Baker in this group and says that after the killing of McCanles, Gordon, and Woods the killers were arrested "but never brought to trial," but they were tried and found not guilty.

This author is another, even at this late date, who has Mrs. McSween playing her piano while her home burned. It was proved long ago that that never happened. Again he is wrong in saying that Billy the Kid raided the Mescalero Indian Reservation, ran off a lot of horses, and killed Morris Bernstein. In his account of the killing of Pat Garrett, the author says, "There is a vague possibility that Carl Adamson and Jim Miller might be the same person." The possibility is vague indeed; Adamson was a well-known rancher, and Jim Miller was a well-known hired killer. He is also mistaken in having Gus Bobbitt a city marshal when Miller killed him.

He leaves the impression that Jim Murphy committed suicide, but we know this to be untrue. He says that L. G. Murphy died of pneumonia, but he died of consumption. He has Luther Mitchell and Ami Ketchum lynched and burned by the Olive gang and leaves the impression that they were buried immediately after they were burned, but that was not the case.

He has the Sundance Kid killed in Bolivia, South America, and Butch Cassidy committing suicide rather than be captured. But Butch's sister has recently written a book entitled *Butch Cassidy: My Brother* in which she claims Butch returned to this country and lived out his life. He knows about this book but ignores her claim. She should know for he visited the family several times and she would gain nothing by lying about it. [Publisher's note: See also *In Search of Butch Cassidy*, by Larry Pointer (Norman, University of Oklahoma Press, 1977).]

This author has Belle Starr born in Washington County, Arkansas; she was born near Carthage, Missouri. He does not say where he got this information. He has her going to school in Carthage and mastering "the use of

Latin, Greek and Hebrew," which I very much doubt. It would be most unusual for a small country school to include these subjects in its curriculum. He also has Belle living two years in Galena, Kansas, as a common-law wife of Bruce Younger and from that referring to her daughter as Pearl Younger. He is also wrong in having Sam Starr "killed in a dance-hall brawl." He was killed at a country dance at the home of Aunt Lucy Surratt.

The author is another who has Ben Thompson in Sweetwater, Texas, and coming to the aid of Bat Masterson during his trouble with Sergeant King. Altogether there are too many errors in this "encyclopedia" to depend upon it as a reference.

137. McPHERREN, IDA. Imprints on pioneer trails, by Ida McPherren. Boston, Christopher Publishing House, [1950]. Cloth.

This author, like many others, says that Calamity Jane died August 2, 1906; she died August 1, 1903.

138. MADDOX, WEB. The black sheep, by Web Maddox. [Quanah, Texas, Nortex Press, 1975]. Pict. fabricoid.

There are chapters on Bonnie Parker and Clyde Barrow, John Wesley Hardin, Sam Bass, and Belle Starr. In his chapter on Sam Bass the author has Dodge City in Iowa and has the Union Pacific train robbery taking place on September 19, 1877, but it was on September 18. He writes that Leech "was able to direct officers to Berry," but Leech did not arrive in Mexico, Missouri, until after Berry was killed. He also misspells Heffridge's name as Hefferidge.

Of Bass's first Texas train robbery at Allen, the author says that "approximately $1,400 was taken," but the take was $1,280. When the Bass gang started for Round Rock, the author says, Murphy was thrown from his horse and injured, and the "band left him behind to recover and it took him two weeks to locate them again." Though I think I have read every book about Bass, I have never seen that before. It never happened.

The author tells about the gang's stop in Rockwall, where "Sam spied a gallows standing some distance away. It had been used in an execution and had not been dismantled." But there never was an execution on that gallows. It was erected to hang George Garner for the murder of the sheriff of Rockwall, but before the hanging Garner and his wife were found in his cell, both dead from morphine that Mrs. Garner had smuggled into the jail.

The author is also mistaken in saying that in Round Rock Murphy sought out Deputy Grimes and described to him Bass, Barnes, and Jackson. That is not true. When the three passed Grimes on the street and crossed over to enter Koppel's store, Moore, another deputy, noticed the bulges on their hips. He went up the street to where Grimes was standing and told him of his suspicion. The two followed the gang into the store, where the battle started.

The author then writes, "Spurned by all, and overcome with remorse, Jim Murphy committed suicide less than a year later." That tale has been proved false so many times that one is astonished to find writers of this late date perpetuating it.

In his chapter on Belle Starr the author has her brother Preston living in Scyene, Texas, but he lived in Collin County, farther north. He also has Cole Younger fathering Belle's daughter, Pearl, but Cole always denied it. He seems to have Belle robbing Watt Grayson without help from others, and says that Grayson was a hermit. Grayson was married, and when the gang began torturing his wife, he gave in and revealed where the treasure was hidden. The author is greatly mistaken in having the Youngers in prison in Stillwater, Oklahoma. It was Stillwater, Minnesota. He also has Belle Starr robbing "any number of banks," but that is not true. He also repeats the tale about Blue Duck losing some of her money "while Belle was relaxing in Dodge City" and then going to the gambling hall and robbing it to get her money back, "taking a little extra for her time and trouble."

The book tells nothing new, only perpetuates false history of which we already have too much.

139. MAJOR, MABLE, and T. M. PEARCE. Southwest heritage. A literary history with bibliographies, by Mabel Major and T. M. Pearce. Third edition, revised and enlarged. Albuquerque, University of New Mexico Press, [1972]. Stiff wrappers. Also publ. in cloth.

There is some mention of such gunmen and outlaws as Clay Allison, Sam Bass, Billy the Kid, Wyatt Earp, Pat Garrett, John Wesley Hardin, Wild Bill Hickok, Doc Holliday, Tom Horn, Black Jack Ketchum, and Belle Starr. The authors say that Billy the Kid was "the most feared" outlaw in the Southwest. This is not true. Billy had many friends, especially among the Spanish-speaking inhabitants. They also repeat some of the tales Sister Blandina Segale told about her contacts with the Kid. They do admit that most of the books written about the Kid are mixtures of fact, fiction, and legend, "with fact the least of the ingredients."

In writing about Sam Bass they say that "he not only gave gold to the poor, but, so the folk still believe, he buried it in caves all over the state." We know that he did not have such amounts of money. He had spent his last gold piece on his way to Round Rock. As historians they should have corrected that legend. They speak of Wild Bill Hickok as "the prodigious killer, marshal of Fort Hays, Kansas, and later of Abilene, Texas." Of course, he was marshal of Hays City, not Fort Hays, and it was Abilene, Kansas, not Abilene, Texas. They are also wrong in having Billy the Kid attending the funeral of John Tunstall. He was being held by the Murphy crowd. They should also have corrected the error that Berry Ketchum, Black Jack's older brother, was an outlaw. He was a respectable rancher.

140. MALONE, JOHN WILLIAMS. An album of the American cowboy, by John Williams Malone. Illustrated with photographs. New York, N.Y., Franklin Watts, Inc., [1971]. Pict. cloth.

This is largely a picture book without any text of value. The author is mistaken in having Wild Bill Hickok a marshal of Hays City after he was marshal of Abilene. It was just the reverse. He is also mistaken in saying that Billy the Kid's real name was William H. Bonney, and he follows the legend that Billy killed his first man when he was twelve years old for insulting his mother and that he had killed twenty-one men by the time he was twenty-one.

141. MARTIN, CY. Whiskey and wild women. An amusing account of the saloons and bawds of the Old West, by Cy Martin. New York City,

Hart Publishing Company, Inc., [1974]. Pict. cloth.

Of many recent books about the women of loose morals in the early West, perhaps this one is the most nearly complete. The author makes some errors. He has Kid Curry's escape from the Knoxville prison all wrong, saying that Curry used a wire, "probably smuggled to him by Fannie Porter," to pick his cell lock. He used a wire he secured from a broom, tolling the jailer to the bars, placing the wire around his neck, and forcing him to unlock his cell. The author also credits Fannie with being there with two horses, but that is not true. He misspells Longabaugh's name as Longbaugh.

He admits that there are many stories about how Calamity Jane got her nickname and says, ". . . but the one most logical is that her paramours were visited by some venereal calamity." This is the first time I have seen such a claim. He has her married to Burke September 25, 1891, in Deadwood, but she was married to him in August, 1885, in El Paso, Texas. He says that Cole Younger found an old acquaintance in Texas, Myra Belle Shirley, whom "he knew back in Jasper County, Texas," but the author must have meant Jasper County, Missouri. He has her becoming pregnant by Cole, though Cole always denied it. He has Belle living in Dodge City and her husband, Sam, losing $2,000 at a gambling casino and then has Belle holding up the place and getting her money back, plus another $5,000. Most other writers claim that the money was lost by her lover Blue Duck. The whole story is only a legend. After Belle's death, the author says, Edgar Watson was accused of her murder, "but the charges were dismissed." The charges were not

dismissed; Watson was tried in Fort Smith and found not guilty.

The author repeats the legend about the Rose of Cimarron carrying a gun and ammunition to her sweetheart, Bitter Creek Newcomb, during the battle at Ingalls, but she was not in town that day. He also mentions a robbery of the National Bank of Cimarron, Kansas, by Doolin and his gang in the spring of 1893. I wonder whether he does not mean the bank robbery at Spearsville on November 1, 1892. After the battle at Ingalls, the author says, the Rose of Cimarron nursed her wounded sweetheart, but that is not true. He also has her living with Newcomb for four years, but that never happened either.

He continues to spell Henry Brown's name as Hendry and misspells Fannie Garretson's name as Barretson, but the latter could be a typographical error, though it is spelled incorrectly in the index also.

142. MASON, HERBERT MALLOY. The Texas Rangers, [by] Herbert Malloy Mason, Jr., New York, Merideth Press, [1967]. Boards.

Aside from the modern outlaw Clyde Barrow, about the only North American outlaws the author mentions are, as he says "such killers as John Wesley Hardin and Sam Bass. He evidently does not know the true history of Bass, or he would not call him a killer. If Bass ever killed a man, he did it at the end of his life in the fight at Round Rock, and no one knows for sure that he killed anyone there.

143. MAYNARD, LOUIS. Oklahoma Panhandle. A history and stories of No Man's Land, by Louis Maynard. [N.p., privately printed], 1956. Pict. wrappers.

This book contains some information about the outlaw William Coe and his character. There is a section on Black Jack Ketchum, as well as a mention of Billy the Kid. The author is mistaken when he says that Black Jack committed fifteen murders, including a mother and her daughter.

144. MAZZULLA, FRED, and Jo MAZZULLA. Brass checks and red lights. Being a pictorial pot pourri of (historical) prostitution, parlor houses, professors, procurors and pimps, [by] Fred and Jo Mazzulla. [Denver, 1966], Privately printed. Pict. col. wrappers. Also publ. pict. col. cloth.

The authors are mistaken when they say that Madame Goul "married a half brother of Billy the Kid." He had no half brother, only an older brother, Joe.

145. MAZZULLA, FRED, and Jo MAZZULLA. Outlaw album, by Fred and Jo Mazzulla. Denver, A.B. Hirschfield Press, [1966]. Privately printed. Stiff wrappers.

In this little book of short sketches and pictures the authors say Calamity Jane died on August 2, 1908, but she died on August 1, 1903. They also say that Billy the Kid killed his first man when he was twelve, and repeat that legend that he had killed twenty-one men by the time he was twenty-one years old, a common error. They have his true name as William H. Bonney, and they also misname Edward O. Kelly as Ed O'Kelly and misspell Con Wagner's name as Wager. They say that the James family paid Kelly $5,000 to kill Bob Ford, but that is an error. They have Black Jack Ketchum holding up a Union Pacific train in Wyoming, but the trains he held up were Colorado and Southern trains in New Mexico.

They are careless with their dates, having Jesse James killed on April 2; he was killed on the 3d. They also have the O K Corral fight September 26, 1881, but it was on October 25 of that year. They have Kelly convicted of Bob Ford's death on July 8, 1892, but it was July 13 of that year, and they have Kelly killed in Oklahoma City on June 13, 1904, but he was killed on the night of January 13 of that year.

146. METZ, LEON C. Pat Garrett. The story of a western lawman, [by] Leon C. Metz. Norman, University of Oklahoma Press, [1974]. Cloth.

This is perhaps the best and most thoroughly researched book on the life of Pat Garrett. The author tells of many little-known events in Garrett's life that I have not seen in other books. He makes a few mistakes in the telling, most of them apparently from preceding books. On page 10 he has the Bowie County, Texas, line "snuggled tightly against the Louisiana border," but it is in West Texas.

He has Billy the Kid carrying a six-gun the night he was killed. That is perhaps taken from Garrett's own book, but most historians claim that no gun was ever found. He does not have Robert Widenmann in the group when Tunstall was killed—that is, he fails to call him by name but says "another man." He also says that Dick Brewer "and another man" went off to chase some turkeys, but again the "other man" was Widenmann. He is also wrong in having Jesse Evans doing all the shooting when Tunstall was killed.

He is wrong in placing Wildy Wells, the scene of the Garrett–Oliver Lee gunfight, in Texas. It is in New Mexico. He also says that the names of the men behind the gate when Brady and Hindman were killed "were not definitely known," but they have been listed many times. His is also the first account I have seen listing John Long in the party with the sheriff. He names five men at the Blazer Mill's fight (Billy the Kid, John Middleton, Charlie Bowdre, George Coe, and Frank Coe) and says, "There may have been more." Indeed there were others, and he does not even mention Dick Brewer, the leader of this group, whom Roberts killed at the time. He does not mention that Middleton was wounded but says that a bullet grazed Billy the Kid's arm, the first account of that I have seen. He has Brewer and Roberts buried "In *a* coffin" as though it were the same one. Brewer was buried one day and Roberts the next.

He is also wrong in saying that during the battle at the McSween home "two-thirds of McSween's forces deserted across the Río Bonito. This left alone the lawyer [McSween] and about fourteen fighting men bottled up in his home." Colonel Dudley did order some Mexicans out of town, but some of McSween's men were still at the Tunstall store and other buildings. He has the Kid one of the first to leave the burning McSween house, while most accounts have him among the last to leave. At the killing of lawyer Chapman he has the Kid "slipping away" just before Chapman was shot, but the Kid witnessed the killing.

He is also mistaken in having the mob in Las Vegas demanding Dave Rudabaugh when they arrived in town from Stinking Springs in a wagon. It was the next day, after Garrett and his prisoners had boarded a train for Santa Fe, that they made this demand. He does then have the mob at the train, but his account is different from any other I have seen. He states that "Olinger strolled across the street to Worley's Restaurant," but other accounts have him taking a bunch of prisoners over there for a meal.

He has Billy the Kid "bounding up the steps" after securing a pistol that a friend had hidden in the outdoor privy, but, since the Kid was leg-ironed, I fear that he would have found it difficult to do much bounding. When the Kid made his escape, this author has him stopping "long enough to shake hands with some awed Lincoln citizens." I doubt that very much.

On the whole, in spite of the few minor errors, this is the best and most reliable book on Pat Garrett to date. The author has dug up much material that no other biographer has mentioned, and for that he is to be complimented.

147. MILLER, FLOYD. Bill Tilghman, marshal of the last frontier, [by] Floyd Miller. Garden City, New York, Doubleday & Company, Inc., 1968. Cloth.

This author claims that Bat Masterson was "elected sheriff and took office on January 1, 1878," but he was elected in November, 1877, and assumed office on January 14, 1878. He did act as sheriff for the opening of the January term of the district court on January 3.

The author is mistaken in calling Wyatt Earp "a Texas cowboy who spent more time in saloons than he did in the saddle." Earp was not from Texas, nor was he a cowboy. In fact, he had no use for that species. The author has Ben Thompson, "a printer by trade," killing thirty-two men and Doc Holliday killing twenty-six men, neither count correct. He has Mysterious Dave Mathers riding into Dodge City once a month to get drunk, but he was a citizen of Dodge.

He continues to speak of Tilghman as Sheriff Tilghman when he was only a deputy sheriff under Bat Masterson. He has Ingalls, the scene of the battle between the Doolin gang and the marshals, in Kansas, but it was in Oklahoma Territory. He makes it appear that the marshals first went to Mary Pierce's hotel, but they did not go there until the battle was over and then only to capture Arkansas Tom, the only outlaw captured.

The author is mistaken when he writes: "Heck Thomas headed a posse which found him [Doolin] outside of Lawson [Lawton] and in the gunbattle that followed, Doolin was shot dead." There was no battle. Thomas killed Doolin with a shotgun blast as the latter was trying to move his family to another state.

On page 206 the author says that Al Jennings was sentenced to five years when convicted, but he was sentenced to a life term on February 17, 1899. Through the interventon of friends President William McKinley commuted his life sentence to five years on June 23, 1900, and he was released November 13, 1902.

The whole book is loaded with conversation that no one recorded. Though it makes for more interesting reading, it has no place in a historical biography.

148. MILLER, RONALD DEAN. Shady ladies of the West, by Ronald Dean Miller. Los Angeles, Westernlore Press, 1964. Cloth.

The author gives a rather thorough review of prostitution in the West and includes information on such familiar characters as Belle Starr, Calamity Jane, Cattle Kate Watson, and Pearl Hart.

He has Belle Starr studying Greek, Latin, and Hebrew at the age of eight, a most doubtful statement. He has her father closing his tavern in Carthage because of the frequent raids by Lane and Quantrill, but he quit the tavern business when the town was destroyed by fire during the Civil War. He misspells the name Scyene as Sylene, but that could be a typographical error.

The author is mistaken when he writes: "Then on Saint Valentine's day, the James and Younger brothers invented bank robbery in Liberty, Missouri." That claim has been disproved. He is also mistaken in saying that Belle's brother Ed had ridden with the James gang and was a member of Quantrill's band when he was killed. He also writes, "Belle sent her [daughter Pearl] to Siloam Springs to have her illegitimate baby," but it was Pearl's mother-in-law who took her there. He also says of Belle, "Her main occupation was prostitution," but that is untrue. She did live with common-law husbands, but that would not brand her as a prostitute.

The author makes it appear that Calamity Jane arrived in Deadwood some time before Hickok, but they went there in the same party. He also has the date of her death wrong, August 2, instead of August 1.

He writes that "twenty cattle kings" hanged Averill and Cattle Kate, but there were only six. He is also mistaken in saying, "Months after the grand jury had voted indictments for murder, witnesses began to disappear." The four witnesses to these hangings began to disappear mysteriously before the grand jury met.

149. MILLER, THELMA B. History of Kern County, California. With personal sketches of their wonderful men and women, past and pres-

ent, who have builded the glamorous empire within an empire, by Thelma B. Miller. Illustrated. Chicago, S. J. Clarke Publishing Company, 1929. Cloth.

There are chapters on Joaquin Murieta and Tiburcio Vasquez, as well as other lesser-known outlaws of California. The author is mistaken in saying that Billy the Kid, "who usually plied his trade in Arizona, came to Kern County for a brief stay at one time when Arizona became too hot to hold him." Billy the Kid never went to California, and New Mexico was where he "plied his trade," not Arizona.

150. [MISSOURI]. North Kansas City, Missouri, now 1962, then 1912. ₁Kansas City, Missouri, 1962₁. Stiff wrappers.

A publication for the celebration of fifty years of Kansas City history. There is some material on the James boys and their parents and the killing of Jesse by Bob Ford. The author is mistaken in having the James boys taking part in the Liberty bank robbery, but he admits that "to this day no one knows for sure who did it." He is also wrong in saying that the large reward for Jesse was offered by the railway and express companies. It came from the Governor. He also says that Bob Ford "was killed in a saloon brawl in Colorado." There was no brawl. Ed O. Kelly walked into Ford's own saloon and shot him down.

151. MOORE, DANIEL G. Enter without knocking, [by] Daniel G. Moore. Tucson, Arizona, University of Arizona Press, ₁1969₁. Cloth.

A history of the state penitentiary of Arizona and many of the states criminals

and outlaws. It mentions Pearl Hart and Buckskin Frank Leslie, but the author is mistaken when he writes: "Buckskin Frank Leslie, a former deputy at Tombstone during its heyday as a rip-roaring silver camp, serving a sentence there for killing a woman with whom he had been living." Leslie was never a deputy of Tombstone, and the author fails to tell about his pardon and his life after he left prison.

152. MORGAN, E. BUFORD. The Wichita Mountains. Ancient oasis of the prairie, [by] E. Buford Morgan. ₁Waco, Texas, Texian Press, 1973₁. Cloth.

The author tells a wild tale about $2 million in loot being buried by the James boys "somewhere along the old road between Fort Sill and the Keechi Hills north of Cement." The James boys never got that much money in all their robberies combined, and what they did get they rapidly spent. He has Frank James coming to that country after Jesse's murder and digging up the money, but Frank died a poor man. The author is also mistaken in calling the Marlow brothers outlaws. They were victims of false charges.

153. MORRISON, WILLIAM BROWN. Military posts and camps in Oklahoma, by William Brown Morrison. Oklahoma City, Harlow Publishing Corp., 1930. Pict. cloth.

On page 21 the author is mistaken in saying that Belle Starr was sentenced in Judge Parker's court in 1833. That would be fifteen years before she was born. This could be a typographical error. He also says, "She began her downward career as a spy for Quantrill during the Civil War, and at its close came to the Indian Territory . . . ." She went to Texas with her parents after leaving Carthage, Missouri, before the war was over, and was never a spy for Quantrill. The author says that she "probably met her death at the hands of her son." That is just a supposition.

154. NAHN, MILTON C. Las Vegas and Uncle Joe. The New Mexico I remember, by Milton C. Nahn. Norman, University of Oklahoma Press, 1964. Cloth.

This author leaves the impression that he believes the skeleton hanging in Dr. Desmarais' office in Las Vegas was that of Billy the Kid. He writes: "Now for the logical approach to the problem: The Kid was shot on July 14, 1881. According to the *Optic,* his body was brought to Las Vegas some five days later. Both statements imply that Billy was unquestionably dead as a doornail, whever he was buried or whether or not his body was thereafter exhumed. Yet Billy the Kid's name appears on that warning posted by the vigilantes in Las Vegas on March 24, 1882. Along with other thugs and bunco-steerers, he was urged to leave town by midnight under threat of lynching. Here, surely, is the proof that Billy the Kid *was* in Las Vegas after the sheriff shot him in the wishbone in Fort Sumner. The trouble is that no one has ever doubted that Garrett put the bullet where it did the most good and that Billy lay dead that night of July 14, 1881, in a room in Pete Maxwell's house. There would thus appear to be no point in ordering a man from town if he had been shot dead eight months before and a hundred miles away. But, appearance to the contrary notwithstanding, I hold that this is the nerve of the case that Billy the Kid rested . . . in Las Vegas in Desmarais' office. To put the issue pithily, he had

to be in Vegas in order to be ordered out of the town." Does this author really believe that the Kid was alive in Las Vegas?

He says that the Kid and his gang were captured at Stinking Springs after a battle, but there was no battle. Bowdre was killed as he stepped outside to feed the horses; the posse shot him without provocation or warning. The author also says that Billy Claiborne killed two men because they refused to call him Billy the Kid. It is true that he wanted to be called by that name, but he never killed anyone for refusing to do so. He also repeats the legend that the dead Kid's trigger finger brought $150.

He says that the Kid escaped jail by starving himself for a few days to reduce the size of his hands and wrists so that he could slip off his handcuffs, "after which he seized a shotgun, killed Bob Ollinger [*sic*], his jailer, and fled." He does not mention the killing of Bell, and, because the Kid's wrists were larger than his hands, he had no trouble slipping his handcuffs; he had no need to starve himself.

The author is also mistaken in writing that "old man Chisum got started in the cattle business by winning a ranch on four sixes." That is the tale told about Burk Burnett and his 6666 cattle brand.

155. NASH, JAY ROBERTS. Bloodletters and badmen. A narrative encyclopedia of American criminals from the pilgrims to the present, [by] Jay Roberts Nash. New York, Published by M. Evans and Company, Inc., Distributed in Association with J. P. Lippincott Company, Philadelphia and New York, [1973]. Cloth.

This huge volume deals with most of

the outlaws and gunmen from those of the early West to the city muggers of more recent days. In telling about the early outlaws of the West, the author merely repeats the many false accounts and follows the legends to be found in romantic writings.

This author has Clay Allison an outlaw and gunman hired to kill "various cattlemen of New Mexico." He has Chunk Colbert and Allison "sitting down to dinner one night at the Clifton House at Red River in Texas." But it happened at noon in Cimarron, New Mexico. He also has Colbert's killing wrong. He has Allison's death incorrect when he writes, "While on his way to kill John McCullough, a neighbor, Allison got drunk and fell out of his wagon." He was not on his way to kill anyone but was driving a loaded wagon for a friend. Neither was he killed "when the heavily loaded vehicle rolled over his neck." His head hit a front wheel, and he died of a concussion.

The author is wrong in having the Apache Kid a scout on the San Carlos Reservation in New Mexico. It is in Arizona. He seems to have him roaming New Mexico, but his territory was Arizona and Old Mexico.

The author is wrong in having Sam Bass robbing the train at Allen, Texas, February 23, 1878. The train was robbed on the 22d. He also robbed three other trains in Texas, not two as the author states. He has Bass racing his mare in Old Mexico, but that never happened. Bass went only as far south as San Antonio. He has Collins persuading Bass to use his six-gun, saying that all he had to do "was draw it from its holster and earn big money." But what Collins suggested was that they gather a herd of cattle and drive them north to Kansas. He is also wrong in saying that when they got to Kansas "Bass and Collins

deserted and entered the Black Hills." They sold the cattle and then went to the Black Hills, and, though most of the money they received for the cattle belonged to some Texas ranchers, they spent it lavishly.

He claims that it became Bass's trademark to give his victims a dollar "for breakfast" after each robbery, but that is just an imaginary thought of the writer. He also says that, as soon as this happened, the victim they had robbed was told that it was Sam Bass who robbed them. He states that Collins, for the Union Pacific robbery, gathered the toughest outlaws in Nebraska, but these men were not from Nebraska, and they had been with Collins in South Dakota. He is also wrong in saying that they robbed this train in the morning; it was 10:48 at night when the robbery took place. Neither did they stop the train "as it was going up a hill." They halted it at the station after forcing the station agent to flag it down. The author is also wrong in having Collins and Heffridge "wounded several times," having Collins saying, "I'm going down with my six-gun," and then fighting until the death of both. Another mistake he makes is saying that Nixon and Berry "were trapped outside of Mexico, Missouri." Nixon was not with Berry. Again, he is wrong in saying that Nixon took most of Berry's money and that the Pinkertons hunted Nixon for years.

He has Bass and Davis riding "through Texas dodging lawmen all the way." As we know, these two had no trouble with the law until Bass organized his Texas gang, and by that time Davis had made his way to South America.

He has Jim Murphy being offered a "considerable reward" for turning in Bass, but Murphy promised to do it to get his father and him out of jail. He has

Murphy, as the gang rode to town from their camp near Round Rock, saying that he was "going to look around for lawmen," and disappearing; He stopped off at Old Town, telling the others that he was going to buy some horse feed.

The author has the killing of Bass all wrong, saying that a local farmer came into town that night and told the authorities that "an outlaw was dying on his front porch." Bass was on no one's front porch, but in the brush. He also intimates that Bass died soon after reaching town, but he was shot on the 19th and did not die until the 21st.

The author's account of the Benders is also unreliable. He follows that old false tale about Billy the Kid and his family moving to Coffeyville, Kansas, in 1862. That was before the town was established. He then says that the family moved to Colorado, where his mother married, but his mother went from Kansas to New Mexico upon the advice of her doctor. Like many others, he credits the Kid with having killed twenty-one men "by the time of his twenty-first birthday." He is also wrong in having the Kid killing "an unknown gunfighter in Coffeyville when he was fourteen." He gives the Kid credit for killing everyone who got shot in New Mexico, it seems, including Baker, Morton, Buckshot Roberts, Joe Grant, Sheriff Brady, Deputy Hindman, Jimmy Carlisle, Morris Bernstein, Beckwith, and of course Bell and Olinger (the latter's name misspelled Ollinger).

He has the Kid killed by Pat Garrett "on the Maxwell ranch *near* Fort Sumner," but it happened in Maxwell's home *in* Fort Sumner, not on a ranch. He admits that "of all the legends of the Old West, that of Billy the Kid is the most confusing and impenetrable, so laced is it with dime novel romance, heroic embellishments, and fabulous fiction

created by his own friends and enemies." Yet he does nothing to correct the legends, only perpetuates them. He repeats the legend about the Kid's mother marrying in Colorado, but she married Antrim in New Mexico. He is also mistaken in saying that there were no schools in Silver City and says that "Billy's education consisted of petty thefts, bloody knock-down street fights and visions of violent drunken men shooting each other to death." Billy did go to school, and he was a good pupil.

The author accuses the writers of pamphlets about the Kid as being "fanciful and unreliable," and yet he repeats most of their writings. He repeats the preposterous legend about the Kid killing a man who insulted his mother. He is also wrong in stating that McSween owned a "gigantic ranch." McSween was not a rancher but a lawyer. He is also mistaken in saying that Tunstall was killed "as he was returning to his ranch from Lincoln." We know that he was killed as he and four of his friends were driving a band of horses *to* Lincoln. He is again mistaken when he says that the Kid watched Tunstall being "lowered in his grave." It is well known that the Kid was unable to attend Tunstall's funeral because he was under arrest by the Murphy crowd.

It is surprising how this author could make so many mistakes when there are books correcting them. He has the killing of Morton and Baker wrong, saying that the Kid killed them with "one shot each," and he is just as mistaken in describing the battle at Blazer's Mill. He writes, "The doomed man [Roberts] just before the Kid's gang rode up picked this unfortunate moment to answer Nature's call and he found himself surrounded in an outhouse. Roberts, however, hadn't neglected to take his rifle and six-gun with him and he put up a great fight from the unlikely bastion. Brewer was killed outright. Bowdre and Coe were wounded. Such was the intensity of Roberts' gunfire that he actually drove off the band, but Billy fired a parting shot which proved lucky and fatal to Buckshot Roberts." This account is entirely wrong. Roberts received his death wound from Bowdre before Roberts retired to a room in the house, not an outhouse. Bowdre was not wounded; Roberts' shot hit his gunbelt buckle and ricocheted to take off one of Coe's fingers.

He very definitely has the Kid the only one killing Brady and Hindman: "Billy took aim at Brady's back and then fired several shots into the sheriff who toppled forward, dead. Hindman was next and the Kid's shots hit him several times." He seems to be unaware that Billy's companions were shooting too. Then he has Matthews shooting the Kid in the hand, but he was shot in the buttocks. Again he is mistaken when he writes that the Kid was stealing horses at the Mescalero Indian Reservation when he killed Bernstein. The Kid did not kill Bernstein, nor was he there to steal horses, though Bernstein perhaps thought that he was.

The author is also mistaken when he says that the Kid rode to Governor Wallace to tell what he knew about the murder of lawyer Chapman. He did go to meet Wallace, but at the request of the governor. The author also makes the ridiculous statement that, when Jimmy Carlisle stepped out to negotiate with the Kid, Billy shot him dead. That is far from the way it happened, and there is no proof that the Kid shot Carlisle at all.

This author seems to have a talent for getting every detail wrong. He says that Charlie Bowdre was killed at Stinking Springs as he fired a shot from a window in a heavy battle between the Kid's gang

and the Garrett posse. Bowdre was killed as he stepped outside in the early morning to feed the horses. He is also wrong when he writes that the Kid was sentenced by Judge Bristol to be hanged for the murder of Buckshot Roberts. He was tried and sentenced for the killing of Sheriff Brady, not Roberts.

When the Kid killed Bell (and this author seems uncertain about the true circumstances), Olinger heard the shot when he was across the street at the hotel feeding some prisoners. This author has him "drinking beer in a local bar down the street." He is also mistaken in having the blast from the shotgun that killed Olinger "hurtling him far into the street." In his summary before his text the author has the Kid escaping from jail at Mesilla when he killed Bell and Olinger, but he seems to be correct in the text. He has a "handyman" giving the Kid an ax to break his leg irons, but it was a miner's pick.

He closes his account of the Kid: "Whether or not Billy the Kid killed twenty-one men in his twenty-one years is no longer important; neither is debate over his slayings and his fast draw. What is important is that history, in his case, insists upon a legend gigantic and solid, romantic and dashing. So be it." He is certainly doing his part to uphold the legends written about our western outlaws, but there are a few conscientious historians who insist upon the truth rather than romantic falsehoods.

His short account of Curly Bill Brocius is unreliable, and his killing of Reuben Burrow is wrong. In his account of the Daltons he has Charley Bryant shooting up Hennessey, and immediately being arrested by Ed Short, but Short arrested Bryant while he was ill in an upstairs room at a hotel. He is wrong in spelling the Dalton boys' father's first name Louis; it should be Lewis. His account of the Daltons, though unreliable, is more accurate than most of his other accounts. He is wrong, however, in saying that Bill Dalton was killed "as he was playing with his young daughter on the front porch of his farm house." He was killed near Ardmore, Oklahoma, as he jumped out of a window trying to escape.

The author states that Bill Doolin was the only member of the Dalton gang to survive the Coffeyville raid. He forgets that Emmett Dalton survived to serve a prison sentence. Naturally Doolin survived—he was not with the gang in this raid. The author is mistaken in saying that Bill Dalton forsook his family in California to join the Doolin gang.

The author writes that Doolin's largest haul was $40,000 taken from a bank in East Texas. The only robbery in East Texas was at Longview, and this was done by Bill Dalton with a few companions strictly on their own, and there was nothing like that amount taken. He is also mistaken in writing that Bill Tilghman captured Doolin in Eureka Springs "after a slugfest." There was no slugfest; Doolin surrendered quietly. The author claims that Red Buck was killed while robbing a bank, but he was killed on March 15, 1896, when citizens chased him to a dugout near Arapaho.

In the account of John Wesley Hardin the first mistake the author makes is saying that Hardin "was born in Bonham County." He was born in the town of Bonham, Fannin County, Texas. He is mistaken in saying that Hardin killed his first man, a Negro, "at [age] fifteen while living with his family in Bonham." He killed the Negro far from Bonham, near Moscow, Texas, in Polk County, while visiting his uncle.

The author writes as though Hardin went to work for a rancher named William C. Cohron immediately after killing three Yankee soldiers and that he chased a cattle rustler named Juan Bideno for killing Cohron. But this happened much later when Hardin went to Kansas with a herd of cattle. The author calls Ben Thompson "the scourge of the plains," though we fail to see why. His accounts of Hardin's capture and of his death are both unreliable.

He is mistaken when he says that Pearl Hart "convinced a town drunk, Joe Boot, to help her rob the local stage." It was Boot who suggested the robbery. He also makes some doubtful statements about Tom Horn, among others that "dozens of men fell before his guns, victims of his clever bushwhacking."

In his long article about Jesse James he follows the old legend about the James boys robbing the bank at Liberty. Likewise he repeats that threadbare legend about Jesse paying off a widow's mortgage and then robbing the collector of the money. He admits that that tale has been told about every important outlaw of the West but states that "most historians attribute the act to Jesse." Most historians say that the story is a hoax.

The author is also mistaken in having the Youngers and the James boys cousins. Here again he merely repeats some false history. He says that Jesse, to prove he was absolute leader of the gang, "threatened his own brother, Frank." I had not seen this statement before. In this chapter too he writes that Belle Starr was in love with Cole Younger and lived in Collin County on a ranch owned by her father. Belle lived with her father on a small farm just east of Dallas in Dallas County. His account of the James boys' robberies seem to have been taken from the dime novels, and he has the killing of banker Heywood in Northfield entirely wrong.

In writing of Al Jennings, the author has the Jennings boys cowboys, but they were lawyers like their father. He has the circumstances of the killing of Ed Jennings by Temple Houston wrong. He is also wrong in saying that "both Al and Frank Jennings were given life sentences." Frank was sentenced to only five years. The author claims that Al returned to Oklahoma after serving five years and then went to California to brag about his deeds, but he does not mention that Al ran for county attorney in Oklahoma City in 1910 and for governor of Oklahoma in 1914, being defeated both times. This shows that he was in Oklahoma for several years before he went to California.

The author has Black Jack Ketchum "born and raised in New Mexico," but he was born and raised in West Texas. He is also mistaken in saying that Black Jack robbed the same train four times and mistaken in having these robberies committed on the Santa Fe Railroad. It was the Colorado and Southern. He is also wrong in saying that Sam Ketchum was sometimes called Black Jack. He is wrong in saying that after Black Jack killed two miners in Arizona he was tracked to Turkey Canyon, where a fierce battle followed. The battle was between Sheriff Farr and his posse against Sam Ketchum, Carver and McGinnis; Black Jack was not there. The fight followed a train robbery in which Black Jack had not taken part because the gang had quarreled with him.

The author is wrong in having Sam Ketchum robbing trains after Black Jack was in prison. Sam had died from a wound received in the battle before Black Jack was captured. He has Sam shot by conductor Harrington while he was holding up a train, but it was Black Jack who was attempting to hold up the train as a one-man job and who was

shot by Harrington. He even has Sam's arm being amputated because of the wound and says he died of shock. He has Black Jack saying things on the scaffold just before he was hanged. No one else has recorded them. The entire account is confused.

Concerning Wyatt Earp in Ellsworth, the author repeats that well-worn tale about Wyatt backing down Ben Thompson after the killing of Sheriff Whitney. When this killing took place, Earp was not even in the town. That is one of the yarns Earp told Stuart Lake while dictating his autobiography. The author is wrong in having Earp marshal of Wichita. He was only a city policeman. He is also wrong in having him "chief deputy" of Dodge City. He states that a $1,000 reward was offered to anyone who would put Wyatt in Boot Hill and that George Hoyt [Hoy] was trying to collect the reward when he was shot. No such reward was placed upon Wyatt's head, and the shooting of Hoy did not take place under these circumstances.

The author seems to make mistakes in every detail of his accounts. He writes that Wyatt left Dodge in 1878 and rode to Arizona "at the request of Sheriff John E. Behan." That is preposterous, for Behan was sheriff at that time, and when Wyatt arrived in Arizona, they became bitter enemies. He has Behan asking Wyatt to serve as his deputy, but that is not true. He also has Curly Bill Brocius killing Fred White on purpose, but this killing was proved to have been an accident, and the victim himself admitted as much before he died. Again he is mistaken in having Wyatt paid $1,000 a month to protect the Oriental Saloon in Tombstone.

He tells about Big-Nose Kate sitting up all night drinking with the Clantons and in parenthesis has her "later Doc's lover." She had been Doc's woman for several years, and before he went to Arizona. His account of the O K Corral fight is very unreliable, as is the killing of Morgan Earp. He even has Wyatt killing Johnny Ringo.

He has Frank Canton heading the Red Sash gang of "outlaws" and says the "war [I assume he means the Johnson County War] "became so bloody that it reduced the hardened Frank Canton to a nervous wreck." That is news indeed.

Like all his other accounts, his chapter on the Renos is undependable. And in his chapter on Joseph Slade he misnames Jules Reni as Jules Beni. He also has the killing of Reni all wrong. He even has the killing of Soapy Smith wrong.

In his section about Belle Starr the author writes that her father, Judge Shirley, moved his family to Scyene, Texas, near Dallas, "to avoid the violence of the border wars between Redlegs and slaveholders," but he left Carthage because the town had been burned, including his tavern. The author is also mistaken in having Ed Shirley fighting *with* the Redlegs; he was a southerner fighting *against* that group.

"In 1869," the author writes, "Belle, Reed and the others rode to California and, hearing that a wealthy prospector living near the North Canadian River, had a large cache of gold hidden in his shack, attacked him one night and tortured him into telling them where his riches were hidden. The band rode off with about $30,000 in gold." He leaves the impression that this happened in California, but it happened on the North Canadian in Indian Territory. The man they robbed was an Indian named Watt Grayson, and the accumulation of money in his possession was the government's annuity for the Creek Indians.

The author is wrong in saying that

Sam Starr arrived at Younger's Bend, when Belle married him. Sam married Belle before there was a Younger's Bend. He has Belle's death incorrect too when he writes, "Alone on the trail, Belle was shot from her horse by an unknown gunman lying in ambush. Some said he was one of her many lovers Belle had discarded. Hours later a traveler found Belle and took her home. She died in her daughter's arms." We know that it was her daughter who discovered the body after Belle's horse arrived home riderless, and it was not "hours later."

He also has the killing of Henry Starr wrong. He tells a tale I have not seen before, writing that Charley Storms was playing poker with Wild Bill Hickok in Deadwood when Hickok was killed by Jack McCall. He also says that Storms got Hickok's gun and that that was the gun with which he tried to kill Luke Short.

In his chapter on Ben Thompson he repeats that falsehood of Stuart Lakes about Wyatt Earp arresting Thompson in Ellsworth. However, he does say that "no records, newspaper accounts or official testimony exists to support this story, other than the heady narrative penned by Lake."

In the account of Cattle Kate Watson he states that "a large vigilante group showed up at Kate's bordello and caught her off guard," but there were only six men in the group, and her corral was not "crowded with cattle with brands of other cattlemen," nor were Kate and Jim Averill "stealing cattle on the wholesale basis." Finally, like all his other accounts, his chapter on the Wild Bunch is unreliable.

In this modern day, when so much has been written by conscientious historians trying to correct the many legends about the western badmen, it is regrettable that the author chose merely to repeat the tales of the early dime novelists.

156. NEWMAN, TILLIE KARNS. Coffeyville, Kansas, centennial souvenir historical booklet, by Tillie Karns Newman. ₁Coffeyville, 1961₁. Stiff illus. col. wrappers.

The author of the principle article of this book quotes two of the most unreliable accounts of the arrival of Billy the Kid's family in Coffeyville in 1862 and in saying that his father, William H. Bonney [sic] died there, "leaving his young widow and two baby sons. . . . The widow disposed of all the property except a wagon and team of horses and joined a party of emigrants heading for Pueblo, Colorado." She then has the Kid's mother marrying Antrim and moving to Santa Fe, New Mexico, where they opened a restaurant, and says the Kid was still under five years of age. We know that she married Antrim in Santa Fe, that Mrs. McCarty never went to Calorado, and the Kid was nearer 14 years of age instead of under five. She is also mistaken in having his mother marrying Antrim "in the summer of 1863." It was March 1, 1873.

157. OLSSON, JAN OLOF. Welcome to Tombstone, by Jan Olof Olsson. Translated from the Swedish by Maurice Michael. London, Elek Books, ₁1956₁. Cloth.

In this book there is quite a bit of material on Wyatt Earp. Through a character called Hassayamper, the author says that Wyatt became famous for arresting the Clements brothers in Ellsworth, Kansas. He is evidently thinking of Lake's tale that Earp had trouble with the Clements in Wichita. The author has Clements "a brutal chap, dirty and fat and nasty and he shot and killed people like nothing."

He says that Earp then became city marshal of Dodge City, which is not true. He was only a deputy marshal at Dodge. He says that after Earp won the office, "as he always did when he got a police job, he arranged things suitably and looked after himself. He bought himself into a gaming-bank and acquired a number of building sites, thus becoming a capitalist." All this is untrue. The author also has Earp serving as city marshal a second time. He has Mannen Clements born in London and misspells Rudabaugh's name as Roudabaugh. He is also mistaken in saying that Earp and the mayor of Dodge City "drew up a list of prohibitions" to be enforced in Dodge. Earp had nothing to do with passing such laws.

He has Hassayampa say: "In the cattle-towns and mining-towns and in every hole in the West you would find in those days a woman called Katie With the Nose—or one of her establishments. She was a beautiful blonde with a rather big nose." I suppose he means Big-Nose Kate, but she was not a blond or a beauty, and she ran no saloons with gambling tables. He is certainly in error, too, when he claims that Nellie Cushman ran a brothel and is mistaken in having Big-Nose Kate running a dance hall in Dodge. He repeats that Lake tale about her buying a piano and failing to pay for it until the mayor sent Wyatt Earp to repossess it.

He says that the reason Wyatt and Doc Holliday were such good friends is that Doc saved Wyatt's life in Wichita, Kansas. According to Stuart Lake that happened in Dodge. He is mistaken in having Wyatt owning building sites and houses "throughout the whole of the wild West," in such towns as Dodge City, Wichita, Deadwood, Laramie, and

Tombstone. He is wrong, too, in having Doc Holliday in Tombstone before Wyatt arrived there. He has Wyatt writing to Doc about property values and asking if it was the sort of town in which he should invest his money. The author also has Virgil Earp already town marshal of Tombstone before Wyatt arrived there, but they went to Tombstone together.

He is mistaken in having the governor of Arizona appointing Wyatt federal marshal. He was appointed U.S. marshal much later by Crawley P. Dake. He also has Wyatt buying shares in the gaming rooms in the Crystal Palace and the Oriental Saloon. That never happened either, though he was given a small interest in the Oriental in return for protecting the place. Some of the stories about the robberies of stagecoaches (which he calls diligences) are wrong, and the author has Clum, the editor of the *Tombstone Epitaph*, shooting one of the robbers with a "little pocket revolver." He has Sheriff Behan "an intriguer and a thoroughly nasty character" who was in cahoots with the crooked cowboy outlaws. He states that "Wyatt realized that Behan was in on everything the cowboys did and that he received a percentage of the proceeds from all robberies of diligences and thefts of cattle." That is a rather broad accusation.

The author is also wrong on the date of Wyatt's death. He died not in 1930 but on January 13, 1929. He is also wrong in having Earp returning to Tombstone a year before he died, though he does say that he only went to visit Boot Hill and there requested Hassayampa to visit him for a talk. He is also wrong in saying that Wyatt got rich in oil in California. He has Morgan Earp killed in Campbell's billiard parlor, but it was in Hatch's place, and he is mis-

taken in saying that Wyatt "killed every cowboy who was with the Clantons and the McLowerys [*sic*]. Altogether, though this book has some interest, it is historically unreliable. Like some others, he misspells the McLaury brothers' name as McLowery.

158. O'REILLEY, HARRINGTON. Fifty years on the trail. A true story of western life, by Harrington O'Reilley. London, Chatto & Windus, Piccadilly, 1889. Cloth.

This nineteenth-century author misnames Joseph Slade as Dan Slade and Jules Reni as Jules Berg (Julesburg was the town named after Reni). He is inclined to exaggerate his statements, such as that forty or fifty were killed at the battle on Beecher's Island; there were six killed and eighteen wounded. The author had a reputation for "stretching the blanket." He claims that General McKenzie sent for him when he needed advice, and though the author lived among Indians, he did not seem to know a Sioux from a Cheyenne. There is also some material on Doc Middleton and Fly-Speck Billy.

159. PAINE, LAURAN. Texas Ben Thompson, by Lauran Paine. Los Angeles, Westernlore Press, 1966. Cloth.

In his first chapter the author makes this statement: "The gunman Tom Horn, a native of Missouri who died on the gallows up in Wyoming, never recovered from his brief sojourn in Texas. He walked to his death with a smile, and a Texas swagger, affecting to his last breath the mannerisms of Texas." Horn's sojourn in Texas was so brief that he could not have acquired many of its mannerisms, and it is news that Texans "swaggered" any different from other people.

I think he is mistaken when he says, "Many a drover bought cattle for a dollar a head in Texas and later at the rails' head up in Kansas, sold them for a hundred and fifty dollars a head." In those days cattle never brought such prices. In a footnote on page 103 the author claims that, after he left Abilene, Wild Bill Hickok became embroiled in a fight with Tom Custer and was asked by the town marshal to resign. The fight with Custer happened before he went to Abilene, and Hickok was the town marshal.

He is also mistaken in saying that Bill Thompson, after he accidentally shot Sheriff Whitney, made the statement that he would have shot him "if he had been Jesus Christ." I was glad to see, however, that he does not have Ben Thompson being arrested by Wyatt Earp, as Stuart Lake claims.

He writes that Ben Thompson sent for his wife and son to visit Abilene. When they arrived, he took them for a buggy ride. He writes: "The streets of Abilene were deeply rutted. In some places there were chuck holes nearly three feet deep. One of the wheels of Ben's rig dropped into such a hole, upsetting the buggy atop its passengers." The author says that the boy's foot was crushed, Ben's leg broken, and his wife's arm crushed. The trouble with these statements is that all of this happened in Kansas City, where Ben had gone to meet his family. His accounts of the killings of Ben Thompson and King Fisher are also unreliable.

160. PAINE, LAURAN. Tom Horn. Man of the West, [by] Lauran Paine. London, John Long, [1962]. Cloth.

Though of interest, this book is filled with errors. The author has Sam Bass in Leadville, Colorado, but Bass was never in Colorado. He misspells Bat Masterson's middle name as Barkley instead of Barklay. The reason he gives for the outbreak of the Lincoln County War is incorrect, as is his information about the lynching of Cattle Kate and Jim Averill. He says that John Clay was at the lynching, but Clay was not among those present. There are many other errors.

161. PARRISH, JOE. Coffins, cactus and cowboys, by Joe Parrish. [El Paso, Texas, Superior Publishing Co., 1964]. Stiff wrappers.

This tells the story of Dallas Stoudenmire and his short reign as marshal of El Paso. The account of the killing of this officer is entirely wrong. The author includes John Wesley Hardin, John Selman, Bass Outlaw, George Scarborough, Jeff Milton, Wyatt Earp, and even Billy the Kid because, the author says the Kid made one brief excursion into El Paso. In this account he follows the long-disproved legend about the Kid rescuing his friend Segura.

The author is also mistaken when he says that Hardin's first victim was a Negro, whom he killed "to avenge a fancied slight." The true story is that the Negro, a freed slave named Mage, lost a wrestling match to Hardin, and when he wiped his face and saw blood where Hardin had scratched him, he became very angry and said that no white boy could draw blood from him and live. The next morning, when Hardin started for his home after spending the night with his cousin, he met Mage, who was carrying a stick and who threatened the boy. Hardin tried to explain that he had had no intention of scratching him, but the Negro continued to try to beat him, and so Hardin shot him several times.

Mage did not die until the next day, but the act put Hardin on the run from the "Yankee law." The author is also mistaken in having Hardin facing down Wild Bill Hickok in Dodge City. That happened in Abilene.

He is also mistaken in having John Selman shooting Hardin in the Acme Saloon with a rifle. He shot Hardin with a six-gun, and he did not shoot him "again and again." He is also wrong in saying that Selman "had been working his way West for some time and arrived in El Paso in 1881, or 1882." Selman had already been farther west, in New Mexico, where he was active during the Lincoln County War in 1878.

162. PARSON, MABEL. A courier of New Mexico, by Mabel Parson. [N.p., n.d.]. Cloth.

This book contains some material on Billy the Kid. The author is mistaken in saying that the Kid was the "fighting foreman of a big ranch." She also continues that legend about his having killed twenty-one men by the time he was twenty-one years old.

163. PATCH, JOSEPH DORST. Reminiscences of Fort Huachuca, by Joseph Dorst Patch. [N.p., n.d.]. Pict. wrappers.

The author is mistaken in saying that "Wyatt Earp was sheriff of Tombstone, and his brothers and Doc Holliday were his deputies." He has a poor opinion of Earp, saying that both he and Doc Holliday "were professional gamblers and generally shot their victims when they didn't have a chance." He also says that when Earp left Tombstone "the town was more lawless than it was when he first arrived."

164. PENFIELD, THOMAS. Dig here! by Thomas Penfield. San Antonio, Texas, Naylor Co., 1962. Cloth.

The author writes on page 108: "You believe this bunk if you wish. The writer has no intention of passing it off as anything else." The note was in reference to a story entitled "Lost Mine of the Silver Stairway," but it can be applied to most of the other stories in the book. He is careless with geography and dates. He is mistaken in saying that the Santa Clara Mountains are southwest of Tucson and that Tucumcari is on the east bank of the Santa Cruz River, and he is mistaken in having Solomon Warner a merchant of Phoenix in 1850; Phoenix was not founded until a few years later. Geronimo arrived at Fort Sill not in 1886 but in 1894, and the Camp Grant Massacre took place not in 1861 but ten years later.

He writes that Tom and Sam Ketchum worked for a cow outfit in Arizona, but they spent most of their time in New Mexico. He says that Tom "bore a striking resemblance to a petty badman known as Black Jack Christian who had just been killed." In Bisbee one day Tom was mistaken for the dead man, and he decided to take the name Black Jack. That is something I have not seen before. Nor have I read elsewhere the author's claim that each member of the Ketchum gang "had to wear, as a kind of badge of trade, a plain gold ring on the third finger of the left hand." He credits Black Jack Ketchum with fifteen murders, but the number is greatly exaggerated.

The author has Black Jack burying a lot of treasure, though he admits that the evidence "is pretty thin." When Black Jack was shot in the arm during an attempted train robbery, the author says, he "took off into the timber afoot" and was "caught a few days later." Black Jack stayed on the railroad right of way and was captured the next morning, Ketchum himself flagging the crew of a passing freight train. He says that Sheriff Cicero Stewart of Eddy County was sent for to make a positive identification of Black Jack, but my late friend Bob Kennon, about whom I wrote a book, was working for Sheriff Rhome Shields of Tom Green County, Texas, at the time, and he told me that Shields was sent for for this purpose and that he went with Shields.

One of the chapters is entitled "The Many Treasures of Sam Bass," but except for the money from the robberies of the Union Pacific, Bass never had enough money to pay anyone to bury it. All his later robberies were largely failures. The author has Bass burying treasure in seven locations in Texas (1) near Springtown, Parker County, amount unknown; (2) northwest of Denton, Montague [sic] County, $30,000; (3) in a cave near McNeil, Travis County, $30,000; (4) near Dallas, Dallas County, $30,000; (5) in a cave on Packsaddle Mountain, Brewster County, amount unknown; (6) near Boston, Wise County, $200,000; (7) near Costell, Llano County, $5,000. The author writes: "With part of his loot reportedly buried in so many locations in Texas, was any of it ever recovered? No one can be sure. Henry Chapman, who lived near Springtown, Parker County, came close to it. One day he was riding a mule through the woods from Harrison's gin, ... to Miller's place near the mouth of Salt Creek. At a point near Sheen's Peak, his mule shied and broke the saddle girth. While he was dismounted, mending the girth, he discovered a pile of fresh earth covered with brush. He supposed at first it was the grave of a

slain person, but he was curious and removed the brush and fresh earth.

"Within a few minutes, Chapman uncovered a wooden box big enough ... to hold a bushel and a half. It was filled to the top with gold and silver coins, many of them $20 gold pieces. He was filling a sack with coins when he looked up and saw eight riders approaching in the distance. He hastily mounted and rode away. He never saw them again, but he was sure they were surviving members of Sam Bass' gang." Such tales are simply wild efforts to create a legend. The author also says that Bass wanted to rob the bank at Round Rock because he could not recover his buried treasures. It is strange that he would be watched at all those places.

He is another who has Bass and his companions selling their herd of cattle in Deadwood. They were sold in Kansas, where there was a market. He has Collins and Bass gambling away the entire proceeds of the cattle sale overnight in Deadwood. He intimates that Bass planned the Big Springs robbery and was the leader of the gang, but the leader was Joel Collins. He also says that the $60,000 they got in $20 gold pieces was in a pouch, but it was in wooden cases. He says that Collins was overtaken and killed and that $25,000 was found in his saddlebags. He does not mention that Heffridge was killed with Collins, and if the latter was carrying $25,000, he certainly had more than his share of loot.

Collins and Heffridge had their money in the legs of a pair of old pants, not in a saddlebag. The author has just said that the loot was evenly divided, but he has only five men in this holdup. There were six, and since the loot was $60,000, each man got $10,000. He has

Bass escaping to Texas alone, but Davis went with him.

He has Jim Murphy joining the Bass gang just before the bank robbery at Round Rock, but Murphy had joined them sometime back at Denton. "With with of his loot reportedly buried in so many locations in Texas, was any of it ever found?" asks the author. I would answer in the negative because there wasn't any to be found. Bass had spent the last of his Union Pacific gold, and his other robberies hardly realized enough to keep him in food and horse feed.

He has a Red Curly (who he says was Sandy King) caught with Russian Bill and the two hanged in Shakespeare, but not because, as he says, they had robbed the mint at Monterey, Mexico. He is also mistaken in having Augustin Chacon captured on "Arizona soil." He was captured in Old Mexico. The book contains little real history but is founded upon legends.

165. PHARES, Ross. Bible in pocket, gun in hand. The story of frontier religion. By Ross Phares. Garden City, N.Y., Doubleday & Co., Inc., 1964. Cloth.

This author spells Tascosa as Tasco. He is mistaken when he says that Clay Allison was killed when, in a drunken stupor, he rolled off a loaded wagon and was crushed to death under its wheels. The wheel of Allison's wagon struck a grass clod, and he lost his balance and fell. His head struck a front wheel, which fractured his skull. Such errors may be considered minor ones, but it is easy to get history correct.

166. PIERSON, JAMES R. The Pony Express trail, 1860–1861, by James R. Pierson. St. Joseph, Mo., published by Pony Express Productions, [1960]. Stiff col. pict. wrappers.

There is a mention of Rock Creek Station and an account of the killing of Dave McCanles by Wild Bill Hickok, but the author is mistaken in saying that "the incident over which the killing occurred was the alleged theft of livestock belonging to the Central Overland California and Pikes Peak Express Co. He does, however, admit that the theft was "alleged."

167. POINDEXTER, C. A., and BRACKEN FITZPATRICK. The historical background, setting and synopsis of "Jesse James." Filmed at and near Pineville, Missouri, By C. A. Poindexter and Bracken Fitzpatrick. Pineville, Missouri, Printed by the Pineville Democrat, [n.d.]. Stiff wrappers.

This book has a chapter on Jesse James and another on his death, as well as a synopsis of the movie of his life. The authors misspell Dr. Samuel's name as Samuels and Quantrill's name as Quantrell. They say the first bank robbery Jesse James committed was at Liberty, Missouri. He was not in that robbery but recovering from a wound in the lungs. They are also wrong in saying that "two of them [the Younger brothers], Jim and John died in the penitentiary." Only one died there; the other committed suicide after his release. They write, "It is said that Cole Younger became a preacher and that he preached at Springfield, Missouri." That will be news to the historians. They have Governor Crittenden a friend of the James boys who tried to get them to surrender so that he could pardon them, but that was not the case.

The synopsis of the movie is full of errors of fact. They have Mrs. Samuel killed by the bomb a villain threw into the house. She lost an arm but survived. They have Bob Ford tipping off the law that the James gang was preparing to raid the Northfield Bank, and they repeat the old legend about Jesse saving the widow's home from the cruel mortgage holder.

168. PRAGER, GLENN B. Roswell. A fond look back, by Glenn B. Prager. ₁Roswell, Great Western Printing, n.d.₁. Stiff wrappers.

In a section on Lincoln County and Billy the Kid the author leaves the impression that the Kid's mother married Antrim in Kansas, but she married him in Santa Fe, New Mexico. He also follows that old tale about the Kid stabbing "a man who he fancied had insulted his mother." He is also mistaken in saying that the Kid and his companions were captured at Stinking Springs "after a gun fight." There was no fight. Garrett killed Charlie Bowdre when he came out the door the next morning to feed the horses. The author also has the killing of Bell and Olinger confused. He says that the Kid had a gun in his hand when he was killed by Garrett, but Billy was unarmed.

169. PRASSEL, FRANK RICHARD. The western peace officer. A legacy of law and order, [by] Frank Richard Prassel. Norman, University of Oklahoma Press, ₁1972₁. Pict. cloth.

This is a scholarly and unusual handling of the subject and shows serious research. The author, however, is mistaken in saying that John M. Larn "ended his career as a peace officer on a vigilante rope." Larn was shot, not hanged, by the vigilantes. He also errs in saying that Jim Courtright was a "well-known

Southwestern desperado," and he also misspells his name as Courtwright both in the text and in the index. He is mistaken in saying that the Pinkertons tracked down John Wesley Hardin in Florida. A Texas Ranger tracked him down. In another error he states that Charles E. ("Black Bart") Bolton was recruited by Wells Fargo as an operative to keep him from robbing their stagecoaches. It was said that they paid him a salary to quit robbing them, but he was never an operative of theirs.

170. PRATHER, H. BRYANT. Come listen to my tale, by H. Bryant Prather. Tahlequah, Oklahoma, Pan Press, ₁1964₁. Cloth.

When this author writes about Sam Bass, he makes many mistakes, such as having Ranger June Peak securing the services of an informant. He is here referring to Jim Murphy, but Peak had nothing to do with Murphy's treachery. He has Bass wandering all over the country before reaching Denton after the Union Pacific robbery. He writes as though Bass's first Texas robbery was at Cement City, "just west of Dallas." That was his third Texas train robbery, and it occurred at Eagle Ford. After the battle at Salt Creek, in which Arkansas Johnson was killed, the author says, "Murphy was later located in a boarding house on Ross Avenue, Dallas, Texas." That is untrue, as is the statement that he told officers "just how and when the bank at Round Rock was to be robbed."

171. PRATHER, H. BRYANT. Echoes of the past, by H. Bryant Prather. Dallas, Texas, the Trumpet Press, Inc., ₁1968₁. Cloth.

The author of this little book claims that Sam Bass made his headquarters in

Springtown, Parker County, Texas, for some time, but he is mistaken. He says that Bass "by choice became a bank robber," but Bass never robbed a bank. He was preparing to rob one when he was killed.

172. PREECE, HAROLD. The Dalton Gang. End of an outlaw era, by Harold Preece. New York, Hastings, [1963]. Cloth.

This author's account of the Northfield raid is unreliable. He writes of the Doolin gang robbing a train in Spearville, Kansas, but it was a bank they robbed there. In one of his footnotes he has Chris Evans, of the Sontag-Evans gang, "the younger brother of Jesse Evans," a statement far from the truth. This is a well-written book, but the author includes conversation that no one recorded. Though it makes far more interesting reading, it is out of place in an historical work.

173. PRICE, S. GOODALE. Black Hills, the land of legend, by S. Goodale Price. Los Angeles, De Voors & Co., 1933. Cloth.

Like most books about the Black Hills, this one has some information about Wild Bill Hickok, Poker Alice, and Calamity Jane, none of it very reliable. The author writes that Wild Bill was paid $1,000 a month at Abilene, Kansas, to serve as marshal. That is incorrect, as is the author's claim that Hickok drove the outlaws from the streets of Abilene. He also has the slaying of Wild Bill wrong; he says that Hickok was killed in the Melodian Saloon "after an argument over a gold dust wager."

174. RAY, SAM HILL. Border tales. Stories of Texas-New Mexico, by Sam Hill Ray. [El Paso, Commer-cial Printing Co., 1964]. Stiff pict. wrappers.

The two chapters on Billy the Kid follow the Griggs account, a book full of errors (see *Burs Under the Saddle*, page 221). In an account that is far from the truth, the author has the Kid's father a mining engineer who came to Kansas in answer to an ad in a Philadelphia paper, and he has the wife named Rachael, a daughter, Jeannie, and a son, William (Billy). He has the Kid's father killed in Topeka by the Apaches. It seems that Jeannie fell in love with a miner and when the Kid tried to make the miner marry her, the miner confessed that he was already married and had six children in Texas. The Kid got a gun and killed him. The miner was thus the Kid's first victim. This is exactly the same story as Griggs's, but we know that it is incorrect. The author is also mistaken in having the Kid's grave marker read: "William H. Bonney, alias Billy the Kid. Died July, 1880." He was killed in 1881. He says that Billy the Kid boasted of twenty-one killings, but this boasting has been done by the would-be historians who followed him. This author is another who tells the imaginary tale about the Kid riding eighty-one miles to San Elizario to free his friend Segura from prison.

175. RAYFIELD, ALMA COCHRAN. The West that's gone, [by] Alma Cochran Rayfield. New York, Carlton Press, 1962. Cloth.

This author, in writing about her father's experiences, gives an inaccurate account of the robbing of the bank at Medicine Lodge by Henry Brown and Ben Wheeler. In a later chapter she tells of the attempted train robbery by Black Jack Ketchum. In this chapter, however, she is mistaken in saying that

Ketchum shot off a passenger's jaw when he stuck his head out the window and then shot another passenger in the jaw. Ketchum shot only one man, and that was the express messenger. She calls conductor Frank Harrington by the name Ed. There is an unreliable account about Harrington guarding Ketchum that I have not seen before.

She is mistaken in saying that Bat Masterson's brother went to Dodge City from the East to be Bat's deputy and is also mistaken in saying that Bat was out of town when his brother was killed.

176. REA, RALPH R. Boone County and its people, by Ralph R. Rea. Van Buren, Press-Argus, 1955. Cloth.

The author erroneously says that the Youngers were followers of Sam Hildebrand. Henry Starr was killed at Harrison, Arkansas, by W. J. Myers, while robbing a bank. Glen Shirley says that Myers was the bank's cashier, but this author says that he was the bank's former president.

177. RENNERT, VINCENT PAUL. The cowboy, [by] Vincent Paul Rennert. New York, Crowell-Collier Press, [1966]. Cloth.

Most writers about cowboys do reasonably well until they start writing about the outlaws of the period. Then they tend to follow often-repeated legends instead of doing some research of their own. In writing of the Lincoln County War, this author says that the sheriff's posse went out to Tunstall's ranch, seized him, and on the way back to town killed him, but that is far from the way it actually happened.

He says that the war was waged between John Chisum and Murphy and his business partners and intimates that it was a cattle war, but it was an economic war to gain the upper hand between two mercantile businesses, the Tunstall, McSween and Chisum store and bank and the Murphy, Dolan and Riley Company. It erupted when the former began encroaching on the latter's business and influence.

When Morton and Baker were killed, this author has them "cornered in a dugout," where, he says, they held out until their ammunition was exhausted. They were captured in the open. He says that the battle at the McSween home lasted three days, but it lasted five, and he has only one man killed on the Murphy side. In the battle in which Buckshot Roberts was fatally wounded at Blazer's Mill, the author has fourteen men in Brewer's party, and he says they *fled* after Roberts was wounded. Though they left the scene after Brewer was killed, they did not flee. He writes that there were ten men in the party that hung Jim Averill and Cattle Kate, but there were only six.

178. RENNERT, VINCENT PAUL. Western outlaws, [by] Vincent Paul Rennert. New York, Crowell-Collins, [1968]. Cloth.

In the chapter on John Wesley Hardin many of the author's statements are true, but others are unreliable, especially the account of Hardin's capture in Florida. He misspells Mannen Clements' first name as Manning. In his chapter on Sam Bass he has Jim Berry killed, but he says that "Collins and Heffridge were killed *later*." These latter two were the first ones killed after the Union Pacific robbery. He is also mistaken in saying that Bass, in his first Texas train robbery, at Allen Station, got $3,000. Only $1,280 was taken in this robbery. He is also mistaken in having the express messenger at the Hutchins robbery "shooting it out rather than surrender" and being wounded before giving up. There was no resistance. He has many more battles between the Bass gang and the law than there actually were.

In his chapter on Billy the Kid he has Mesilla in Texas instead of in New Mexico, and he has Jack Long in the sheriff's party when Brady and Hindman were killed. This is the first account I have seen in which Long was included. He has McSween a lawyer and rancher, but McSween owned no cattle. During the battle at the McSween home, he has Beckwith killed by two Mexicans hiding in a chickenhouse, and he says that they too were later killed. He is also wrong in saying that Garrett was *appointed* deputy sheriff to catch the Kid. He was duly elected sheriff. The author is also mistaken in saying that after the Kid mounted a horse to escape "he went over to Olinger and fired the second barrel into him." He did that immediately after the first shot. After the Kid's escape, the author says, "for several months Garrett seemed uninterested in the Kid's case or reluctant to go after him." Garrett was very much interested in the Kid's case, but there were plans to be made and information to obtain.

In telling of the battle at the McSween home in Lincoln, the author says that Billy the Kid was in the group, the first to leave the burning home; but he was in the last group to leave. He says that Carlyle was killed by his own men when he jumped through the window of the Greathouse Station, but the more conservative historians do not believe this. Like so many others, too, this author says that the Kid was going to Fort Sumner to see his sweetheart when he was killed.

Among other unreliable statements in

his chapter on Butch Cassidy and the Wild Bunch, he says, "Ben Kilpatrick and an outlaw named Howard Benson tried to rob the Southern Pacific Express near Sanderson, Texas." The outlaw with Kilpatrick at that time was a former cellmate named Ole Beck. He says that the Wild Bunch got their name because of their drinking and carousing, but that is not true. He spells Longabaugh's name as Longbaugh, as well as misspelling other proper names.

He says that Jesse James's mother divorced her second husband, but he died before she got the divorce. He does, unlike most, have Jesse at home with a lung wound when the bank at Liberty was robbed. He misspells the name Samuel as Samuels. In the account of the bank at Northfield, he has Pitts smashing Heywood "over the head with his gun butt," but no westerner used the butt to strike a man. If he wanted to hit someone over the head with a six-gun, he used the barrel. He has the James gang robbing a train in Muncie, Indiana, but the train was at Muncie, Kansas, a few miles out of Kansas City. Like his other chapters this one, too, is unreliable. One of the pictures purporting to show the James and Younger gang is not of those men. Though some of his information is true, there is no excuse for the errors listed here.

179. RICKARDS, COLIN. Bowler hats and Stetsons. Stories of the Englishmen in the wild West, [by] Colin Rickards. London, Ronald Whiting and Wheaton, [1966]. Cloth.

This author is another who claims that Jesse James was in the Liberty, Missouri, bank robbery. Jesse was at home recovering from a wound in his lungs. The author is also mistaken in having Ben

Thompson saving Bat Masterson's life when Bat killed Sergeant King and incurred the anger of some of King's troopers. I can find no record that Thompson was ever in West Texas. The author says that this happened at Fort Elliott, but most other writers say that it happened in Sweetwater, Texas (the name was later changed to Mobeetie), near Fort Elliott. He also has Ben, his wife, and his son hurt in a runaway while Ben was taking his family for a ride, but the accident was not caused by a runaway but happened when a wheel of the buggy struck a hole. Of course, this is an error of small consequence, but it is just as easy to have the account correct.

The author incorrectly gives the name No. 10 Saloon to Bob Ford's saloon in Creede. That was the name of the saloon in which Wild Bill Hickok was killed in Deadwood. He says that Ed Kelly killed Ford because he wanted to be known as "the man who killed the man who killed Jesse James." He has Poker Alice sitting at a table when Ford was killed, but I have not seen that detail elsewhere.

He calls Billy the Kid "a bucktoothed, effeminate little gunfighter from the New York slums," but the Kid was a baby when his parents left New York. He has the posse that killed Tunstall shooting first at Billy the Kid, Dick Brewer, John Middleton, and Robert Widenmann, but that never happened. They just surrounded Tunstall and shot at him. The author is mistaken when he writes that "Dick Brewer and twelve of his men *ambushed* crippled gunfighter Andrew L. Roberts." Roberts was not so crippled that he could not be out bounty hunting, and all the men were in plain sight when the shooting took place; there was no ambush. The author also has Sam Bass killed by Dick

Ware, but it has never been proved who really shot Bass.

180. RICKARDS, COLIN. Buckskin Frank Leslie, gunman of Tombstone, by Colin Rickards. Drawings by Russell Waterhouse. El Paso, Texas, Texas Western Press, 1964. Pict. cloth.

On page 16 of this short history the author is mistaken when he writes that Billy the Kid "had been killed in a gunfight." He was killed in the dark by Pat Garrett, and there was no gunfight since the Kid did not have a gun.

181. RITTENHOUSE, J. D. Maverick tales. True stories of early Texas, [by] J. D. Rittenhouse. [New York], Winchester Press, [1971]. Cloth.

This author is mistaken in saying that Clay Allison killed Chunk Colbert "in an argument over breakfast." Their quarrel dated much earlier. He repeats the old legend about Allison pulling the dentist's teeth because the dentist had pulled a wrong tooth for Allison, only this time the incident occurred in Las Vegas, New Mexico. This stunt has occurred—in legend—all over the West. He is also wrong in having a wagon wheel crush the life from Allison. He did fall from the wagon, but his head hit a front wheel, and he died of a fractured skull.

Of the O K Corral fight the author says, "There were four Clantons there, and only one fell in the Earp-Clanton fusillade." True, only one Clanton, Billy, fell. But the McLaury boys were Clanton men, and both of them were killed. He has Billy Clanton fifteen years old at the time of this battle, but he was older than that. He tells of the hanging of Russian Bill and Sandy King, but misspells Russian Bill's name as Tettenborn instead of Tattenbaum, and says that Bill's mother was the daughter of a Scots sea captain and his father a German subject of the Russian Czar.

He is also mistaken in saying that the Northfield Bank robbery was Jesse James's first holdup killing. Jesse killed John W. Sheets during the holdup of the Gallatin Bank in 1869. He says that the Bass gang "perhaps held up four trains." They did hold up four Texas trains, and there was no "perhaps" about it. The author also says that the Collins gang robbed two stages in South Dakota, but they held up more than two. He also says, "When Sam was buried, a stranger rode up swiftly after the ceremony and threw handsful of earth on the grave. People still believe it was Frank Jackson." This too is untrue.

182. ROBERTS, PAUL H. Them were the days, by Paul H. Roberts. San Antonio, Texas, the Naylor Company . . . , [1965]. Pict. cloth.

This author writes, "It has been written that Sheriff Commodore Owens of Apache County, Arizona, killed Ike Clanton on Black River in the White Mountains," but he later cites many characters who deny this, and they are correct. Owens did not kill Clanton. In one place he mentions "the killing of Grat Dalton, working for the Hashknife under the name of Joe Crawford." Yet later he admits that Grat was killed in the Coffeyville raid in 1892. I have never seen evidence that Grat was in Arizona at any time, and of course he was not killed there.

In a letter to Roberts, William V. Morrison, coauthor with C. L. Sonnichsen of *Alias Billy the Kid,*" a postscript says: "I believe Rudabaugh broke jail

and moved into Mexico where he died on a ranch." Rudabaugh did not die on a ranch; his head was severed from his body by a gang in Parral, Mexico, where his body lies buried.

183. ROBERTSON, FRANK C., and BETH KAY HARRIS. Soapy Smith, king of the frontier con men, by Frank C. Robertson and Beth Kay Harris. New York, Hastings House, 1961. Cloth.

This is an interesting and well-written book, but there are a couple of statements I must question. One is that Calamity Jane and Wild Bill were ever in Creede, Colorado. The other is that Dave Rudabaugh was ever there. The period about which the authors write was in the early 1890's, and Rudabaugh was killed in Old Mexico on February 18, 1886. Unlike many others, they spell Ed O. Kelly's name correctly and not as Ed O'Kelly.

184. ROCKWELL, WILSON. New Frontier. Saga of the North Fork, by Wilson Rockwell. Denver, Colo., World Press, 1938. Cloth.

In his information on Billy the Kid, the author states that Pat Garrett led thirteen men in the posse that pursued the Kid after his escape from the Lincoln jail. Only John Poe and Kip McKinney accompanied Garrett.

185. ROLLINS, GEORGE W. A sermon in wax, $65,000 art exhibit . . . , [by George W. Rollins, Houston, Bastains's, n.d.]. Pict. wrappers.

This is a catalog of a wax exhibit of some noted lawmen and outlaws, seemingly written by George W. Rollins. Like so many other accounts of the outlaws, it is filled with errors. The author has Jesse James killing fifty-seven men, and says that the killings were inspired by the bombing of his home "in which he was hiding," but the James boys were not at home when the bombing took place. He says that Henry Starr "robbed more banks and trains than any other man," but he never robbed a train, only banks.

He has Sam Bass "landing in San Antonio" when he came to Texas, but he first landed in Denton. He also has Bass driving cattle to Omaha, but that herd was bossed by Joel Collins, and the cattle were driven to Kansas, not Nebraska. He has Bass organizing a band of ruffians who went "robbing numerous places of business, persons and banks," but Bass never robbed anything except stagecoaches and trains. The author is certainly mistaken in having him robbing a gambling hall in Waco, Texas, and securing $27,000. He has a half dozen killed or wounded at Round Rock and says that Bass was "buried where he fell." As we know, Bass did not die until two days after he was shot, and he was buried in the city cemetery.

The author writes: "It is a shame that books of fiction so defame our national characters with literature that is false and poisonous to the minds of our younger generation." Yet his accounts of these characters are full of errors. He has Wild Bill Hickok an officer in Fort Dodge—meaning, I suppose, Dodge City—Hickok was never an officer there. He has him killing nine men from the time he arrived there at 11 P.M. to daylight the next morning. And the author has Wild Bill killed in Cripple Creek, Colorado, and says, "At his side sleeps his only sweetheart, Calamity Jane." We know all this to be untrue.

He has Bill Doolin a drunken loafer and says, "he died at the hands of one whom he had robbed," but he died at the hands of Heck Thomas. He writes that Thomas, while an express messenger on a train running through Texas, was robbed by Doolin, but that was one of the Bass gang robberies. He has the capture of Doolin all wrong and says that Henry Starr went into Cherokee Bill's cell during Bill's attempted jail break and in a hand-to-hand struggle wrenched the pistol from him and locked him behind the door of his cell." Nothing like that happened; Starr merely talked Bill into giving up his gun.

He also says that Belle Starr was buried where she fell, but we know that she was buried in her own yard and not where they found her murdered. He has the Coffeyville bank raid entirely wrong, even to having one of the robbers named Tim Evans. It will always be a mystery to me why some writers insist upon writing about the western outlaws when they know so little about them and do not attempt to learn the truth about them.

186. ROSA, JOSEPH G. The gunfighter, man or myth? by Joseph G. Rosa. Norman, University of Oklahoma Press, 1969. Cloth.

This well-written book deals with the western six-gun and the men who used them, both for and against the law. The author calls Jules Reni by the name of Bene. On page 161 he writes that Ben Kilpatrick and Howard Benson "held up a train at San Angelo and were killed by a Wells Fargo messenger." This happened on the Southern Pacific near Sanderson, Texas (far from San Angelo), and Kilpatrick's companion was a former cellmate, Ole Beck. He misnames Henry Newton Brown as George Hendry Brown, spelling Henry with a "d", as so many do, and he writes that Brown was "believed to have been a former associate of Billy the Kid." He was indeed a former associate of the Kid.

He does not seem to know that Kip McKinney was also with Garrett and John Poe at the killing of the Kid. He says that Phil Coe was a "former partner" of Ben Thompson's when he was killed, but he was still his partner when this happened. He says, "Hickok's friend, Mike Williams, ran into the line of fire and was killed," but Williams came running from behind a building and was killed when Hickok shot him, thinking he was a friend of Coe coming to kill him.

He has Bill Thompson killing Sheriff Whitney on purpose, but most historians claim that this was an accident by a drunken man. He says that Ed Masterson, when he was shot by Alf Walker and Jack Wagner, "was helped to his room where he died within half an hour," but Ed made his way alone across the street to Hoover's saloon, where he died.

I do not think the author is correct when he says that Frank Stillwell "tried to kill Wyatt in front of the Union Pacific [sic] depot." Most historians say that he was gunned down without warning at the Southern Pacific Depot, the Union Pacific being thousands of miles north. In a footnote on page 186 he has the name Jack Roban; it should be Jack Rohan.

187. SANDERS, GWENDOLINE, and PAUL SANDERS. The Sumner County story, by Gwendoline and Paul Sanders. North Newton, Kansas, Mennonite Press, 1966. Pict. cloth.

This book tells about Luke Short's killing of Jim Courtright and of his own death at Gueda Springs, Kansas. The authors are mistaken in saying that

Short met Bat Masterson for the first time at Wyatt Earp's Oriental Bar in Tombstone. Earp did not own the Oriental, and the two men had become friends in Dodge City much earlier.

In writing of the Daltons, the authors quote a character named Sherman Teal, who misspells several of the Dalton's names, such as Grant for Grat, Emit for Emmett, and Bradwell for Broadwell. The author also tells of the killing of Mike Meagher by Jim Talbot and about the bank robbery at Medicine Lodge by Henry Brown and Ben Wheeler. They write: "Some authorities say that the trusted marshal Brown was, in former years a saddle partner of Billy the Kid." Indeed he was.

188. SANDOZ, MARI. Love song of the plains, by Mari Sandoz. New York, Harper & Brothers, 1961. Cloth.

Of the Hickok-McCanles "fight" the author says, "Hickok shot down an unarmed Southerner, McCanles, when the first anger of the Civil War was breaking over the West with the news of the first defeats and the lengthening casualty lists." That was not the cause of the murders. The author does not give the real cause of this shooting, and she intimates that it was Wellman who owed McCanles for the stage station, but it was the stage company. She states that Wild Bill earned his name from the wild tales he told when he was tried for the killing of McCanles, but he was practically unknown at that time. It was Colonel Nichols in *Harper's Magazine* who gave him this reputation.

She accuses Wild Bill of following "the army, some say into the usual path of the petty bad man of the period into the army, some say into the more profitable business of raiding and bushwhacking." She says that the Collins-Bass gang, after the Union Pacific robbery at Big Springs "scattered down through Kansas with the money," but some of them did not get far.

Of the Johnson County War she says, "Settlers were shot down and hanged, but not even the hanging of Jim Averill and Cattle Kate seemed to stop the rush of homesteaders or to scare out very many." It was not the incoming settlers that worried the cattlemen but the ones who were already there and rustling cattle.

189. SAVAGE, WILLIAM W., JR. (ED.). Cowboy life. Reconstructing an American myth, edited and with an introduction by William W. Savage, Jr. Norman, University of Oklahoma Press, [1973]. Boards.

This is an anthology of chapters taken from such writers as Joseph McCoy, Charlie Siringo, W. S. James, and Andy Adams. In the chapter by Charles Moreau Harger, the author has Wild Bill Hickok named William Hickok. For the chapter by Baylis John Fletcher, see item 73.

190. SCHOENBERGER, DALE T. The gunfighters, by Dale T. Schoenberger. Illustrated by Ernest L. Reedstrom. Caldwell, Idaho, Caxton Printers, Ltd., 1971. Fabricoid.

This author has done some serious research, but there are a few questionable statements in his text. I think he is mistaken in having Kate Elder in the red-light district of Wichita, Kansas. We first hear of her when she was with Doc Holliday in Fort Griffin, Texas. I think he is also mistaken in saying that Wyatt Earp "pistol-whipped and jailed" Curly Bill Brocius when Fred White was accidentally killed. Wyatt's brother Virgil was the arresting officer. He also states

that Wyatt bought an interest in the gambling concession of the Oriental Saloon in Tombstone, but most historians claim that he was given a small interest for the protection he gave the establishment.

The author claims that Wild Bill Hickok was standing near the Novelty Theater when he heard the shot that Phil Coe fired at a dog, but he was in the Alamo Saloon, his favorite hangout. His account of the killing of Coe is also questionable; he has Coe within eight feet of Wild Bill, and yet his first shot missed, and he turned and killed his deputy before he again shot at Coe, this time hitting him in the abdomen. He says, "Hickok and Coe exchanged several shots until one of Bill's bullets struck Coe in the lower abdomen." I do not think Hickok was that poor a shot at such close range.

He has Harry Young the bartender of Saloon No. 10 in Deadwood when Wild Bill was killed, but according to reliable natives and eyewitnesses the bartender was Anson Tipple. The author says that Ben Thompson was born November 11, 1843, but Thompson's most reliable biographer, Floyd Streeter, claims that he was born November 11, 1842.

He is also wrong in having King Fisher suggest to Ben Thompson that they visit the Variety Theater in San Antonio. It was Thompson who persuaded Fisher to go there with him, unfortunately, to their deaths.

191. SCHRADER, DEL. Jesse James was one of his names, by Del Schrader (with Jesse James III). First printing . . . . Arcadia, Calif., Santa Anita Press. . . . 1975 . . . . Imt. leather.

Anyone acquainted with the stories of

the western outlaws will find most of this author's statements a great surprise and many of them really shocking. It is another of those ridiculous books by authors who claim that the original Jesse James was not killed by Bob Ford in 1882. This one claims that Jesse lived under more than seventy aliases, the last one (when he acknowledged to the world that he was the original Jesse James) being J. Frank Dalton. Though several books have been written pointing out the many errors made by would-be historians about the western outlaws, practically every page of this book is full of errors. Several books have appeared about this Dalton; one of the first was published in 1948, when this character decided to let the world know that he was really Jesse James. The book was *Jesse James Rides Again*, by a couple of reporters named Frank O. Hall and Lindsey H. Whitten. (See item 164 in *Burs Under the Saddle*.) Others have followed, such as *Jesse James and the Lost Cause*, by Jesse James III; *Jesse James the Outlaw*, by Henry J. Walker, in 1961 (both discussed at some length in *Burs Under the Saddle*), and *I Knew Jesse James*, by Randy Turilli, in 1966 (item 214). These books are ridiculously untrue, and Schrader's even more so, being the last straw on the patience of a historian. One can only treat it as deliberate parody or burlesque.

The author has Governor T. T. Crittenden a schoolmate of Jesse James and also his lawyer. He says that one time Jesse needed a good lawyer and sent for Crittenden. After they had done business, Jesse counted out thirty-five thousand dollars and gave it to Crittenden.

" 'You take this Tom,' Jesse commanded, 'I want you to go back to Missouri and run for Governor. I'll give you a draft for another thirty-five thousand on my St. Louis bank. Hell's fire,

seventy thousand dollars should be enough to get you elected Governor.' " Thus writes this author. It is not surprising that Jesse could carry around that amount of money, for the author has him a multibillionaire.

Taking up the fanciful details page by page, we find that Frank James is a doctor named Sylvester Frank James and Cole Younger, *his brother-in-law*, a civil engineer. He has a Charlie Bigelow going under the name Tom Howard and living in St. Joseph, Missouri, on Lafayette Street, where the real Jesse James lived under that name. He has Frank James a "former Confederate Army surgeon." He has a Negro slave killing Bigelow's two brothers. Of course, Jesse killed Bigelow and dragged him to the house and coached Bob and Charlie Ford on what to say to the law, and to say that they had killed Jesse.

The fake Jesse sent for his so-called Aunt Zerelda Samuels [*sic*], but Zerelda Samuel was the real Jesse's mother. He calls Mrs. Bigelow by the name Zerelda Mimms Bigelow. That was the name of Jesse's wife (Zerelda Mimms). There seems to be much confusion in family names. He has a Missouri Jesse Dingus James and Frank James brothers of a different family. Dingus was a nickname for the real Jesse James, as we know.

This author's Jesse says that he threatened Mrs. Bigelow with death if she opened her mouth about this murder and then, always with the generosity of a wealthy man, he gave Mrs. Bigelow $15,000. He has Aunt Zerelda Samuels [*sic*] arriving to view the corpse and Jesse giving her a thousand dollars again with the threat of death if she didn't go along with the plot. "Aunt" Zerelda gave him some anxious moments when she acknowledged to the lawmen that the corpse "beyond a doubt" was the body of "her dear son Jesse Woodson

James." But he says her son was Jesse Robert James, "better known as 'Dingus.' "

He is also mistaken in having the fake Jesse asking to serve as a pallbearer, and he even has him singing in the choir at the funeral. This author also has Jesse composing the song about "that dirty little coward that shot Mr. Howard and laid poor Jesse in his grave." He is also mistaken in having Jesse's real mother born in Georgia. He is mistaken, too, in having "Aunt" Zerelda's right arm "partially blown off as the result of some devilment by Pinkerton detectives many years before." This, as we know, happened to Jesse's real mother. The author also writes that J. Frank Dalton later poisoned "the troublesome old witch." Nothing like that ever happened. It seems that back in those days it was no trouble to hire someone to "stand in" for another, and J. Frank Dalton hired his cousin A. B. Ford to stand in for Bob Ford.

The author has Major John Edwards none other than Jesse's brother, Dr. Sylvester Frank James. He seems to think that perhaps it was Crittenden who went to St. Paul, Minnesota, to "arrange for the three Dodson brothers of Kansas City to stand in in 1876 for the three Younger brothers in Stillwater Prison after the Northfield bank fiasco." Now who would stand in for some life-termers for any amount of money? That is ridiculous.

Throughout this book we find J. Frank Dalton, during his life of 107 years, most generous with his billions. It seems that he had gold and other monies buried in practically every state west of the Mississippi. He had more gold than Fort Knox. He backed Buffalo Bill's wild West show, made other generous uses of his fortune. The author has Robert E. Lee recalling some years later "he

was disturbed by the fact that Buffalo Bill, when he had been drinking, openly introduced his sharp-shooter as the real Jesse James . . . ."

Now comes another shocker. Dalton told reporters that "on September 5, 1914, at the age of 67, he enlisted in the Canadian army and fought four years in Europe, emerging a lieutenant-colonel, "and more incredible he learned to fly and spent the final 22 months of World War I in the Royal Air Force." He has a Colonel James R. Davis "in reality the deadly Cole Younger, consigned to his grave many years before by historians." He has all the old gang alive many years after they were laid to rest.

He has J. Frank Dalton a first cousin of Jim Corbett, the heavyweight champion, and has him financing Corbett while he trained. The historians, the au-seems to say, are the only ones who make errors. He says, "Historians are guilty of another gross error. They not only list Frank and Jesse James as the sons of the Rev. Robert James and Zerelda Cole, but they kill off Rev. James in the California goldfields. Actually, Rev. James, Captain George James' brother, changed his name to Jim Reed, remarried and died while bravely fighting for the Stars and Bars."

This author has his Jesse knowing such great southern generals as Robert E. Lee, Stonewall Jackson, J. E. B. Stuart and J. O. Shelby on a first-name basis. But Jesse was no soldier; he was a guerrilla. The author also says, "One of the best known women spies was Myra Belle Shirley, the daughter of a Missouri judge, John Shirley. Because she went under the alias Belle Starr, historians have often confused her with another Belle Starr, the murderous woman outlaw." Shirley was no judge, but an inn-keeper, and Belle was not a spy. Neither was Starr an alias; she married Sam Starr, though she was not married to him at the time this author is writing of her.

He says that the James boys went to school with Myra Belle Shirley, which is not true, and that Belle took care of Jesse when he was wounded by some Yankee soldiers. He says that Belle and a woman friend were raped by some Union soldiers and that when Jesse and Cole Younger, whom he says had married Jesse's sister Rebecca, heard this they went to the courthouse dressed as farm boys and proceeded to shoot down many of the soldiers. He says that Jesse was trained as a cavalryman in the army and at eighteen was "elected first captain by his troop and rose to full colonel before he was captured while badly wounded near the end of the war." Jesse was never in the army, nor was he "elected" to any office by his "troop."

He has Dalton saying that when battles were fought "the Confederate Command kept borrowing my men." Again he says, "By the time Jesse W. James was 20 he had been *elected* a full colonel." Again, Jesse was no soldier. He then has Jesse's gang robbing a Union boat on the Mississippi River of fourteen million dollars in gold.

He says that his Jesse was outlawed "because he did not do his war-time 'stealing' out of uniform," and he has one of Jesse's Indian men robbing two soldiers of $500 and at another time robbing two majors of $300. We wonder what soldiers were doing with so much money when their pay was so low. He then has Jesse wounded and Myra Belle Shirley nursing him again, and this time they fall in love. He has them married by Myra's father, "Judge" Shirley. He also claims that Jesse could speak Spanish, French, and German. I wonder where he learned those languages.

The author also has Jesse rescuing Emperor Maximilian from Mexico and later going back to rescue the emperor's treasure of gold and jewels. These treasures were buried in Live Oak County, Texas. He has the emperor shot with some others, but not killed, rescued, and taken to Texas, where he joined Jesse's gang. Jesse had the treasure dug up and placed in a cellar Jesse had prepared. He then has Jesse and his body guard, the Negro Trammel, going to Washington and then to New York and sailing for Europe in search of the emperor's wife. When they returned with the empress, the emperor gave Jesse five million dollars and twelve and a half million for the Knights of the Golden Circle, an organization preparing for a second Civil War. He has Jesse's grandson, Jesse James III, saying that he was a very rich man before he started robbing banks, but we know that is false. He also says that he was only twenty-three years old when he was made a millionaire by Maximillan. All of this is pure bunk.

The author has Jesse wounded fifteen times during the Civil War. He has him gun running, supplying guns to the Indians who wiped out General Custer's command at the Battle of the Little Big Horn. Of the Custer debacle he says, "Fifty years after the battle, Colonel James verified Custer's suicide, saying, "The Indians had him disarmed and captured. He asked for the return of his pistol so he could die like a soldier. After a brief pow-wow, the Indians gave it back to him and he shot himself in the heart."

This author has Grat Dalton a first cousin of Jesse and Frank James and has him named the Sundance Kid. We know that Harry Longabaugh was the Sundance Kid and a member of the Wild Bunch. He also says that his Jesse and his men had gone to Wichita, Kansas, "to help build railroad beds and grades," where they met Wild Bill Hickok when he was marshal of that town. But Hickok was never marshal of Wichita, and why would Jesse, with all his money, want to do such heavy work? Because Hickok had threatened one of his men, this Jesse went into a parlor house, bribed a Negro maid with a twenty-dollar gold piece, and then went upstairs and kicked a door in. He then marched Hickok down the street in his "red drawers and stockinged feet" to "a point just beyond the edge of town." Nothing like that ever happened.

He writes, "History records that Wild Bill headed west to Dodge City and then north to Hays, Kansas," but Hickok did not ever go to Dodge. Again he writes, "Historians and pulp authors, completely ignoring the facts, relate that Hickok . . . was shot in the back on Wednesday night, Aug. 2, 1876, while playing poker with his back to the door, in a Deadwood saloon." That is the first time I have ever read that he was shot at night. It is strange that all historians and eyewitnesses were wrong about it. He claims that Saloon No. 10 was "an ex-Confederate hangout where the damnyankees feared to tread," but they found the Yankee Hickok there drinking at the bar. He has Hickok behaving like a coward when James faced him, spilling his drink, "his face chalk white and suddenly dripping perspiration." He then proceeds to have Jesse kill Hickok and his men drag him over to a table and "place a 'dead man's hand' of cards on the table." That is indeed news to historians everywhere.

He then has Jack McCall, "a young teamster from Nacona, Texas," sidling up to compliment James on his shooting. He then has Jesse giving McCall his gun, telling him, " 'Let it be known from

now on that you are the man with the gun that killed a spying, damyankee sonuvabitch.' " And thus it is known to the world that McCall killed Wild Bill. When he has an officer come to arrest McCall, the author has his hero whisper, " 'Don't you worry, McCall, we'll get you out of this.' "

The author also has Wild Bill married to Calamity Jane "on September 1, 1870," just two days before her daughter was born. When this Jesse told her about the killing of Wild Bill, she only said, "You mean somebody finally shot that no-good varmint?" (Use your own judgment about the truth of that.) After McCall was exonerated in the death of Wild Bill, this author has him heading back to Texas on one of Jesse's freight wagons. But McCall went to Cheyenne and Laramie, Wyoming, not to Texas. He also has this Jesse giving Calamity Jane a thousand dollars for letting him take her daughter and leave Deadwood on a stagecoach accompanied by a matron hired by Jesse to get the child out of a bad environment. Then he has the child being taken to the home of Cole Younger's wife in Maryland. Cole had no wife, nor was he married to Jesse's sister, Rebecca. For that matter Jesse had no sister, though this author has him with a twin sister. He also says that Jesse had taken care of Calamity's daughter until she married a man named McCormick.

Getting back to 1876 and Jack McCall, he writes, "Jesse and Frank James said farewell to their cousin, the Sundance Kid, at dawn one morning in Deadwood and headed east into the rising sun." Then he tells of a swamper "much older than the teenage Jack McCall, was suddenly charged with the murder of Wild Bill because he, too, was named McCall." He says that this man was tried, convicted, and hanged before he knew what was going on. From this book we learn some strange history indeed.

This author also says that the robbery of the bank in Northfield was Cole Younger's idea. He claims that the First National Bank was "Spoons" Butler's bank. I have never seen that name in any other account. To differ from other writers, this one says of the battle after the robbery that Charlie Pitts was killed in a Medelia, Minnesota, gunfight, that Stiles was not killed but wounded and some Swede was buried in his place, that Clell Miller recovered from his wounds and died a natural death in Murray, Arkansas, and that Stiles died of old age in California in the late 1930's. We learn something new on practically every page. He also makes the ridiculous statement that "the Youngers never served a day in the Stillwater prison. They licked their wounds on a ranch near Leadville, Colorado." Then he claims that the three Dodson brothers "stood in" for the three Youngers for $300 a month. He has Jesse saying "I should know—I was the one who paid them." You would never make me believe that any man would agree to serve a life sentence for someone else for any amount of money. What good would the money do them in prison for the rest of their lives?

Here is another shocker. The author has his Jesse telling of the suicide of Jim Younger because of a love affair. He says that the victim was not Jim Younger but one of the Dodson brothers. Then he says that Dodson did not commit suicide: "I killed him and made it look like a suicide. You see, after getting $300 a month from me for 25 years, this Dodson was trying to blackmail me for $50,000. I just wouldn't hold still for that—so I shot him." He claims that one reason for the failure of the North-field raid was that all of them were drunk the night before and had a terrible hangover the day of the robbery.

He has Jesse quite a Midas and a keen student of law, setting up a system of trust funds "which drained a myriad of corporations." His relatives estimated his wealth to be from one or two billion to ten billion. He has Jesse having children, legitimate and otherwise, scattered throughout the West, but the true Jesse only had two, and they were legitimate. He also has him with more brothers than the world knows about, such as Morgan, Peter, Levi, and still another unnamed one, as well as a twin sister.

You will also be surprised to learn that this rich Jesse "was one of Henry Ford's original backers and many of Jesse's livery stables became early Ford automobile dealerships." This Jesse lived under many aliases, and he backed many businesses for he had money to burn. He backed the Hughes Tool Company of Howard Hughes. Under the alias of J. W. Gates he was one of the founders of the Texas Company and of Sour Lake. As Dave Moffat, a Colorado banker, he backed the building of the Denver, Pacific & Northwestern Railway. As J. J. Corley he built a narrow-gauge railroad from Colorado City to Cripple Creek. He was also a large stockholder in the San Pedro, Los Angeles and Salt Lake Railroad. Under the name Roy Hewitt he ran a large freighting business in Colorado. "Bet-a-Million" Gates was another of his many aliases. He owned the principal stock in the Moffat Brothers Construction Company in Colorado, an eastern race track and other tracks around the country, including a block of stock in the Santa Anita track in California. He even helped develop the breed of San Gertrudis cattle in Texas, naming them for his daughter, Gertrude. The rest of the world is laboring under the impression that this breed of cattle was developed at the King Ranch in Texas by the Klebergs.

It seems that Jesse's wealth was unlimited. His freight and stagecoach lines became bus and railroad lines; his livery stables became automobile agencies. He owned vaudeville houses in St. Louis, Chicago, Salt Lake, Denver, and Kansas City, even "taking a fling at making early-day motion pictures." He invested in railroads, circuses, wild West shows, and rodeos and owned a dozen ranches scattered throughout the West. He seems to have had a part in nearly every important event that took place in the West, even to competing with Jay Gould, who "tried to grab the Royal Gorge of the Arkansas River." He intimates that Jesse owned the Denver and Rio Grande Railroad which was fighting for that right of way, and he later outfoxed Gould out of two million dollars. His mines produced gold, silver, copper, lead, zinc, and coal. He owned lumberyards, brickyards, river steamers, and ocean-going freighters.

This author also has his Jesse, after World War I, rounding up a bunch of Wobblies in Utah, trying them, and executing them. Nothing like that ever happened. He writes: "And Jesse was a mean opponent when pushed. He was right in the middle of the Johnson County War in Northern Wyoming in 1892." He seems to have been everywhere and into everything. He says he imported gunmen from Texas, Idaho, and Colorado and "placed a former army officer in command." Guess who this "officer" was. Nobody but old Jesse James. He tells of the killing of Nick Ray and Nate Champion and then has the gang marching on Buffalo, which they never did. He says that Colonel Van Horn of Fort McKinney "brought the war to a screaming halt." Then he says that "all charges were dropped against Jesse's Regulators, but U.S. troops stayed in Buffalo until tempers cooled." No troopers were in Buffalo; they arrested the invaders at the T.A. Ranch.

He says that Jesse met Thomas A. Edison under the alias Colonel Carr and that they became lifelong friends. He also invested a lot of money in the Wright brothers' airplanes. In fact, there was not much going on that he did not have a finger in. He made a fortune in Texas oil, "hitting at Spindletop, Sour Lake, Breakenridge, Burkburnett, Iowa Park, Ranger, Desdemona, Mexia and Coleman County," as well as in Wyoming, Montana and Oklahoma.

One of the most ridiculous of the author's claims is that one of Jesse's aliases was Senator William A. Clark, the copper king. The author says, "On his deathbed, old Jesse admitted he was William A. Clark. The author also claims that the James family records show that Jesse and his daughter went to England in 1925 and stayed a year. Jesse built the daughter a ninety-room mansion near Liverpool.

He has Jesse telling his grandson that Bob Ford never killed anyone, "and he wasn't killed by some idiot named O'Kelly at Creede, Colorado, in 1892." Of course, a stand-in was the one who was killed. He says, "Bob was my comptroller for years when I was copper king of the world." And he has Bob's son elected governor of Montana and has Bob buried in Georgetown, Texas.

The author has Dr. John Samuel, the son of Dr. Reuben Samuel and Zerelda Samuel, a half brother of the real Jesse and Frank James and has him dying in Wyoming in 1960. Then he says that Samuel was killed at a country dance near Kearney, Missouri, in his early twenties—a most confusing statement. Dr. and Mrs. Samuel only had one son, Archie, and he was killed when he was very young by the bomb that wounded Mrs. Samuel. It seems that this John was sent to Vanderbilt University and, after graduation, to Vienna and Germany to finish his studies, all the expenses being furnished by Jesse. He says that John then came West where he was a specialist in gunshot wounds and where there was "a lucrative practice treating members of the Hole-in-the-Wall gang and the Wild Bunch." This Jesse also sent the doctor south to take care of the wounded men in Pancho Villa's army.

The author has Senator Clark mixed up in the Teapot Dome scandal, and it was decided that it was time for another funeral. He has Bob Ford saying: " 'Dr. Samuel here can sign the death certificate, . . . and you just happen to own the undertaking parlor right here in Butte. So what the hell you waiting for?' . . . Thus the world was to learn of the death of the famous capitalist, Senator Clark, on March 2, 1925. It was easy. No muss; no fuss. More important, Jesse James lived to fight another day."

He has Bob Dalton a cousin of the Jameses, but he was not, and he says that many of the crimes blamed on Jesse were committed by Dalton. But history says that Jesse was killed before the Daltons became outlaws. Then he has the Sundance Kid as Grat Dalton and in the Butch Cassidy gang, but we know this to be untrue for Grat was killed at Coffeyville. Some of the other accomplishments of this fake Jesse were his gift of the Clark Library to the University of California and his building in Los Angeles the Philharmonic Auditorium on Fifth Street across from Pershing Square. The author says that

Jesse was an accomplished violin player and a lover of classical music.

In this book I now learn of something happening right under my nose when I read that his Jesse "sold the last of his stock in Sanger Brothers Stores in Dallas, Ft. Worth and Waco." I never heard of the Sangers having a store in Fort Worth, and by the year he mentions (1948), I am sure they had sold the store in Waco. The author says that his Jesse loved children, and "nobody knows how many he fathered." He gave a zoo to the children of Butte. As the head of the J. W. Ely Bridge Company in Jacksonville, Illinois, he built Ferris wheels and merry-go-rounds "so the kids will enjoy" them. He also is said to have built the Angel's Flight, a tourist attraction in downtown Los Angeles.

The author also writes that "by his own admission shortly before his death he [Jesse] had killed 2,000 men and 13 women" and also says that he had a lot of businesses and a lot of wives and mistresses and that women "flocked after him."

Next he has his Jesse killing John Wilkes Booth in quite a story about how he went into Booth's hotel room and gave him a drink of lemonaide into which he had poured arsenic.

This author has his Jesse owning a huge ranch in the Mexican state of Chihuahua and hating Díaz with a passion because he ordered his troops to attack Jesse's ranch, where they slaughtered *two hundred* cowboys. Only Jesse's son, an Indian servant, and Billy the Kid, going under the name Brushy Bill Roberts, escape this massacre. Billy the Kid is the manager of the ranch, having just returned "from an ill-fated tour of South America with a Wild West Show headed by Butch Cassidy and the Sundance Kid."

He also has his Jesse giving Carranza

two million dollars in gold to let him build a railroad in Mexico, with the understanding that he would not be taxed for twenty years and his ranch would be protected. But he writes that "Jesse neglected to inform Carranza that Captain Brushy Bill Roberts, Jesse's *twin sons*, and about 150 of the toughest American gunslingers old Jesse could dig up in Texas and New Mexico, were already secretly drilling at his Chihuahua ranch." He never did things by halves. It seems that the money Jesse had given Carranza was to be used to purchase munitions in Chicago, the money, to be shipped across the Río Grande in a piano box. At the American port of entry the gold suddenly disappeared "in a coup engineered by the old fox, Jesse James."

Although history has Pancho Villa assassinated in 1923, Jesse is right there to furnish him a stand in. He tells Villa, "I invested millions of dollars in you, so listen to me. We're getting you a double. Don't worry, I'll pick up the tab, because I've had plenty of experience in this kind of business. Then we'll smuggle you across the border. I have considerable propery in New Mexico where you can hide out safely." So Villa lived comfortably in America on a trust fund set up by his friend Jesse. Then the author says the double began bragging that he was the real Villa and was shot in the back by an assassin after the real Villa had been living in New Mexico for more than a year.

The author now tells a lengthy version of the legend about how his Jesse helped the widow with her mortgage. To reveal still more about his generosity, the author tells of the time when his Jesse read about the financial plight of a Catholic home for girls, went to visit the school carrying a suitcase, and dumped $50,000 on the desk of the mother superior. He also helped Buffalo Bill Cody with his wild West show when it got into financial difficulties.

He has Jesse and his wife, Myra Belle, and her father, Judge John Shirley, going to Cyene [*sic*], Texas, to establish a home. They lived there as Mr. and Mrs. Dick Reed, but when a horsethief with the same name was hanged, they hastily remarried as Mr. and Mrs. Bruce Younger. The author says that Myra Belle worried about not being able to have babies and began nagging her husband. He began playing around with other women, and so she divorced him. But he has Jesse saying that Myra Belle was the only woman he ever loved. There is not one word of truth in these stories.

The author has his Jesse telling about Myra Belle's love of children and of her "picking up stray kids." She picked up a boy about seven or eight years of age and dressed him up in new clothes. The child said his name was Ollie Roberts. Myra said to him: " 'Ollie, you need a new name. From now on, you shall be known as William H. Bonney. And just to confuse the Yankee soldiers, you tell them you're Billy Bonney and you're an orphan from New York City.' " One day Ollie "disappeared into thin air. But don't worry, the world will hear of William H. Bonney some day."

Since seemingly it was destined that this Jesse be into everything that happened, he was in Canton, Texas, when Wild Bill Longlee [*sic*] was to be hanged. Jesse had a local blacksmith (who had served under him in Louisiana) make a steel ring to encircle Longley's chest and fit under his armpits, having a loop at the back of his neck to which a rope could be attached. To this were to be added two steel stirrups to fit under the feet inside his boots. The next morning Jesse and Cole Younger were there to see Longley hanged. The trap was sprung, and Longley's body was put into a pine coffin and taken to the cemetery, accompanied only by friends. It seems that Longley, in his last words, had told the crowd that he would return and kill them all. Sure enough, he spent the next day on top of Old Red Hill east of Canton, but no Negro soldiers appeared. Late that evening when the sun was red, "He strode into town with two six-guns at his side." A group of Negro soldiers loitering in front of a saloon looked up, saw Longley and panicked. He killed four of them and wounded four others. The true story is that Longley was hanged in Giddings, not Canton, and he really was hanged until dead.

The author claims that Canton was an important Confederate underground center and that Jeff Davis changed his name to John Patterson and moved to Canton, where he was able to locate a billion-dollar cache of Confederate gold reserve. Of course, we know that the Confederacy was not that wealthy. The author then has his Jesse, under another alias, and Jeff Davis, under the name John Patterson, founding several banks, including the First National Bank of Colorado Springs, Colorado. He has the Confederate buried treasure "worth at least $100 billion" and claims that, in addition to the billions of dollars, there are scores of caches filled with arms, ammunition, and coins. He then states that "at least three caches have been opened and emptied in the past 25 years near St. Joseph, Missouri, Guthrie, Oklahoma, and Dallas, Texas, and the contents were eagerly bought by collectors." I have lived in Dallas more than fifty years and have not heard of such a sensational thing happening here or near here. One of Jesse's caches in Wyoming contained, the author says, one thousand 1873 Winchester 44-40 repeating rifles

and almost 100,000 gallons of century-old liquor. Some of his caches also contained pork and beans, condensed milk, and canned beef. When they were opened they were found to be perfectly good and eatable after they were seventy-five or eighty years old.

In this book one never knows what surprise the next page will bring. Now comes the story that Judge Isaac Parker was really John Younger, Cole's brother, and that in 1874 John Younger was reported killed in a shooting scrape in Monagaw Springs, Missouri. "People swore it was John Younger and that's the way it went into the history books." John was not even there. He has Younger changing his name to Parker, moving to Ohio where he became a Republican, "but always remaining a crook at heart." He says that his Jesse and Cole Younger often visited Judge Parker in Fort Smith. Does he really expect anyone to believe this?

He is also wrong in saying that Jesse's mother was a Dalton and that John Younger's mother was also a Dalton. The Daltons were no kin to the Jameses, and the real Jesse James's mother was not a Dalton. The author has the brother of his Jesse, Dr. Frank James, treating Doc Holliday for tuberculosis at Glenwood Springs, Colorado, "but he died anyway in the 1890's." Doc died November 8, 1887, nor was he treated by any Dr. James. The author's Jesse says, "There never was a shoot-out at the O K Corral, that's just hysterical fiction. The Clanton boys were shot down in cold blood on the street. Both Wyatt and Doc told me that." He then tells a wild tale about hiring Wyatt Earp to ride messenger on a stage shipment of gold, tells his driver of his suspicion of Earp, and loads four packages into the stage (which are really four armed men). How he got them into packages is a mystery. Four outlaws tried to rob the coach. The driver unlimbered his guns, and the four packages came alive and killed them. When Wyatt returned to James, he said, "I guess you know, Colonel." What did Jesse do? Have Wyatt arrested? Kill him? No, he passed him an envelope containing a thousand dollars and said, "This should give you a fresh start somewhere. Good luck to you."

This author contends that Grat Dalton died under the name Grover Shropshire outside Cut Bank, Montana, in 1965. He writes: "Historians will be quick to point out that Harry Longbaugh [sic] was the Sundance Kid. He certainly was. Another alias was Ben Kilpatrick. Toss in Grover Shropshire, Enrique Brown and half a dozen more assumed names." Then he quotes Jesse James III as saying: "But they all add up to Grat Dalton. This will come as a shock (indeed it does) to many western buffs used to seeing that worn old photo taken in 1892 at Coffeyville showing Bill Powers, Bob Dalton, Grat Dalton and Dick Broadwell stacked like cordwood awaiting the undertaker. The men identified as Bob and Grat Dalton were corpses of the Christian brothers." He then says, "Bob and Grat Dalton and Bill Doolin and Eugene Robertson [who was he?] were just about to enter Coffeyville from another direction when Doolin's horse threw a shoe. They stopped to nail it back on and this took about ten minutes. By that time the shooting started. The tardy bandits were just in time to help a couple of men escape and then run for it themselves. I'd heard the story two dozen times from Grat Dalton."

He then has Grat in Bolivia with Butch Cassidy. He says that, after getting in bad there while running a wild West show (some of his performers

being Billy the Kid, Will Rogers, and Milt Hinkle), they gave the captain of the Bolivian army plenty of money to have Grat shot in a patio and get Butch "to use his last bullet on himself." He says, "He was damned glad to see the last of us—and the story was blown up back in the States." He has Grat and Butch going to Hollywood and working in the movies.

The author says that Sam Bass had two obsessions: to get rich and to join Jesse James's gang but says that Jesse had no use for him. He tells about Bass and sixteen of his gang (Bass never had a gang of that size) riding into Glen Rose and getting drunk on cheap whisky. He has Bass seeing a group of women washing their clothes in a creek some distance away.

"With a yell," he writes, "Sam and his sixteen men galloped amid the women, each man leaning down out of his saddle and sweeping a girl or woman into his arms. One girl, with an infant in her arms, was seized by Bass himself. When the baby began to cry, Sam tore it from its mother's arms and tossed it to the road." It seems that the Bass gang then took the women to their camp and raped them. The storekeeper where the gang had started drinking sent a Negro boy to tell Jesse James (who always seemed to be handily near), and of course Jesse had no use for Bass and was glad to help. When he and his gang got to Bass' camp, they found it deserted, but there was a plain trail, and so he followed it. They found the new camp some miles down the road, and Jesse called out Bass.

"Jesse got off his horse," the author writes, "and Bass walked up to shake his hand. Instead, Jesse whipped out his gun and pistol-whipped Bass to the ground. A deep hole was then dug, and Sam was placed in it up to his neck with the dirt tamped tightly around him. Then he had Bud Dalton pour honey over Sam's bloody head and face. I think I have read every book about Sam Bass, even the rare ones, in my research, but nothing like this has ever turned up before. It is so far from the truth it is hardly worth commenting upon.

According to this author, Pat Garrett did not kill Billy the Kid and in his later years admitted that he killed "someone else by mistake, but not Billy the Kid." Actually, so the author says, "the man Garrett shot was Billy Barlowe." Then he goes on to say that Pat Garrett was an alias and his real name was George Patterson "according to Confederate Underground Records . . . with a $10,000 price on his head." This author also has Garrett married to Quantrill's daughter and has him a federal marshal, "having been appointed to the post by President Theodore Roosevelt." Roosevelt appointed him customs collector at El Paso, Texas, not federal marshal.

"History," he writes, "cooked up quite a wild story of how a young rancher named Wayne Brazil [sic] gunned down the 54-year-old Garrett over a property dispute on Feb. 29, 1908. But that isn't the way it happened, according to Golden Circle records. Golden Circle agents captured Garrett in a Las Cruces bar and took him to an old house in the Organ Mountains of Southern New Mexico where he faced a drumhead military trial." The jury condemned him, and he was shot. He says Wayne Brazel's real name was Jim Miller and that he was one of the executioners, and that he told his self-defense story and was exonerated. He says that they buried Garrett with fanfare in a cemetery in Las Cruces. Of course, we know that Jim Miller was an entirely different person.

He writes that "Jesse James kept an eye on the young lad of eight whom his first wife, Myra Belle Shirley, rechristened 'William H. Bonney,' throughout Billy's life" and "when Jesse James emerged in 1948, Billy the Kid was with him, but he was greatly ignored because the spotlight was on old Jesse." He says that, "after escaping with his skin from New Mexico, he [the Kid] went to work for Jesse James. In one of his trips to Fort Smith he asked Judge Parker to swear him in as a deputy U.S. marshal but that the judge knew who Billy was and turned him down. Then the author writes, "Billy was just one of the desperadoes who knew Judge Parker was not above sharing loot with badmen of his day." A slanderous statement.

On his way to the Northwest, Billy held up a stage in Idaho and another one in Utah. He later moved to Rock Springs, Wyoming, married, and sired two sons and was now "using the name of Roberts, having been born Ollie Roberts." It seems that Billy the Kid, or Roberts, was made a deputy marshal while in Rock Springs, but he did not like the cold weather, and Jesse advised him to go down to the Indian Territory. There he used his marshal's office. When he called upon Judge Parker, the judge said to him, "Your marshal's badge is good anywhere in my jurisdiction." Then the author says that "wearing a badge turned Billy from an outlaw to a law-abiding citizen."

He also says that Scyene was a boom town and that people were moving in faster than buildings could be erected. The city fathers decided that the town needed law officers—and guess who were chosen for this duty. Jesse James and Cole Younger, of course. But Scyene never was much of a town and was soon swallowed up by Dallas. It seems that Jesse once shot the derby off a preacher's head. That gentleman rode to a Union army camp to report it to Colonel Nichols. The officer led a troop to town, and there was a battle. When Jesse shot the colonel over the right eye, the battle was over, and not a single Yankee survived the skirmish.

Some Confederate suggested that they'd better get out of town, for more Union soldiers would come. Jesse and Cole removed each other's badges and tossed them in a mudhole and joined the mass exodus from the town. Merchants crammed what merchandise they could hurriedly pack into wagons, boarded up their doors, and left. When the Yankee soldiers arrived the next day, they found Scyene a ghost town.

In writing of the many and various hidden caches under the control of his Jesse James, the author says that Jesse, during the depression, opened one of the Texas caches and took out ten million dollars to save three Texas banks. In spite of his financial empire, he was pressed for cash during the depression. He took $125,000 from a cave near Gad's Hill, Missouri, about $75,000 from a cemetery in Northeastern Arkansas, and $100,000 from the east side of an ancient Indian burial ground on the Bayou Macon, north of Delhi, Louisiana. Though all this money was in scattered places, he got it to a hotel in Shreveport, Louisiana, and then called a banker asking him to bring him $100,000 in bills, an armored car and some husky men to pick up the money. The author does not say what became of the other $200,000.

He gives ninety-nine places where treasure was buried and lists code *A* to Code *G*. Does his code run to Z? If so, the treasure must have been unlimited. He says that when President Jefferson Davis moved to Canton, Texas, in 1867, he brought a billion dollars in gold with him. Billions more were added, and possibly about 70,000 gold bars remained. Another rich depository he mentions was built somewhere off the old Nashville Pike not far from Nashville. It took eighteen professional miners and two parties of Negro laborers eighteen months to build this cache. "According to the records," it contained six hundred million dollars in gold in 1870. From time to time more gold was put into it for ten years, "and the cache today may be worth five billion." Money seems to have been no object in those days.

He has Cole Younger 127 years old when he visited Jesse in 1950. He says that Frank James wrote the verse chiseled on Belle Starr's tombstone (which, of course, is untrue), and Jesse says that he paid to have it done. In his last chapter the author lists a number of women Jesse married, and he seems to have lived with many without marriage ceremonies. He writes: "Old Jesse may have been married at least fifty times. . . . Women were too easy for him to get— he didn't have to marry them or promise them anything." In another place he says, "Jesse and his twin sister, Matilda, were the youngest of 20 children raised by Colonel George James and his wife, the former Mollie Dalton." The real Jesse James was the son of Robert James, and his mother was Zerelda Cole.

In a photo on page 238 there is a legend that reads: "Dodge City, 1880; rear, Belle Starr, Bat Masterson, Luke Short. Front, Jesse James, Billy the Kid, Wyatt Earp." There is no resemblance to any of those characters. The photographs in this book are about as unreliable as the text. On one page there are two portraits the author says are of Jesse James, both said to have been taken in 1870, yet there is not the slightest resemblance in the two pictures. On the next page is a portrait of Bob Dalton and his sweetheart, Eugenio Moore, taken, the legend says, "long after he was 'killed' at Coffeyville." But this picture was taken before he went to Coffeyville. The next page has that common picture of the Wild Bunch taken in Fort Worth and published many times. The legend under this picture is also wrong. It says: "Seated, Bob Dalton, [should be Happy Longabaugh], Grat Dalton [should be Ben Kilpatrick], Butch Cassidy [correct], and unidentified member of the Wild Bunch [should be Kid Curry]." Below a picture showing a frame shack the legend reads: "Secretive even in death, Jesse James died in this shanty at Grandbury, Tex., 1951, and was buried in a borrowed grave." It seems strange that, if Jesse owned all the riches the author claims he did, he did not die in a magnificent home and was not buried in his own grave.

The legends for a couple of photographs on page 211 are all wrong. The first reads: "Kentucky Frank James is buried in [an] Oklahoma grave." The real Frank James and his wife are buried in a little private park on the outskirts of Kansas City, Missouri. I have visited the grave and taken pictures of it. The other legend reads: "Bob Dalton, first cousin of Jesse James, was [a] dead shot." Dalton, as we know, was no kin to any of the Jameses. On page 276 there is a photograph having the legend: "This 1950 photograph shows Cole Younger, left, 127, Billy the Kid, in his 90s, with Jesse James, 106." As a rule outlaws died young. Anyone having anything to do with this author's Jesse lived to a ripe old age, most of them over the century mark.

When I read that rare little book *The Only True History of the Life of Frank James, Written by Himself*, and also *This Was Frank James*, by Columbus Vaughn and Lester and Sarah Snow, I thought that they were the most boldly deceptive attempts at history I had ever read. But this book about Jesse James has them all beat. There is scarcely a page that does not contain some false statement. This absurd burlesque on history is indeed the last straw, and let us hope that no other writer burdens us again with such piece of claptrap.

192. SCHREINER, CHARLES III. A pictorial history of the Texas Rangers. "That special breed of men," compiled by Charles Schreiner III, Audrey Schreiner, Robert Berryman [and] Hal P. Matheny. [Mountain Home, Texas], Published by Y. O. Press, 1969. Pict. cloth.

This is largely a picture book with a limited text. There are many errors, such as the statement that Sam Bass was killed on July 19, 1878. He was shot on the 19th but did not die until the 21st. The compilers also have James Gillett a captain, but he was only a sergeant. They have John Hughes serving as a Ranger continuously from early 1887 until 1915, but he resigned on May 17, 1889, to go to Mexico with Bass Outlaw and Walter Durban to work as a mine guard, and did not reinlist until December 1, 1889.

They also misname Ben Kilpatrick as George and have Tom Hickman a deputy sheriff of Gainesville. A deputy sheriff is a county job. They make the same mistake in having Alfred Allee a deputy sheriff of Beeville. They also have the incorrect date for James Riddle's enlistment in the Texas Rangers, and they have Ira Aten joining in 1880, but he did not join until 1883. In their bibliography they have the title of Gillett's book *The Texas Ranger* instead of *Six Years with the Texas Rangers*.

There are also many misspelled words

and proper names throughout the book. They repeatedly have *marshall* for *marshal*, *chaplin* for *chaplain*, *guerilla* for *guerrilla*, *heard* for *herd*, *big* for *bit*, *guirt* for *quirt*, *priviledged* for *privileged*, *existance* for *existence*. They also made mistakes in proper names, such as Cortinas for Cortina, F. McMahon for Frank M. McMahon, Querrell Carnes for Quirl Carnes, Vaughn for Vaughan, Spears for Spier, Daniels for Daniel, and Razz for Raz Renfro. Otherwise this is a unique and valuable book, making an attempt to preserve the history of this unusual organization.

193. SCOTT, GEORGE RYLEY. Such outlaws as Jesse James, by George Ryley Scott. London, Gerand S. Swann, Ltd., [1943]. Cloth.

This book has chapters on most of the better-known western outlaws, and the author repeats all the old legends, such as having ten men in the McCanles-Hickok "fight" at Rock Springs and the tales about Billy the Kid and Sam Bass. They refer to John Wesley Hardin as Jack.

194. SCOTT, KENNETH D. Belle Starr in velvet, by Kenneth D. Scott, as told by Jeannette Scott. Tahlequah, Oklahoma, Pan Press, [1963]. Cloth.

Jeannette claims that she is the granddaughter of Belle Starr, but she does not seem to know her family tree, for she says that Belle and her brother Ed were twins. Ed was eight years older than Belle. The author calls Quantrill a horsethief, rustler and robber, but he was a guerrilla at war. He has Ed Shirley a captain of the guerrillas and spells Eno's name as Enos. He is another who has the James boys and the Youngers first cousins, though they were no kin. He has Belle joining the Confederate troops in Kentucky after Carthage was destroyed. When Carthage was burned, her father took his family to Texas, and Belle never served in the army as a water boy. The author has her going back to Carthage after she left the army in Kentucky and there falling in love with Jim Reed. All of that is pure imagination.

The author has Preston Shirley, Belle's older brother, going to Texas with Jesse James, "both on the dodge." Preston went to Texas and settled in Collins County during the Civil War and was never closely associated with Jesse James, nor was he an outlaw. The author has Jesse in love with Belle and proposing to her. Jesse loved his wife and family. Again the author has Belle going back to Carthage to marry Jim Reed in a "wedding like no one had ever heard of before!" They were married not in Carthage but in Texas on horseback by an outlaw who posed as a minister.

He makes the statement that Judge Shirley and his son Preston "had built up quite a cow outfit" in Texas, but that is untrue. Preston was not associated with his father; he lived in Collin County and his father in Dallas County. The author has Jim Reed, Blue Duck, and John Middleton holding up the Austin–San Antonio stage, but that too is untrue. After that he has Belle buying a livery stable.

He has John T. Morris a member of the Starr gang, but Morris was a deputy sheriff. He also has the killing of Reed by Morris entirely wrong, saying that he was shot in the back while running from Morris. He also repeats that fable about Belle refusing to identify the corpse to keep Morris from getting the reward, even adding that little Pearl also said, "That's not my daddy." He intimates that after Sam Starr received word of

Reed's death he stole away and secretly killed Morris.

The author has the Clay County Savings Associations, of Liberty, Missouri, robbed a day after the robbery of the bank at Northfield, Minnesota, but the Missouri bank robbery took place on February 13, 1866, and the Northfield robbery on September 7, 1876, more than ten years later. And though he has Jim Reed already killed, he has him in the Northfield robbery and getting away with the James boys. Reed was not in that robbery.

He has Belle going to Virginia City, Nevada, to look it over for Jesse James and Scout Younger, an account I have never seen before. He intimates that Scout Younger is one of the Younger brothers, but they were no kin. He has Scout Younger a member of the James gang and at the Northfield bank robbery and spending a lot of time with the James gang in San Antonio, but Jesse spent very little time in that city. Scout Younger was not a member of the James gang, nor was he at the Northfield robbery.

He also tells a different tale about Blue Duck losing his money at Fort Dodge (evidently meaning Dodge City for there was no gambling dens at the military fort). He has Blue Duck losing his own money, not some borrowed from Belle, as others have it, though both versions are wrong. He claims that Belle named her place Younger's Bend after Scout Younger, whom he claims she married, but Scout Younger does not mention this in his own book. Perhaps he has confused Scout with Cole Younger, though Cole never married her either.

The author says that the gang had attempted to rob the Northfield bank "because Major General Benjamin F. Butler and his son-in-law, Governor J.

T. Ames of Mississippi, were the principal stockholders. Butler had incurred the undying enmity of the South during the Civil War, as commander of the forces occupying New Orleans. They thought this was a good way to even the old score with Butler and get a good-sized chunk of money at the same time."

The author has the Grayson robbery in Dallas County, Texas, but Grayson lived on the North Canadian River, near Eufaula, Indian Territory. He has Tom Starr the son of Ellis Starr, but they were both sons of James Starr. He has Henry Starr living with Sam and Belle Starr and joining Jesse James to rob banks. Jesse did very little robbing after the Northfield fiasco, which happened in 1876, and since Henry Starr was born on December 2, 1873, he would have been a little young for such strenuous work. He has Henry Starr robbing a bank with the James gang in 1884, but he would have been only eleven years old at the time, and Jesse was killed in 1882. He also has Henry with Belle when he was twenty-one, but he was only sixteen when she was murdered. So he is entirely wrong when he has Henry joining Jesse James and Scout Younger to rob banks. He is also wrong in having Belle's son, Ed, joining Henry Starr's gang.

He has Sam Starr killed in a country schoolyard, but he was killed in the yard of "Aunt" Lucy Surratt during a country dance, and he does not mention that Sam killed John West at the same time. He is also mistaken in having Belle's daughter, Pearl, joining Buffalo Bill's wild West show as a trick rider under the name Rose of Cimarron. This name was attached to Rose Dunn, of Bill Doolin's day, and I have never seen any record of Pearl being with Buffalo Bill. He does not mention that she was first a whore in Fort Smith and later a madam of such a house.

He has Belle going to Tucson to look "into the different opportunities along the line of work in which they were interested," but that is incorrect. It seems that she was scouting for opportunities for the James gang.

The author repeats that legend about Belle robbing an old banker in Texas. He also has her doing a large business selling "hot" jewelry in New Orleans, which is very unlikely. He has Sam Starr forming a gang and robbing an Omaha bank that Belle had cased, a tale that is not in any other book about Belle. Neither do I accept his statement that Belle and Judge Parker were good friends.

He has Scout Younger and Belle separating as good friends some time after their marriage and Belle soon afterward marrying Jim July. He calls him Jim Starr, seemingly unaware of the fact that Belle made Jim change his name to Starr after Sam's death when she began living with him. He is also mistaken in having Henry Starr's favorite occupation holding up trains. He was strictly a bank robber.

He has Belle killed on her forty-third birthday, but she was born on February 5, 1848, and killed on February 3, 1889, near her forty-first birthday. He says that her gravestone reads: "Belle Starr Born in Carthage, Missouri, Feb. 3, 1846 Died Feb. 3 1889," but in the illustration in his book her gravestone reads: "Belle Starr Born In Carthage, Mo., Feb. 5, 1848, Died Feb. 3, 1889." One could go on and on listing the errors in this book, but it would only become monotonous. The woman shown on the cover is certainly not Belle Starr.

195. SEIDMAN, LAURANCE IVAN. Once in the saddle. The cowboy's fron-

tier, 1886–1896, [by] Laurance Ivan Seidman. Illustrated with contemporary prints and photographs. New York, Alfred A. Knopf, [1973]. Cloth.

The last paragraph of the short introduction reads: "On this book, Laurue Seidman, drawing from a rich reservoir of little known memoirs and cowboys' autobiographies, tells us something fresh and significant about these people and the historical era that produced them." But I find nothing new in this account; it is mostly composed of quotes from others' writings, practically every page being filled with them.

The author is mistaken in saying that the King Ranch was in San Antonio, Texas, and was owned by an English syndicate. He is also mistaken in having the Lincoln County War in Texas; it was in New Mexico. He also says that the Montana stockmen "rounded up settlers, accused them of rustling cattle and hung fifty or sixty of them without the formality of a trial." But the men they hanged were known and proven horsethieves and cattle rustlers.

He calls Frank Canton by the name Fred throughout. He has only four men in the gang that attacked the cabin of Nate Champion, but there were quite a number of them, local cattlemen and imported gunfighters from Texas. To me this book is a rehash of the subject with a poor account of the Johnson County War.

196. SHERMAN, JAMES E., and BARBARA H. SHERMAN. Ghost towns and mining camps of New Mexico, [by] James E. Sherman and Barbara H. Sherman. Norman, University of Oklahoma Press, [1975]. Cloth. Also pub. in wrappers.

This book contains much history of the ghost towns and mining camps of New Mexico and therefore has some accounts of the various outlaws of that state— Milly the Kid, Joel Fowler, the Ketchums, and many others.

The authors write that Black Jack Ketchum's "life as an outlaw was exposed after the train robbery near Folsom, New Mexico, on July 11, 1899." This was the second Folsom robbery, and Black Jack was not in this robbery. Black Jack had committed many robberies before this one, including some train robberies. It so happened that just before this robbery Sam Ketchum, Elza Lay, G. W. Franks, and others had broken off with Black Jack and had committed this robbery on their own. The authors say here, too, that Black Jack was captured and convicted of killing Sheriff Farr. But Sheriff Farr was killed at Turkey Canyon during a battle with the Sam Ketchum division of the outlaw gang, and Black Jack was not present at this fight. They then have him hanged April 26, 1901, nearly two years after they say he was convicted. As we know, Black Jack was captured after attempting to hold up this same train alone on August 16, 1899. They are also wrong in having William Morton named George and having three other men in the crowd with Sheriff Brady and Deputy Hindman when these two were killed by Billy the Kid's gang. There were only two others.

197. SHINKLE, JAMES D. Reminiscences of Roswell pioneers, by by James D. Shinkle. Roswell, New Mexico, Hall-Poorbaugh Press, 1966. Cloth.

In a chapter by Hary Hudson, largely taken from her book *Pecos Pioneer*, she makes the mistake of calling J. W. Bell by the name George. She has also done this in some of her other books. In another chapter there is the statement that the Lincoln County War was between John Chisum "and all the other cattle owners combined," a statement that, as we know, is untrue.

198. SHIRLEY, GLENN. Outlaw queen. The fantastic true story of Belle Starr—the most notorious gun-girl in the West, [by] Glenn Shirley, Derby, Connecticut, Monarch Books, Inc., [1960]. Wrappers.

This is a typical newsstand pocketbook and though the author in his title writes that it is a true story, like so many others, he follows some of the legends that have grown with his characters. He is mistaken in having the Jameses and the Youngers first cousins and claims they "invented bank robbery" by having them rob the Clay County Savings Association at Liberty, Missouri. Careful historians deny this. He repeats that tale about Belle refusing to identify the body of her husband, Jim Reed, after he was killed by Mòrris, and he is mistaken in claiming that Blue Duck was white. He also repeats that legend about Belle holding up a gambling house in Fort Rodge [sic] after Blue Duck had lost some of her money there. In the first place Fort Dodge was a military post, and there were no gambling points there. Most legends have Blue Duck losing $2,000, but this author has him losing $18,000. He is also mistaken in having John Middleton, Belle's lover, the same person who had been with Billy the Kid. He was a different person. To further fictionalize his story, the author depicts some love scenes between Belle and her amorous companions in a bold and bare manner.

199. SHUMARD, GEORGE (PUB.). The ballad and history of Billy the Kid. Facts and legends. [Clovis, New Mexico, Tab Publishers, 1966]. Pict. wrappers.

It is good that this unknown author put the word "legends" in his title, for he repeats many of those created by Ash Upson, especially about the Kid's early years, such as the one about his family moving to Coffeyville, Kansas, in 1861, "and there was the beginning of Billy's alleged fondness for fast, well-bred horses."

He does not say where Billy's mother married Antrim, but he does say that "they eventually moved to New Mexico and settled in Silver City." They were married in Santa Fe, New Mexico, and did not move to Silver City until they had lived for a time in Santa Fe. The author has Billy's mother begging him to give himself up after he killed his first man, bu the had killed no one before his mother died. The author is also mistaken in having the Kid killing a cowboy and a Negro soldier over a dice game in Tucson. No such thing happened, and Billy was never in Tucson.

He has the killing of Joe Grant all wrong, and I think he is also wrong in saying: "Contrary to many biographers, it is reasonably certain that the Kid did not, at any time, work for the Murphy-Dolan-Riley syndicate," but he did work for them before working for John Tunstall. He has the Kid teaming up with a Mexican gambler, opening a gambling parlor, and, after killing a customer, fleeing with the gambler Mexico, where they killed more men.

He also repeats that legend about the Kid rescuing an immigrant train from an Indian attack and rescuing his friend Segura by riding eighty-one miles to release him from jail. He has the Lincoln County War as a battle between John Chisum and the small ranchers. He is also mistaken in having the Kid kill Beckwith.

He claims that Henry Brown dropped the d from his given name, Hendry, after he arrived in Caldwell, Kansas. But Brown never used the d. It was added in a typographical error in a news writeup, and the author continues to use it. He is also wrong in having Garrett a deputy sheriff when the Kid was captured at Stinking Springs. He was the duly elected sheriff.

Of the killing of Olinger he writes: "Ollinger [sic] was returning from the Wortley Hotel when he was shot, and relates that the Kid leaned out the window and said, 'Hello Bob' and waited until Ollinger [sic] looked up at the window before pulling the trigger." How could Olinger relate what happened when the shot killed him instantly?

He uses the legend of the Kid playing cards with Bell at the time he killed him, and has Henry Brown, during his early days as marshal of Caldwell, killing many men. He follows some others in having the Kid dancing a jig, singing and laughing on the balcony after he had killed Bell and Olinger. His whole account seems to follow Garrett's book closely. He has the Kid killed on July 18 in one place but corrects the date later, so that could be a typographical error. He says that Garrett was killed by an unknown assassin, but most historians now acknowledge that he was ambushed by Jim Miller, a professional killer. The author also continues the legend of the Kid having killed twenty-one men by the time he was twenty-one years old.

In his foreword the author writes: "This book culminates years of research by this writer and is based mainly on newspaper files and clippings of the times." Many of the newspapers of that day were unreliable, a good example being the *Optic*.

200. SHUMARD, George. Billy the Kid. The Robin Hood of Lincoln County, by George Shumard. Mesilla, New Mexico, Mesilla Old Times, [n.d.]. Pict. Wrappers. Cover title.

This author follows the legends about the Kid's parents moving to Coffeyville before that town was established. He also says that after the Kid's mother married William H. Antrim, they "eventually moved to New Mexico," but they were married in New Mexico. He gives the manner of the Kid's killing of a man who insulted his mother, but says, "The fact remains the young lad did become enraged and committed the first of twenty-one killings during his brief twenty-one year life span."

He claims that Billy's mother tried to get him to give himself up after he killed his first man but that he refused and fled to Arizona. His mother was dead before he killed his first man and before he went to Arizona. The author also has the Kid killing two men at the same time in Arizona. Some accounts have him killing F. P. Cahill, and other legends have him killing a Negro soldier there. This author has him killing a Mexican cowboy and a Negro soldier during a session at a dice table.

He follows many of the legends created by Ash Upson, such as having the Kid kill several men in Old Mexico, rescue a wagon train from the Indians, and ride 81 miles to rescue his friend Segura from jail. He has the Kid killing a Texan whom he does not name in Mesilla; I have never seen that story before. Is he trying to tell of the killing of Joe Grant? That killing took place in a saloon, not on the street.

The author claims that the rift between John Chisum and the Kid came when Chisum failed to pay the Kid five dollars for each stolen head of cattle the Kid returned, but most accounts claim that they fell out because Chisum refused to pay the Kid the "fighting wages" he had promised him. The author does not have Robert Widenmann and John Middleton in the crowd accompanying Tunstall when he was murdered. He is also mistaken in having the Kid attend the funeral of Tunstall. He was being detained by the Murphy crowd at the time.

The author has Morton, Baker, and McCloskey killed by the Kid, but others were shooting too, and surely the Kid's bullets were not the only ones to hit these men. He says that the Kid and Tom O'Folliard, at the killing of Sheriff Brady, jumped the fence and rushed to the fallen sheriff to get his guns and that both were shot, but that is incorrect. He is wrong in saying that George Coe and John Middleton were unknown to Buckshot Roberts. He also has the killing of Roberts wrong when he writes: "The Kid managed to move into position where he was able to fire his rifle into the room occupied by Roberts, and after a day and a half, the battle was over with the Kid adding another notch to his pistol." He also has the Kid killing Bob Beckwith, and he is mistaken in saying that George Cleveland was the only Negro of the Kid's gang. George Washington was also on the Kid's side.

The author has Tom Chambers instead of Pat Garrett killing Tom O'Folliard at Fort Sumner, though he soon quotes from the *Las Vegas Gazette* that it was Garrett who shot him. Of the Kid's escape from the Lincoln jail the author writes: "Bell was shot and killed as he fled down the stairs. How the Kid managed to dis-arm and shoot the deputy will forever remain unknown." But it is now conceded that the Kid, instead of disarming Bell, got a pistol from the jail privy where it had been hidden by a friend.

In telling about the Kid's death, the author quotes from the *Las Vegas Daily Optic* of July 18, 1881, that he had a pistol in one hand and a butcher knife in the other, but it has been proved that the Kid did not carry a pistol at the time. This account continues, "The belief is that the 'Kid' had received intelligence of Pat's presence and was searching for him at the time, or that he had gone to murder Maxwell in his bed." But Maxwell was his friend, and the Kid had gone to his house to get some meat for his late supper.

After the "war" was over, the author says, "L. G. Murphy was sick and dying," but he died before the battle in Lincoln. He has Henry Brown and Ben Wheeler shot after the robbery at Medicine Lodge. Only Brown was shot, and both he and Wheeler were then hanged, though Brown was already dead. He is wrong in having Pat Garrett arriving in Fort Sumner after the conclusion of the Lincoln County War. He says that Garrett and the Kid were never close friends, but the records show that they were. He misnames Rudabaugh as Radabaugh. He also has the killing of Grant by the Kid wrong. Again he claims that Tom Chambers killed Tom O'Folliard and calls Kip McKinney by the name Tom.

Several of the last few pages of this book are quotations from various newspapers, all full of errors. Near the end are two pages about Black Jack Ketchum that seem out of place. The account closely follows his preceding book.

201. SIMMONS, A. J., and PAUL G. HOWARD. The amazing outlaw life of Jesse James. With 20 historical photos of the James boys, by A. J. Simmons and Paul G. Howard ... Edited by Gerald H. Pipes. Branson, Mo., published by Jesse James–Confusion Hill, n.d. Pict. wrappers.

This is another of the many pamphlets on the James boys giving sketchy events in their lives. The authors are mistaken in having their mother an aunt of the Youngers. They were no kin. They also misspell Dr. Samuel's name as Samuels. They are also mistaken in having Mrs. Samuel a southern spy, saying that, when she learned something, she would send young Jesse to Quantrill with the information. That never happened.

These authors relate some events that I have never seen before, such as Jesse and Frank stopping in a wild town called Battle Mountain and getting into a card game with some local gamblers, which ended with Jesse killing most of them. The authors write: "The brothers at last felt the pinching need of money. For a long time they had been discussing the possibilities of robbing a train— something that had never been done." They evidently did not know that that train robbery had been carried out by the Reno brothers.

This little book is of no consequence historically. It was written to be sold at the Jesse James Museum at Jesse James–Confusion Hill.

202. SMALL, JOE (ED.). The best of True West, edited by Joe Austell Small. New York, Julian Messner, Inc., [1964]. Pict. cloth.

This is an anthology of articles taken from the first five years of *True West Magazine*. The article on Clay Allison by Norman B. Wiltsey, is filled with errors, such as his version of how Allison was crippled, the legend about his meeting Wyatt Earp in Dodge City and backing down from a fight, as well as that often-repeated legend about his pulling the dentist's teeth because he had pulled the wrong one of Allison's. His accounts of Allison's killing of Chunk Colbert and of his own death are also incorrect.

The author says that Allison's limp was caused by a knife fight done in an open grave when his enemy cut the tendons of his right leg, but the limp was caused by a mule who broke his foot. He is also wrong in having Wyatt Earp a marshal in Dodge City; he was only a deputy marshal.

He has Allison "facing gunman Chunk Colbert across a restaurant table . . . for two hours," but they were eating dinner together, and when Colbert made a move for his own gun, Allison killed him. I have never seen before the story that, at Allison's death, he was riding a wagon loaded with a huge pile of saw logs. According to most historians he was riding a load of feed, and when a wagon wheel hit a large grass clod, he lost his balance and fell. His head hit a front wheel, and his skull was fractured. Wiltsey says that Allison's team was going downhill and that, when he tried to use the brake, his crippled foot gave way, and the jerk of the team when the brake loosened threw him from the wagon seat. The right rear wheel rolled over his head and crushed it. His whole account is most unreliable.

203. STANLEY, F. The Kingston (New Mexico) story, by F. Stanley. Pantex, Texas, F. Stanley, 1961. Privately printed. Stiff wrappers.

The author intimates that the outlaw John Kinney was sent to prison in Leavenworth, but he was sent to the Kansas State Penitentiary. He has Albert J. Fountain boarding a special train at Mesilla on March 25, but he left Las Cruces on March 21. He also has Fountain arresting Irwin and Colville. The latter was a butcher, but the author has Irwin the butcher. He also misspells some names, such as Kinny for Kinney, Asque for Askew, Tomas for Thomas, and Rynerston for Rynerson. He has Toppy Johnson, the outlaw, joining Black Jack, but he does not seem to know Black Jack's surname and says "not Ketchum of a later date, but the outlaw who operated in Western New Mexico and Eastern Arizona."

204. STEELE, Phillip. The last Cherokee warriors, Zeke Proctor, Ned Christie, [by] Phillip Steele, Gretna, La., Pelican Publishing Company, 1974. Cloth.

The first half of this book covers the life of a lesser-known outlaw Zeke Proctor, of Indian Territory, and the second half gives a full account of the life and capture of a well-known outlaw, Ned Christie. The author seems to have done some thorough research on his subject, but he is mistaken when he says that Heck Thomas "had gained a widespread reputation as a lawman for running down the notorious train robber Sam Bass in Texas." Thomas had nothing to do with running down Bass in Texas or anywhere else. He is also mistaken in having Frank L. Van Eaton the author of *Hell on the Border*. That book is an abbreviated reprint of the Harman book of the same title that Van Eaton had printed privately and was peddling in person. I helped him sell some copies in Dallas and accompanied him to prospective buyers.

205. SURGE, Frank. Western lawmen, [by] Frank Surge. Minneapolis, Minnesota, Lerner Publishing Company, [1969]. Pict. cloth.

This little book, written for juveniles, gives brief biographies of some western lawmen. He says Calamity Jane "might have been Martha Jane Cannary and she might have been born in Princeton, Missouri, about 1848, but no one knows for sure." She was born Martha Jane Cannary, and she was born in Princeton, Missouri, but in 1852, not 1848. He also has Calamity marrying Burk in California, but they married in El Paso, Texas.

On the killing of Billy the Kid by Pat Garrett, he writes that "three shots rang out," but there were only two, and both of those from Garrett's gun. He also has Wayne Brazel killing Pat Garrett, but it is now accepted that Jim Miller did the killing. His account of Judge Isaac Parker's sentencing of outlaws is greatly exaggerated.

206. SWALLOW, Alan (ed.). The Wild Bunch, edited by Alan Swallow. Denver, Sage Books, [1966]. Cloth.

This editor is mistaken in having Berry Ketchum an outlaw when he writes: "Berry is said to have trained the other two [Tom and Sam Ketchum] to rob trains in Texas, and after robbing one train of $10,000 took the whole amount, reformed and advised the other two boys to continue their crime careers." He paints Berry in dark colors, but he was an honorable rancher.

He is also wrong in saying that Elza Lay and Sam Ketchum were wounded in the second Folsom train robbery. They were wounded in a battle afterward at Turkey Canyon. On page 78 there is this error: "Several years later,

about 1908, Siringo published his first book *Riata and Spurs*. It was reported that this publication was suppressed. Siringo then published his revised edition in 1912." Siringo's first book was published in 1885. *Riata and Spurs* was his last book, not his first, and it was published in 1927. The revised edition, with changes and omissions, was published later the same year.

The says that, when Black Jack Ketchum was sentenced to be hanged, his brother Berry went out to see him, but Black Jack refused to meet him. That is incorrect. The authorities sent for Sheriff Rhome Shields, of Concho County, Texas, to identify Black Jack. My late friend Bob Kennon went with the sheriff.

207. SYERS, William Edward. Off the beaten trail, [by] William Edward Syers. [Waco, Texas, Texian Press, 1971]. Pict. cloth. Also publ. in wrappers.

This is a collection of tales and legends about Texas. Each section is preceded by a map of Texas with circled numbers to show where each story took place. There is a story about John Wesley Hardin, his early killings and his killing of Charlie Webb, for which Hardin was later tried and sentenced to twenty-five years. His story of Bat Masterson's killing of Sergeant King is entirely different from the other accounts I have read and is incorrect.

In another story he is mistaken in having Sam Bass "dying in his saddle." He died in bed two days after he was shot. He is also wrong in having the Bass gang rob the Texas and Pacific trains three times. They hit this line twice and the Houston and Texas Central twice. He is also mistaken in having Arkansas Johnson "dead by the tracks." We know that

John was killed much earlier in a battle at Salt Fork Creek. He is also wrong in having Sebe Barnes killed in the street at Round Rock. He was killed in the store where they had gone to buy tobacco when the shooting started. In his story of the big fight in Tascosa the author fails to give the names of any of the fighters.

208. TAYLOR, Ralph C. Colorado, south of the border, by Ralph C. Taylor. Denver, Sage Books, [1963]. Cloth.

The author tells of the robbing of the bank at Amity, Colorado, by Henry Starr and Kid Wilson, whom he calls Kit. He is greatly mistaken in saying that Henry Starr was Belle Starr's husband and that Wilson was never caught. He repeats all the mistakes Sister Blandina Segale made in her book, *At the End of the Santa Fe Trail*, and says that Billy the Kid committed 26 murders and that "it might have been 30 if he had not been talked out of violence against four Trinidad doctors by Sister Blandina. He has the Kid a newsboy and bootblack in New York before he landed in Denver [sic] and became an outlaw at the age of sixteen. He quotes Sister Blandina as having the Kid the "head of a large band of thieves, cutthroats and outlaws," and says that he tried being a cowboy but that, "when his mother and step-father" returned to Kansas, "he felt no restraints." Neither his mother nor his stepfather ever returned to Kansas. He also has the Kid's gang murdering travelers for their valuables, but they never committed such crimes.

He has the Kid "extending his outlawry into Colorado" and says that he was killed at the age of twenty-six. Like most writers, he has the Kid killing a man for every years of his life—in this case, twenty-six. The author is also mistaken in having a man named Happy Jack and Bill Schneider members of the Kid's gang. He has one member of the gang betting a dime he could deliver a certain rancher's scalp to the outlaw camp, and "the bet was made and the deed done, all for a dime." He has a mob gathering at the Santa Fe jail after the Kid was captured at Stinking Springs, but the mob was at Las Vegas, and they were after Dave Rudabaugh, not the Kid. He is also mistaken in having the Kid in the Lincoln jail when he was tried. The trial was in Mesilla.

He says that the Kid became a model prisoner and frequently played cards with the guard. He writes, "To facilitate the card playing, the guard removed Billy's handcuffs," and "in an unguarded moment, Billy knocked the guard down, grabbed his gun and shot him through the head." He has the Kid, after his escape, remembering a rancher he hated and riding to his place, killing four of the man's Mexican sheepherders, and sending a note by the fifth to the home of the rancher demanding $5,000. That never happened either.

He has Sheriff Garrett trailing the Kid to the "home of a sweetheart, where he surprised Billy and shot him through the heart." He also says that, while Bat Masterson was still on crutches from the wound inflicted on him by Sergeant King, Marshal [sic] Wyatt Earp sent Bat an urgent call to come to Dodge City and help him enforce the law there. We know that Earp was not the marshal and had no authority to hire anyone. He also has Masterson elected sheriff of Dodge, but sheriff is a county office, and he was sheriff of Ford County. He infers that the Masterson brothers got a contract for grading the new Santa Fe right of way, but that happened before they made Dodge their residence and were elected to office. He is also mistaken in having Bat opening a dance hall and gambling den in Dodge.

He is mistaken, too, in having Ed Masterson, after he was shot by Jack Wagner and Alf Walker, being taken to Wyatt's room and dying there. He made his way to Hoover's Saloon and died there. He is also mistaken in having Bat Masterson returning to Dodge for the last time to help his friend Luke Short because Dodge City had passed an ordinance against gambling. The ordinance banned music in the saloon, and was passed because Short's saloon was drawing more customers than the mayor's, who could not stand the competition.

209. THOMPSON, Mrs. Mary, et al. Clayton, the friendly town of Union County, New Mexico, by Mrs. Mary Thompson, William H. Halley . . . . [Denver, Colorado, Published by Monitor Publishing Company, 1962]. Stiff wrappers.

This book has some material on the Lincoln County War. The authors also tell about Pat Garrett killing Billy the Kid, Tom O'Folliard, and Charlie Bowdre (which they spell Bowdrey). They are mistaken, however, when they say that all three men were buried in the same grave. They were not killed at the same time. There is quite a bit of material about Black Jack Ketchum—his train robberies, and his wounding, trail, and hanging. Like other writers they have him trying to escape by whittling out a make-believe wooden gun, but I fail to see how he could do that with the use of only one hand. They misspell Elza Lay's name as Ezra. They say that Albert Thompson, "who knew more about the Ketchums than anyone, . . . planned to write a history of the gang, but never

did." He did write a history of Black Jack, which was incorporated in a book entitled *The Story of Early Clayton, New Mexico*. The book is now rare; in fact, the copy I once owned is the only copy I have ever seen.

These authors also have Black Jack Ketchum the leader of the Wild Bunch, but he was not, though he was a member of the gang at one time. They also have a character, Bob Lewis, saying that Ketchum killed A. J. Fountain and his little son. That is something new.

210. TILDEN, Freeman. Following the frontier with F. Jay Haynes, pioneer photographer of the old West, by Freeman Tilden. New York, Alfred A. Knopf, 1964. Cloth.

This author is mistaken in having Wild Bill Hickok a city marshal in Deadwood when he was killed. He held no such office there, but it is said that the crooks of that city feared that he would be and so had him killed.

211. TOEPPERWEIN, Herman. Showdown. Western gunfighters in moments of truth, by Herman Toepperwein. Drawings by Charles Shaw. Austin, Texas, Madrona Press, Inc., [1974]. Pict. cloth. Oblong.

This book is composed of biographical vignettes, each facing a full-page illustration of the subject. The vignettes first appeared in the *Texas Parade Magazine*. There are items on Henry Plummer, the Harpes, Jesse James, Clay Allison, Bill Longley, Ben Thompson, John Wesley Hardin, the Cook gang, Wyatt Earp, King Fisher, Billy the Kid, Buckshot Roberts, Jim Miller, John Selman, Black Jack Ketchum, Belle Starr, the

O K Corral fight, Dallas Stoudenmire, Sam Bass, Cattle Kate Watson, Henry Brown, Billy Brooks, Jim Courtright, Luke Short, Tom Smith, Burt Alvord, Tom Horn, and others. The author covers many of the western outlaws and gunmen but offers nothing new. Note the following errors:

In the introduction the author has Doc Holliday dying in a Denver hospital and repeats this mistake in the text. Holliday died in a hospital in Glenwood Springs, Colorado. He is also mistaken in saying that Clay Allison "fell out of his wagon on the way home one day and was crushed to death." It was not his wagon and he was not on his way home, nor was he crushed to death. He had volunteered to drive a loaded wagon for a friend. When a wheel struck a large clump of grass, he was jarred off his seat, his head struck a front wheel, and he died of a fractured skull.

The author has Billy the Kid named Bonney and says that he killed both Frank Baker and Billy Morton. He is also mistaken in having the Kid killed by Garrett on July 13, 1881. He was killed on the 14th. He continues to credit the Kid with twenty-one killings. He gives Buckshot Roberts' first name as Will, but it was Andrew. His account of the fight at Blazer's Mill is unreliable. He has Dick Brewer giving his followers a "pep talk," but that never happened. He is also wrong in having Bud Frazier and Jim Miller fight each other. There was no fight; Miller simply stepped into a saloon where Frazier was gambling and shot him in cold blood as he did all his other victims. He is also wrong in having Wayne Brazel saying that Miller shot Garrett in self-defense. Miller shot him from behind some bushes. In his account of John Wesley Hardin, the author has John Selman a bartender when he shot Hardin, but he was an officer of the law.

He says that Henry Starr was killed in Henderson, Arkansas, while robbing a bank, but that happened in Harrison, Arkansas. He has conductor Harrington "blasting off the outlaw's [Black Jack Ketchum's] right arm," but his arm was not blasted off though it had to be amputated to save his life. He repeats the old legend about Belle Starr making Blue Duck get off his horse and pick up her hat, which had blown off. He is also mistaken in having Doc Holliday a Texan. Texas had enough native gunmen without claiming one from Georgia.

He also continues to spell the McLaury boys' name as McLowery. He misspells Dallas Stoudenmire's name as Stroudenmire throughout. He is another who has Ben Thompson standing up Sergeant King's friends when King was killed by Bat Masterson at Sweetwater, Texas. Thompson was never in Sweetwater. Of the Union Pacific robbery by the Collins gang, he says that they were "seasoned train robbers," but that was the first train they had robbed, and the last for several of them.

He has Sam Bass "cornered by officers at Round Rock" and killed on July 21, 1878. He was shot on the 19th and died on the 21st, and he was not cornered.

The author seems to think that the hanging of Cattle Kate and Jim Averill set off the Johnson County War, but that is not true. It was merely one of the incidents during that trouble. He continues to spell Henry Brown's name as Hendry D. Brown, but his middle name was Newton and his first name was not spelled with a *d*. He also states that Brown was such a good officer in Tascosa that Caldwell, Kansas, hired him away from the town. That is not true, though Brown did wind up at Caldwell. The author is also wrong in having Ben Wheeler arriving at Caldwell and telling his old friend Brown that he was going to rob the bank at Medicine Lodge. This news, the author says, made Brown so angry that he ran Wheeler out of town. This is ridiculous. He then has Brown thinking the proposition over and going to Wheeler's camp and throwing in with him. Of course, as we know, the robbery was a failure. The author says that Brown and Wheeler were hanged by a posse, which is true, but he does not seem to know that Brown was shot to death before he was hanged.

212. TOWLE, VIRGINIA ROWE. Vigilante woman, by Virginia Rowe Towle. New York, A. S. Barnes and Co., London, Thomas Yoseloff, Ltd., [1966]. Cloth.

To begin with, the title is misleading. None of the women in this book were vigilantes. In her chapter on Joseph A. Slade's wife, Virginia, the author describes Slade as "the roly-poly Slade," but such a description does not accord with his pictures or the life he led. In another place she describes him as his wife's "little red-faced, schizophrenic husband." The author does not seem to know the real name of Jules Reni; she calls him variously Reni Jules, Jules Rene, and Jules Beni.

213. TRACHTMAN, PAUL. The gunfighters, by the editors of Time-Life Books with text by Paul Trachtman. New York, Books, [1974]. Simulated padded tooled leather with col. illus. pasted on.

This attractive book deals with the better-known outlaws and gunmen of the early West. The author repeats the legends about the James boys being in the robbery of the Liberty bank and about

Cole Younger testing the carrying power of an Enfield rifle by shooting into a lineup of northern prisoners. He also claims that Belle Starr's daughter, Pearl, was sired by Cole Younger, though Younger denied it. In many places the author calls upon his imagination to fill in details. How does he know that when the James gang approached Northfield before their robbery attempt that they stopped at a restaurant and ordered exactly four eggs each?

He misspells Longabaugh's name as Longbaugh, and he says that Henry Brown, with others, "murdered the county sheriff and cold-bloodedly slaughtered two deputies who were being held prisoners." Only one deputy (Hindman) was killed at that time, and he was no prisoner. The author is also mistaken in saying that King Fisher "once shot a man in the head because he wanted to see if the bullet would bounce off his bald pate." That is another folk tale. He says that Billy the Kid's victims "were either unarmed or plugged from behind."

The author also tells a questionable story that I have not seen before, writing that Clay Allison and Mace Bowman executed a novel duel when they took off their boots, stripped to their underwear and proceeded to shoot at each other's feet as they danced. He also repeats the legend about Allison pulling the dentist's teeth, only this time it happened in Cheyenne, Wyoming. He also has the account of Allison's death wrong.

He repeats the tale about John Wesley Hardin shooting a man in the next room because he was snoring. He has Morton and Baker killed after a five-mile running battle, but that is not the way it happened. He is also wrong in having the Kid's gang killing Sheriff Brady and Deputy Hindman after they had gone to the courthouse to post some notices; they were on their way *to* the courthouse when the killing took place. He has the killing of J. W. Bell by Billy the Kid wrong, and his account of the Kid's entrance into Pete Maxwell's bedroom the night he was killed is different from any other account I have seen. He also has the Kid carrying a gun at the time, but none was found on him.

The author writes that the fight between Nate Champion and the cattlemen's posse took place during a severe snowstorm, but Bill Walker, who was there, said that it was cold and there was a drizzling rain but no snow. Since Walker was being held prisoner at the time, he should have known about the weather. The book does contain some true history, and with its colored plates it makes an attractive addition to one's library. It is one of a series, all attractively bound.

214. TURILLI, RUDY. I knew Jesse James, by Rudy Turilli. Stanton, Mo. . . . , 1966. Pict. wrappers.

This author is another who claims that J. Frank Dalton was the original Jesse James, and he goes to some length to prove his point, including notorized affidavits, but I am still convinced that Jesse was laid in his grave in 1882. The author also says that the mother of Frank and Jesse James was Zerelda Dalton, but her maiden name was Zerelda Cole. The whole book is just one big mistake.

215. TURNER, GEORGE. Murder in the Palo Duro, and other Panhandle mysteries, by George Turner. ₁Quanah, Texas, 1973₁. Fabricoid.

There are accounts of Bat Masterson's killing of Sergeant King, the death of Bat's girl friend, Molly Brenan, and Bat's own wounding. The author writes that "he [Bat] enforced Hickok's established rule against carrying firearms in town" as though Hickok were in Dodge City. Hickok ruled Abilene for a short while, but he was not in Dodge. He is also mistaken in having Bat rescue Bill Thompson from a lynch mob in Dodge. That happened in Ogallala, Nebraska.

In a chapter on Billy the Kid the author corrects some of the stories about the young outlaw, but he makes some errors in his account. He has Sheriff Brady deputizing Frank Baker, Billy Morton, and Jesse Evans to serve Tunstall with a summons, but there was quite a mob of men in that detail. In the battle at the McSween home he has McSween killed by Robert Beckwith and the Kid killing Beckwith. He is also wrong in saying that the Kid was stealing horses from the Mescelero Indian Reservation when Morris Bernstein was killed. That is not true.

He is mistaken in saying that Tom O'Folliard was killed "in a running chase" and "died in the dust." O'Folliard was killed as he approached a house in Fort Sumner, and he fell from his saddle into the snow, not into the dust. The author writes that Charlie Bowdre "was fatally wounded and staggered outside when he was shot" and that Billy and his gang "were starved out." Bowdre was outside when he was shot, and the gang would hardly have starved overnight.

The author also writes that "somehow, by means unknown, Billy got his hards on a pistol and demanded to be set free." It is now pretty well known how Billy got the pistol, and he made no demands. Like so many others, the writer has Billy carrying a gun the night he was killed by Pat Garrett, but that is untrue.

216. TURNER, GEORGE. George Turner's book of gunfighters, [by George Turner]. Amarillo, Texas, 1972. Pict. col. stiff wrappers.

There are twenty-nine brief chapters on various outlaws and gunmen, and most of them are filled with errors. It seems that these historically worthless little books will never cease to be printed. In the author's first chapter, on Billy the Kid, he says, "Mrs. Bonney migrated to Colorado where she married William Antrim," but we know that she married him in Santa Fe, New Mexico. The author repeats the tale about the Kid at the age of twelve killing his first man for insulting his mother. Then he says, "Only hearsay exists to chronicle the next several years of Billy's life, although a great deal of purple prose has been written about deadly encounters in which crooked gamblers, Mexican brigands and a Negro soldier fell prey to Billy's guns." He does not give the details.

He is wrong in saying that Sheriff Brady deputized a posse to bring in John Tunstall for stealing some of Murphy's stock. That is not the reason they were after Tunstall. He has Evans and Morton killing Tunstall and the Kid later killing Morton and Baker, but who knows who killed whom? Others were shooting too. He has Charlie Bowdre and George Coe wounded at the battle of Blazer's Mill, but one of Buckshot Roberts' bullets struck Bowdre's belt buckle and richocheted, taking off Coe's trigger finger. The author also has the Kid stealing horses when Bernstein was killed. In these statements he follows Pat Garrett's tale. He says that the Kid "was supposed to have killed one Joe Grant," but there was no supposition to it. Like so many others, he misspells Olinger's name as Ollinger. He is also another who has the Kid carrying a pistol the night he was killed by Garrett.

In his chapter on Jesse James he is mistaken in having Jesse "Quantrill's right hand man." Jesse was never with Quantrill; he was with "Bloody Bill" Anderson. The author is also mistaken in having the Younger boys cousins of the James boys. They were no kin. He claims that in the years of raiding they had "amassed more than $250,000 in loot, and subsequent events indicate that Jesse and Frank managed to save some of it." This, too, is very doubtful. In the chapter on the Younger brothers he tells of the robbery of the bank at Northfield. The next chapter, on the Ford brothers, says that they visited Jesse on the morning of April 3, 1882, but they had been at Jesse's home for some time. He spells Governor Crittenden's name as Crittendon, and, like so many others, in telling of Kelly killing Bob Ford, he misspells Edward O. Kelly's name as Edward O'Kelly.

In his chapter on Wild Bill Hickok the author says that McCanles, Woods, and Gordon "were killed in a fight at the way station." But there was no fight; it was murder, for McCanles and his party were unarmed. After Hickok had killed a soldier in Fort Hays, the author says, "Hickok lit out, pursued by a cavalry detachment with orders to get him dead or alive. He didn't return until the cavalry headed north." Hickok never did return but made his way to Abilene. The author also has the killing of Phil Coe wrong.

In his chapter on Butch Cassidy he says that while he and the Sundance Kid were in South America the Sundance Kid was killed after an all-night battle and Cassidy, "unwilling to be captured, killed himself." Here, again, the author is careless with his research. In his chapter on the Sundance Kid, he misspells Longabaugh as Longbaugh, and again he has him dying with Butch Cassidy in Bolivia. [Publisher's note: See also *In Search of Butch Cassidy*, by Larry Pointer (Norman, University of Oklahoma Press, 1977).] In his chapter on Kid Curry, the author tells of Curry's killing of George Scarborough and misspells the latter name as Scarborragh. There are chapters on Harry Tracy, Charley Hanks, Joaquin Murieta (which he spells Murrieta), and Black Bart.

In his chapter on Wyatt Earp the author is mistaken in having him marshal of Ellsworth, Kansas, and town marshal of Wichita. He was never an officer in Ellsworth and only a city policeman in Wichita. Then he has Wyatt, "after innumerable encounters with gunfighters," becoming marshal of Dodge City, but he was only assistant marshal there. He is also wrong in having Wyatt meeting Doc Holliday in Dodge. They met before then. He states that Wyatt "killed one gunfighter, George Hoydt [*sic*], and ran the notorious Clay Allison out of town." Hoy, the man he shot, was no gunfighter, but a cowboy, and Wyatt did not run Allison out of town. He is also wrong in having Wyatt the owner of the Oriental Saloon and having Bat Masterson and Luke Short his employees. He has Fred White the sheriff, but he was only the city marshal of Tombstone. Like so many others, he spells the McLaury brothers' name as McLowery. He is also mistaken in having Wyatt a policeman in Los Angeles in his later years and saying that he "married a rich Jewish widow."

Then follows a short chapter on Doc Holliday, after which the author writes about Bat Masterson. He says that after the battle of Adobe Walls Bat returned to Dodge City, "where Wild Bill Hickok was sheriff trying to ride herd on the boisterous cowboys," but Hickok was

never an officer in Dodge. He then says, "Bat was hired as one of Wild Bill's deputies and despite his youth, replaced Wild Bill when the famed lawman moved on." That is careless reporting. He is also wrong in having Bat killing Alf Walker and Jack Wagner, who had killed Bat's brother Ed. Ed, after he was shot, killed both his attackers before he died.

In his chapter on John Wesley Hardin the author has Hardin killing "a Negro boy after an argument." The Negro was a grown man, and the trouble resulted from a wrestling match in which Hardin brought blood from a scratch on the Negro's face. He is also wrong in saying that, when Hardin was killed by John Selman, Selman entered the Acme Saloon and "walked up behind Hardin and shot him in the back of the head." Selman shot Hardin from the doorway.

There is more unreliable history on the Dalton gang, and he spells the father's first name as Louis; it should be Lewis. In his chapter on the Doolin gang he has Rose of Cimarron a female outlaw, but she was not. He also repeats that tale about her helping Bitter Creek Newcomb escape during the battle at Ingalls. He is another who says that Raidler was shot by Bill Tilghman, sent to prison, later pardoned, and finally "became a well-known author." He must be confusing Raidler with O. Henry. He also has the killing of Bill Dalton wrong.

His chapter on Black Jack Ketchum is just as unreliable. He writes that the Ketchum gang was cornered in Turkey Canyon. There was a battle, and Sheriff Farr was killed and Sam Ketchum wounded. He leaves the impression that Black Jack was present, but he was not in this robbery or in the battle. When Black Jack later tried to rob this train alone, conductor Frank Harrington mangled Black Jack's arm with a shot-gun blast. This author says, "Sheriff Pinard, of Clayton, picked up the trail and captured the seriously injured out-law the next day." Black Jack stayed on the railroad right of way; and there was no trail to follow. Harrington himself told his brother that Ketchum surren-dered the next morning to the members of a freight train who saw him waving a rifle with a white flag on it.

Next we find a chapter on Sam Bass. There the author says that after the Big Springs robbery "Collins and Heffridge were challenged by lawmen and soldiers near Fort Hays, Kansas, and when Col-lins went for his gun they were both shot to death." It was not as simple as that. There was a battle, and it was fought near Buffalo Station. He is also wrong in saying that "Jim Berry and Tom Nixon ran into Sheriff Walter Glasscock at Mexico, Missouri, and Ber-ry was killed. Nixon escaped with $7,000 of the loot." Berry did not "run into" the sheriff. The sheriff sought him out, Nixon did not stop in Mexico, and he had his share of the $60,000. He also has the Bass gang robbing stages, trains, and banks from a stronghold near Den-ton, but Bass never robbed a bank. He was planning to do so when he was killed. When the gang was in Round Rock, the author says, Murphy left the others "at Koppel's Store," but he left them on their way to New Town, saying that he wanted to buy horse feed in Old Town. The author is also wrong in hav-ing Moore a sheriff. He was only a depu-ty. Like so many others, he has Jim Murphy committing suicide. He writes, "Eleven months later [after Bass's death] his betrayer, Murphy, terrified of the Denton townspeople, who rather liked Bass, committed suicide by poison."

Following are chapters on Henry Plummer and on the Catfish Kid, in which the author tells about the big fight in Tascosa.

In his chapter on Belle Starr the au-thor is mistaken in saying that her broth-er was a member of Jim Lane's Redlegs. He was a rabid southerner. He also has the James-Younger gang robbing the bank at Liberty, Missouri, but, as I have said many times, that is not true. He says that Jim Reed, one of Belle's "hus-bands," was killed by one of his cohorts, but he was killed by Morris, a deputy sheriff. He seems to think that Belle was killed by her son, Edward, and that "it appears that an incestuous relationship existed between Belle and Edward." The last six chapters, on Ben Thompson, King Fisher, Bill Longley, Jim Court-right, Luke Short, and Big Nose George Curry, are unreliable.

217. VAUGHN, COLUMBUS, SARAH SNOW, and LESTER SNOW. This is Frank James, by Columbus Vaughn, Sarah Snow, and Lester Snow. Philadelphia, Dorrance & Company, [1969]. Cloth.

These authors claim that J. Frank Dalton proved beyond a doubt that he was the original Jesse James. Mrs. Sarah Snow, Vaughn's daughter, says she was really the daughter of Frank James. Frank James never had a daughter. The authors also claim that Frank James was the father of a man named Carl G. Clark, who told Mrs. Snow that "a man named Weim signed the pardon for the Dalton boys after their stay in prison." Emmett was the only Dalton in prison, and he was pardoned by the governor in 1907.

Of course, since they claim that Jesse James lived to be an old man, they say that he was not killed by Bob Ford as history has it. They also claim that Frank and Jesse were half brothers, but that is also untrue. They refer to two unreliable books, *Jesse James the Outlaw*, by Henry Walker, and *The Truth About Jesse James*, by Phyllis Argall, saying that "these publications present undisputable evidence that the Dalton claim was the absolute truth." Back in those days, it appears, stand-ins were popular and readily available. The authors claim that a man named Charles Biglow [sic] was substituted for Jesse and a Sam Collins surrendered for Frank James. It seems that after Jesse's death Governor Crittenden offered "the proposition . . . that if Frank would come in and surrender, he would be given a trial by a Missouri court, and regardless of how the verdict went, the governor would step in and pardon him." But Jesse and Frank feared a frameup, and, "after weighing the matter for some time, they came up with a plan of their own. They would find a double for Frank and he would surrender." After they offered Sam Collins a large sum of money, he "filled in" for Frank. They seem to think that Governor Crittenden was in on the deal and say that "Sam Collins collected around thirty-five thousand dollars from the James boys, assumed the name of Frank James and settled down on the Kearney farm as its owner." All of this is ridiculous.

They claim that Jesse himself killed Bigelow and had Bob Ford present the body and split the reward, and they also have Mrs. Samuel identifying the body and claiming it for burial so that Jesse could go free. They claim that members of the Home Guard, not the Pinkertons, were the ones who threw the bomb into the Samuel home, and they have the James boys turning outlaw because of this bombing, which is entirely wrong. They are also in error in saying that Frank James never lived on the Samuel farm near Kearney, but he did live there much of the time after he was pardoned.

They name the leaders as the men who "shot the father of the James boys." If the authors are referring to their real father, he died in California where he had followed the gold rush, but he was not shot. Neither was their stepfather. They say that these same men dragged the boys "by the necks and clubbed and beat them so that they carried the scars to their graves."

The authors are also wrong in claiming the James boys had a sister. There were no girls in the family. They have Frank James (Joe Vaughn) riding to Arkansas to join an old friend and "recalling times they had spent together as boys in Oklahoma. Frank James did not spend his time in Oklahoma. They have Joe Vaughn telling his daughter about a one-armed woman who he said was Jesse and Frank's stepmother and saying that the boy with her was his own son "born to his Indian sweetheart Ann Raulston [sic]. Ann Ralston was Frank's real wife, and she was not Indian. They have her the wife of Sam Collins "the man who surrendered in Frank's place." They have this Frank James "always talking about his brother Bill," but the real Frank James had no brother by that name.

They also have Frank James with several sons by a woman named Nancy and have him sending one son to Camp Woods, Texas, to dig up some money buried there long before. They have Frank living in fear of every stranger, but the real Frank James had nothing to fear, for he had been pardoned. These authors do not mind telling about their mother's loose behavior and having her giving birth to two illegitimate children before she married Joe Vaughn.

The entire first half of this book is just a continuation of that legend claiming that J. Frank Dalton was Jesse James and Vaughn was Frank James, none of which can be true if we are to believe the records.

The latter part of the book is a reprint of that ridiculous little book *The Only True Story of the Life of Frank James,* originally published in 1926. In *Burs Under the Saddle,* I devoted some space to the original edition, and some of my comments are repeated below.

This is one of the most brazen pieces of writing it has been my experience to read. The author claims to be Frank James, although he says that his mother's name was Agnes Collins and his father's name was Nelson. In the latter part of the book he says that his father was Ed Reed, a brother of Jim Reed, and that he "was a base begotten child." The real Frank James was pardoned and restored to full citizenship as soon as he surrendered; yet this claimant to the name lived in Newton County, Arkansas, for forty years under the name Joe Vaughn, trying, he says, to hide his identity. According to his account, most of his life was spent among the Indians of Indian Territory.

Among other unbelievable things he writes: "Readers, I know it will be hard to make people believe I am the only Frank James, that the boy Frank James was none other than Edd Reed." He further states that "the world thinks that Robert Ford killed Jesse James, but I will say right here that the James boys never were captured." The real Frank James died on the Samuel farm in Missouri on February 18, 1915. It is well known that after his pardon he worked as a shoe salesman in Missouri and Dallas, Texas, that he was employed in St. Louis as a doorkeeper at the Standard Theater, and that at various times he worked as a starter at the fairgrounds in St. Louis. He did not have to hide out

on a farm in Arkansas afraid to reveal his identity.

The author makes the ridiculous statement that after the Northfield bank raid he and Jesse returned to Indian Territory and "there stayed a while in peace" and that in the same year "Quantrell [*sic*] was recruiting his band together fixing for another battle." This is strange because the Northfield raid was in 1876, and Quantrill had been shot in January, 1863, near Louisville, Kentucky, and had died in February of that year.

The author says that his book was finished on December 10, 1925, ten years and ten months after the real Frank James died (the author of this book died on February 14, 1926). This worthless little book was published by his daughter, Sarah E. Snow, who, of course, upholds her father's claims. The book is also full of typographical errors, misspelled proper names, and confused geography. He says, "A short time after Jim Reed died Belle starr married Henry Starr. Henry Starr was killed in a pistol duel by a U.S. Marshal." Henry Starr was a mere boy when Belle was murdered, and he was not killed by a federal marshal. He was killed while trying to rob a bank in Harrison, Arkansas. The author then has Belle married to a John Starr. He says she knew that Watson had killed a man in *Kentucky,* but that happened in Florida. He adds that Belle had dinner with the Watsons the day she was killed, but that also is untrue. The author further claims that a man posing as Frank James surrendered to Governor Crittenden, but the author would not reveal his true name since he might still be alive today (1925). Of course, we know that Belle did not marry Henry Starr, nor did she marry any John Starr.

He says that Belle Starr was a native

of Kansas, but we know that she was a native of Missouri. Neither was she known as a bronco buster, as he says she was. Although he uses no names, he tells about Belle's escape from General Eno to warn her brother Ed and says that this took place in Kansas, where, he says, she got her reputation as a bronco rider.

He is further mistaken in saying that after Jim Reed married Belle they were run out of Illinois and Iowa and that they went to Texas, where Reed was killed a short time later. He is also mistaken when he says they had only one child, Edd Reed, and has him both a United States marshal and an outlaw at the same time.

Burton Rascoe, in his *Belle Starr, the Bandit Queen*, had this comment to make concerning this book: "It is maudlin, illiterate, vague, confused, pathetic." Yet a few paragraphs later Rascoe wrote, "It is quite probable that, when he [Frank James] was on his uppers, he wrote this story of his life as it was published eleven years after his death. . . . There is something so pathetic about its general style and information that I have a deep suspicion that Frank James may actually have written it and that no 'ghost' or collaborator helped him out in the least."

I fail to see how Rascoe could possibly have arrived at this conclusion if he had actually read the book. Frank James was an educated man who could quote Shakespeare and the classic poets, and Rascoe recognized that this book was written by an uneducated man. Certainly Frank James, as has been pointed out, did not hide out, nor did he have to do so after he was pardoned. Much trash has been written about the James boys, but both Frank and Jesse would turn over in their graves if they knew about this one.

218. VIRGINES, George E. Saga of the Colt six-shooter, and the famous men who used it, by George E. Virgines. Illustrated by Ernest L. Reedstrom. New York, Frederick Fell, Inc., [1969]. Cloth.

This book has sections on Bat Masterson, the James boys, Cole Younger, Belle Starr, Emmett Dalton, Billy the Kid, and John Wesley Hardin. The author has the Kid named William Bonney and says that, by "cutting a wide swath of terror through Texas, Arizona, New Mexico and the Mexican border states, he established himself one of the most ruthless and blood-stained reputations of the Southwest." He has the Kid captured at Stinking Springs "after a battle," but there was no battle, only the killing of Bowdre and of a horse. Of the killing of the Kid's jailers, he says, "After making someone knock his irons off, the Kid confiscated two .44 Colt SA's, stole a horse and rode away." He divided his leg irons himself with a miner's pick and did not get them entirely off until later at a friend's home.

The author has Calamity Jane having "her own show," a statement I have never seen before, and he is mistaken in saying that Belle Starr's "crimes included robbery, horse and cattle stealing and murder." Robbery was committed by her cohorts, and she was never accused of murder except in the legends created about her.

219. WAGONER, Jay J. Arizona Territory, 1863–1912. A political history, [by] J. J. Wagoner. Tucson, University of Arizona Press, [1970]. Cloth.

This author gives a detailed history of Arizona in its territorial days until statehood. There is a chapter on law and order and the Arizona Rangers in which he tells about Mossman, Billy Stiles, Augustin Chacon, Burt Alvord and other outlaws. Like some others, the author is mistaken in having Lon Bass a brother of Sam Bass. Sam only had two living brothers, John and Denton, and a half brother, Charles, and none of them was ever in Arizona, nor were they outlaws.

220. WALLACE, BETTY. Gunnison country, by Betty Wallace. Denver, Sage Books, [1960]. Cloth.

In telling of the killing of Bob Ford by Ed O. Kelly, the author is mistaken in saying that Kelly "served three years of a twenty-one year sentence before being paroled." He had served ten years of a life sentence when he was paroled. She also says that he killed a Negro in Pueblo after getting out of the penitentiary "and fled to Texas. There he encountered someone faster on the draw than he was." But Kelly's death came about not because his opponent (an Oklahoma City policeman) was faster on the draw but after a long, desperate physical struggle. Like so many others, too, she spells Alferd Packer's first name as Alfred.

221. WALLER, BROWN. Last of the great Western train robbers, by Brown Waller. South Brunswick, N.Y., A. S. Barnes Co., London, Thomas Yoseloff, Ltd., [1968]. Cloth.

This book is about Harvey Logan and his train-robbing activities. The author follows Logan's career very closely; however, he misspells proper names such as Longbaugh for Longabaugh, Barry Ketchum for Berry Ketchum, Mount Morich for Mount Moriah, and Point Rock for Paint Rock, though the last is probably a typographical error, since he later spells it correctly. He is mistaken

in having Black Jack Ketchum born in New Jersey. He was born in San Saba County, Texas. The author has him in the military service at Fort Whipple and says that he inherited $1,500 from a New Jersey relative. That is news to historians.

He writes: "The gang robbed a through California flyer on the Southern Pacific near Losier, Texas, where Ben Kilpatrick was killed in 1912. After taking $40,000 from the Wells Fargo safe, they fled across Texas ahead of a posse led by Federal Marshals, but as usual they escaped." No such robbery occurred, and when Kilpatrick was killed, only he and his former cellmate, Ole Beck, were in the robbery, which took place near Sanderson, Texas. Both men were killed, and obviously did not succeed in getting any money.

The author is also mistaken in saying that "Seven Rivers south of Roswell, was the lower extremity of the Chisholm Trail." He says that George Scarborough died on "April 4, four years to a day from the time he had killed John Selman." Scarborough was wounded on April 5 and died on April 6. He is also mistaken in saying that Ed Welsh was Ben Kilpatrick's companion when the two were killed trying to hold up the Southern Pacific. He is also wrong in having "12 or 14" men in the gang that hanged Jim Averill and Cattle Kate Watson.

222. WALTRIP, LELA, and RUFUS WALTRIP. Cowboys and cattlemen, by Lela and Rufus Waltrip. New York, David McCay Co., 1967. Pict. cloth.

These authors have fourteen men in the McSween house during the battle at that place. They say that Alexander Grzelachowski was a friend of Billy the Kid, but he was not, because the Kid kept stealing his horses. They also say that the Kid and James Dolan "were the only surviving leaders of the opposite forces in this cattle war," which is not true. They further state that the Kid "became a fugitive of the law and was finally hunted down and slain by Pat Garrett in 1881, after killing a deputy sheriff." He killed two deputies, not one, Bell and Olinger.

The authors are mistaken in saying that white fugitives from Texas entered into an alliance with "white Comanches" and eventually fought each other "and embroiled the entire community in the infamous Lincoln County War."

Their account of the battle at the McSween home is unreliable. They say, "McSween was killed in the final charge," but there was no charge at any time. "Mrs. McSween," they continue, "employed another partner for the bank, who was also an attorney, and Murphy promptly had him killed." She had nothing to do with the bank, and I cannot imagine who the attorney was unless they mean Chapman, but Murphy was dead before Chapman was killed. They have the Kid joining the Chisum Ranch after the murder of Tunstall, but that is untrue. They have the Kid killing twenty-one men, but their version of the legend is a little different: they have him "noted for the twenty-one notches on his favorite rifle, each notch representing a man he had killed."

They are also mistaken in saying that "the Lincoln County War actually began in the courts when McSween, an attorney, refused to defend the cattle rustling cowboys of Major Murphy." That is far from the truth.

223. WAY, W. J. ("Jack"). The Tombstone story, by W. J. ("Jack") Way. The astonishing tale of "the town too tough to die." [Tucson, Arizona, Livingston Press], 1965. Stiff wrappers.

Writing about Wyatt Earp's first entry into Tombstone, the author is mistaken in saying, "Accompanying him, or soon to follow, were his second wife, Mattie, his brothers Virgil, Morgan, James and Warren." Virgil and his wife and Wyatt and his wife went to Tombstone from Prescott together. The author also says that Wyatt bought a quarter interest in the Oriental Saloon. A small interest was given to him in exchange for his protection of the place.

224. WELLMAN, PAUL I. The blazing Southwest. The pioneer story of the American Southwest, by Paul I. Wellman. Published for the Fireside Press by W. Foulsham & Co., Ltd., London, New York, Toronto, Cape Town, Sydney, [1961]. Cloth.

This little known book covers much of the history of the Southwest, from Indian troubles to outlaw troubles. His account of Billy the Kid and the Lincoln County War contains the same errors that occur in all his other books about outlaws. He writes: "There is so much legend surrounding them [the outlaws] now that the truth probably never will be discovered." Yet he repeats the legends as history. He names Billy the Kid as William H. Bonney; has the family going to Coffeyville, Kansas, when the Kid was a baby and before the town was founded. After his father's death, he has the Kid's mother going to Colorado and marrying Antrim. He repeats all the legends about the Kid killing his first man at the age of twelve for insulting his mother and has the Kid killing Morton and Baker, "two shots from him, two dead." He is wrong in having Sheriff Brady, Deputy Hindman, and two others going to the courthouse to "open Court." They were going to the courthouse to post a notice of a delay in opening court. He definitely gives the Kid credit for killing Brady.

The author says that Brewer's gang were searching for Buckshot Roberts and "found him at Blazer's Mill," but Roberts rode to the Mill to do a little bounty hunting and arrived after Brewers' men had been there for some time. The author has Brewer and Roberts buried on the same day, but Brewer was buried the day he was killed, and Roberts died and was buried the next day. The author has the battle at the McSween house lasting three days, but it lasted five, and he is wrong in having the Kid killing Beckwith. He is also wrong in having Governor Wallace offering the Kid amnesty "if he would leave the country."

The author has a regular battle taking place between the Kid's gang and Garrett's posse at Stinking Springs and says that both Bowdre and O'Folliard (whose name he spells O'Falliard) were killed there, but only Bowdre was killed then. He is also wrong in having Bell killed with his own gun. Bell was killed with a gun the Kid had got from the outdoor privy where a friend had left it.

The author writes: "With a Winchester in his hands, taken from the jailer's gun rack, the Kid cowed the crowd of people that gathered at the shots [when he killed Olinger], made someone free him from his manacles and leg irons, and, commandeering a horse, rode away." That is not quite the way it happened. He is also wrong in saying that the Kid went to Pete Maxwell's house to see his sweetheart the night he was killed. Like most others he has the Kid killing twenty-one men.

In his chapter about the Earps he has Wyatt serving as an officer at Ellsworth, but he was never an officer there. He is also wrong in having Wyatt a deputy U.S. marshal when he first arrived at Tombstone. He has Wyatt's brothers joining him "shortly after his arrival," but Virgil arrived with him. He misspells the McLaury boys' name as McLowery throughout.

He has Fred White asking Wyatt to help him arrest Curly Bill Brocius, but it was Virgil who did the helping. He then has Wyatt knocking each member of the gang in the head one at a time and jailing them, and he is also wrong in having the Clantons sending word to the Earps to come down to the O K Corral and fight it out. The Clanton crowd were preparing to ride out of town and had gone to the Corral to secure their horses.

225. WERSTEIN, IRVING. Marshal without a gun. Tom Smith, by Irving Werstein. New York, Julian Mesner, Inc., [1959]. Cloth.

This story of Tom Smith, written for juvenile readers, is full of conversation that no one recorded. In fact, the whole book is a piece of fiction, telling of things that never happened, such as use of the United States Cavalry to subdue Abilene and round up a gang the author says was operating under a man named Monahans after Smith had been fired as marshal of Abilene. Smith was still on the job when he was killed.

This author does not even have the death of Tom Smith correct. He states that he was killed "by a drifter from Texas, wanted for horse stealing." But we know that Smith was sent to arrest Andrew McConnell for murder and that he, with his neighbor, Moses Miles, killed Smith, not some Texas horse thief.

226. WESTERNERS BRAND BOOK (DENVER POSSE). Brand Book of the Denver Westerners, edited by Francis B. Rizzari. Illustrated by Guy M. Herstrom. Vol. XX. Boulder, Colorado, Johnson Publishing Co., 1965. Cloth.

In a chapter entitled "Hero Makers of the West," the author says that Billy the Kid was living in Silver City at the age of eight, but his mother and stepfather did not move to Silver City until after they were married in 1873. Thus, if the Kid was born in 1859, as the author says, he would have been fourteen years old when they married. He has the Kid killing not only a gambler in Arizona but a Negro soldier as well. The author also repeats that old legend about the Kid killing a blacksmith who had insulted his mother. He also has the Kid murdering Indian trappers for their pelts and doing some killing in Mexico. He says that it was the Kid who shot Frank Baker and Billy Morton "out of the saddle while trying to escape," though others were shooting at them too.

In another chapter, entitled "Outlaws of the Southwest," the author has Code Younger for Cole Younger and says that he was killed during a train robbery on October 2, 1896, but he was killed on October 22 of that year (both of these errors could be typographical ones). He also has Black Jack Ketchum robbing the Union Pacific, Denver and Gulf near Folsom, New Mexico, but it was the Colorado and Southern Railway.

227. WHITLOCK, V. H. (OL' WADDY). Cowboy life on the Llano Estacado, by V. H. Whitlock (Ol' Waddy). Norman, University of Oklahoma Press, [1970]. Cloth.

An interesting book of personal reminiscences with some mention of Billy

the Kid, Clay Allison, Black Jack Ketchum and Sam Ketchum, Pat Garrett, and the Lincoln County War. The author is mistaken in saying that it was in Las Cruces that Billy the Kid was tried, convicted, and sentenced to hang. He was tried in Mesilla. He is also mistaken in having Bill Morgan in a posse "that shot it out with Black Jack and Sam Ketchum across a ravine in Northeastern New Mexico," adding "Sam was gut-shot and later died of lead poison." When Sam was shot, he was not with Black Jack. He was shot during the battle with Sheriff Farr's posse in Turkey Canyon.

228. WILLIAMS, BRAD, and CHORAL PEPPER. The mysterious West, [by] Brad Williams and Choral Pepper. Cleveland and New York, World Publishing Company, [1967]. Cloth.

There is a chapter on Joaquin Murieta (spelled Murrieta by the authors), and they make many statements that I have not seen elsewhere. They repeat the legend about Billy the Kid having killed twenty-one men by the time he was twenty-one years old, and they claim Murieta killed more than three hundred, which is not true. It seems that Murieta had a special hatred for Orientals and "more than 200 of his victims were Orientals." They repeat many of the other legends created by John Rollin Ridge.

229. WINFREY, DORMAN H., ET AL. Rangers of Texas, [by] Dorman H. Winfrey et al. Foreword by Colonel Wilson E. Speir. Introduction by Rupert N. Richardson. Original paintings by David Sanders. Waco, Texas, Texian Press, 1969. Two-tone cloth.

In a chapter on Ranger John B. Jones,

the author, Billy MacJoneś, has some material on Sam Bass. He makes many errors in his account. He has a man named Morris Murphy, a Round Rock law officer, thinking he saw one of the Bass gang carrying a gun. In no other account have I ever seen a mention of this character. He has Sebe Barnes shooting Grimes after he had asked if he carried a gun, but it was Bass he asked and no one seems to know just who shot Grimes. If it was Bass, Grimes was the first man he killed.

He is also wrong in saying that Jones fired at the outlaws "as he rushed from the telegraph office." The telegraph office was two blocks away, and Jones ran back to the business section of town before firing at the outlaws. Like so many others, too, he has Murphy later committing suicide. He is also mistaken in saying that Bass had a "spectacular four year career as a highwayman." Bass held up his first stagecoach in 1876, and was killed in 1878. He also misspells Koppel's name as Kopperel.

230. YOST, NELLIE SNYDER (ED.). Boss cowman. The recollections of Ed Lemmon, 1857–1946. Edited by Nellie Snyder Yost. Lincoln, University of Nebraska Press, 1969. Cloth.

In a footnote on page 24 the editor says that when McCanles went to Rock Creek Station to collect a debt Wild Bill Hickok "stepped to the door and, without provocation, shot and killed McCanles," but Hickok shot from behind a curtain farther back in the room.

She has Lemmon saying that there were seven men in the robbery of the Union Pacific at Big Springs, but there were only six. She says that the gang had trailed some cattle to Custer City, South Dakota, and that the "seventh man in

the holdup crew was not from Custer City." They trailed the cattle to Kansas, where they were sold. Her subject is also mistaken in saying that the holdup take was $70,000. It was $60,000. She also tells of the killing of Joel Collins and a man he thinks was named Burns at Buffalo Station. It was Bill Heffridge who was killed with Collins. She is also mistaken in saying that all the robbers "were run down to earth and died with their boots on." The only ones who were killed soon after the robbery were Collins, Heffridge, and Jim Berry.

She is the only one, I know of to claim that Joel's brother Joe was his twin. She says that Joe gave Joel six hundred cows and that they were the ones he drove up the trail, but that is not true. She has Leech finding the masks of the robbers and identifying them as torn from some cloth he had sold to them earlier, but he had sold them bandanas.

The editor in a footnote on page 128 is mistaken in saying that the sheriff of Lincoln County sent "twenty armed deputies against Tunstall, killing him and most of his men." She further writes: "Following the fight in which Tunstall was killed, men on both sides . . . were dry-gulched one by one." There was no fight; it was a cold-blooded murder.

For this information the editor seems to have depended upon Paul Wellman, a most unreliable source. Tunstall was the only one killed, and she is also mistaken in saying that Billy the Kid "was absent at the time of this attack" and that he had "killed nineteen men before he himself was gunned down by Pat Garrett."

In another account the editor misspells Mobeetie, Texas, as Mobita. She says it was "the wickedest town in the country except for Yellow Canyon," but the latter was not a town.

In the latter part of the book her subject, in telling of the death of Johnny Slaughter, says that he was killed by Heffridge of the Collins gang, but he was killed by Robert ("Little Reddie") McKemmie, who, for this deed, was run out of the gang. She does, however, cite in a footnote my preface to Charles L. Martin's *A Sketch of Sam Bass, the Bandit* (a reprint by the University of Oklahoma Press), wherein I relate this incident as it really happened.

She makes the statement that Quantrill's "most infamous attack" was on Leavenworth, Kansas, but it was on Lawrence. She has the Neutral Strip of Oklahoma opened for settlement on April 29, 1889, but it was opened on April 22 of that year. She also seems to be careless with the spelling of some proper names, such as Sansamon for San Simon, Demming for Deming, W. C. Green for W. C. Greene, and Bake Thompson for Babe Thompson, though these could be typographical errors.

231. YOST, NELLIE SNYDER. The call of the range. The story of the Nebraska Stock Growers Association, by Nellie Snyder Yost. Denver, Sage Books, [1966]. Cloth.

The author tells of the Union Pacific train robbery by Joel Collins and his gang, but she is mistaken in having a John Underwood in this robbery. There was no Underwood with Bass until Henry Underwood joined him after his return to Texas. She also tells how Sam Bass "was supposed to have confessed to burying his share of the Big Springs robbery loot there and [fleeing] south. Though hordes of people moved mountains of earth in the vicinity, no U.P. gold was ever found, so far as is known." That is not surprising, for no U.P. gold was buried. Bass had spent his last gold piece on his way to Round Rock just be-

fore he was killed. The author writes: "When Sam Bass was dying at Round Rock, Texas, he was supposed to have confessed to burying his share of the Big Springs robbery loot there as he fled south." Bass carried his money with him after the robbery and used it to tempt some of his friends to join him in a life of crime.

She has a Curly Jack a member of the Jack outlaw gang (Big Jack, Fat Jack, Long Jack, and Curly Jack) of Nebraska turning out to be Jack McCall, who later killed Hickok. That is something new.

232. YOST, NELLIE SNYDER. Medicine Lodge. The story of a Kansas frontier town, [by] Nellie Snyder Yost. Introduction by Don Russell. Chicago, Swallow Press, Inc., [1970]. Cloth. Also publ. in stiff wrappers.

The author continues to spell Henry Brown's first name as Hendry and says that during the Lincoln County War he "was one of the men who tried to defend the McSween home in Lincoln against the Murphy-Dolan forces during the climatic hours of that bitter war." Brown was not at the McSween house but at the Ellis store. She is also wrong in having the Fritz life-insurance policy one of the causes of the Lincoln County War. True, it was the cause of some trouble, but not the war.

She has Henry Brown marshal of Tascosa, Texas, before he became marshal of Caldwell, Kansas. Though he was a law officer at Tascosa, he was not the marshal. She also has him deputy sheriff of Oldham County, but he was only a policeman. For some of her material on Henry Brown and Ben Wheeler she seems to rely on articles in the so-called men's magazines, but such articles are rarely dependable. They are written to sell by authors who have little interest in history. Yet she gives about the most complete account we have of the robbery of the Medicine Lodge bank by Brown and Wheeler.

233. ZURHORST, CHARLES. The first cowboys and those who followed, by Charles Zurhorst. New York, London, Abelard-Schuman, [1973]. Fabricoid.

This is mostly a cattle book, but the author does have some material on John Slaughter as a sheriff and Burton C. Mossman as a peace officer. Of Wild Bill Hickok he writes, "His eyes were as tender and gentle-appearing as those of a woman in love. And although he is credited with having shot and killed more than one hundred men, it is claimed that no one fell except in the interpretation of the word justice." That is quite an exaggeration.

He also calls Wyatt Earp "the famed cowboy-turned-marshal," but Earp was never a cowboy, and he hated the breed. He is also wrong in writing of him that "perhaps more than any other marshal in history, he managed to outwit and 'talk in' criminals without resorting to gunplay."

AFTERWORD

****

And so, in compiling this work, I find that people are still writing on subjects they know little about and are blindly following early legends that have been told as history. Let us hope that some day before this century has passed, such writings will be discontinued and historians who know how to do research will take over.

INDEX

****

All index numbers refer to items, not to pages. Authors are arranged alphabetically in the text and are not repeated in the index. Even though the entry is not mentioned in the discussion of the item, it is included in the work.

Abbott, Teddy Blue: 11, 231
Abilene, Kansas: 14 ,19, 33, 34, 55, 56, 61–63, 66, 71, 74, 83, 93, 94, 105, 108, 129, 133, 139–41, 159, 190, 195, 205, 216, 225, 231
Adams, Andy: 189
Adams, Ramon F.: 80
Adamson, Carl: 37, 146
Adobe and Iron: 106
Album of the American Cowboy, An: 140
Allee, Alfred: 192
Allen, Joe: 100
Allison, Clay: 13, 33, 37, 44, 45, 61, 62, 78, 80, 89, 98, 99, 102, 115, 127, 128, 136, 139, 155, 165, 181, 190, 202, 209, 211, 213, 216, 227
Alvord, Burt: 36, 108, 109, 136, 181, 211, 219
Amazing Outlaw Life of Jesse James, The: 201
America in Legend: 51
American Cowboy, The: 132
American Cowboy in Life and Legend: 133
American Folklore: 50
American West, The: 127
America's Western Frontier: 94
Angus, Red: 48, 53, 93, 112, 195, 230
Antrim, Mrs. William Harrison: 21, 85

Antrim, William Harrison: 16, 44, 53, 54, 156, 199, 200
Apache Kid: 54, 61, 67, 86, 107, 114, 127, 136, 153, 179
Arizona: 2, 4, 8, 19, 21, 22, 33, 44, 54, 67, 68, 89, 91, 93, 99, 106, 112, 115, 118, 125, 133, 151, 155, 163, 182, 186, 190, 219, 223
Arizona: A Short History: 67
Arizona Territory, 1863–1912: 219
Arkansas: 1, 176
Armstrong, John : 28, 74
Around Western Campfires: 4
Aten, Ira: 3
Autobiography of Frank Tarbeaux, The: 38
Averill, James: 55, 61, 66, 99, 112, 132, 136, 141, 148, 155, 160, 177, 188, 211, 221

Baca, Elfego: 98, 99, 114, 128, 136, 146
Badmen of the West: 61
Baker, Cullen: 61, 136
Baker, Frank: 13, 21, 39, 44, 53, 54, 83, 95, 109, 117, 128, 136, 146, 155, 177, 179, 196, 199, 200, 211, 215, 216, 226
Baldwin, Skeeter: 56, 211
Ball, Eve: 117

Ballad and History of Billy the Kid, The: 199

Bandit Belle, The: 15

Banister Was There: 26

Bank Robbery: 7, 8, 17, 18, 21, 56, 61, 97, 134, 150, 156, 178, 185, 201, 206, 211, 216, 218, 232

Barnes, Seaborn: 3, 9, 51, 62, 64, 109, 113, 136, 207, 216, 229

Barter, Rattlesnake Dick: 57, 155

Bass, Sam: 3, 7, 9, 17, 26, 28, 29, 32–34, 36, 38, 42, 48, 50, 51, 56–58, 61, 62, 64, 65, 69, 73, 80, 84, 87, 89, 94, 109, 113, 114, 116, 129, 134, 135, 136, 138, 139, 142, 155, 160, 164, 170–72, 174, 178, 181, 185, 188, 193, 204, 207, 211, 216, 224, 229, 231

Beck, Ole: 27, 61, 178, 186, 206, 221

Beckwith, Robert: 21, 44, 53, 54, 109, 128, 136, 155, 179, 196, 199, 200, 215, 224

Behan, John: 19, 54, 61, 67, 68, 106, 108, 109, 115, 118, 119, 129, 133, 136, 155, 216, 224

Beidler, John X.: 66, 89, 108, 109, 179

Bell, J. W.: 2, 16, 34, 46, 54, 108, 109, 127, 128, 155, 168, 197, 213, 215, 216, 222

Bell, Tom: 57, 179

Belle Starr and Her Pearl: 95

Belle Starr in Velvet: 194

Bernstein, Morris J.: 21, 61, 107, 109, 146, 155, 199, 216

Berry, Jim: 3, 26, 38, 42, 48, 57, 61, 66, 73, 84, 138, 155, 178, 216, 230, 231

Best of True West, *The*: 202

Bible in Pocket, Gun in Hand: 165

Bigelow, Charlie: 191, 217

Big Springs: 17, 32, 42, 48, 51, 64, 66, 73, 84, 113, 134, 188, 216, 230, 231

Bill Tilghman: Marshal of the Last Frontier: 147

Billy LeRoy: 46

Billy the Kid: 2, 5, 9, 11, 13, 14, 19, 21, 29, 30, 33–37, 39, 44–46, 50, 51, 53, 54, 56, 58, 59, 61, 66, 70, 72, 75, 80, 81, 83, 85–87, 89, 91, 93, 95, 99, 100, 102, 107–109, 117, 119, 127–31, 136, 139, 140, 143–46, 149, 154–56, 161, 162, 168, 169, 172, 178–80, 182, 186, 191, 193, 196, 199, 200, 205, 208, 209, 215, 216, 218, 222, 224, 226–28, 230, 232, 233

Billy the Kid: The Cowboy Outlaw: 72

Billy the Kid: A Date with Destiny: 16

Billy the Kid: The Robin Hood of Lincoln County: 200

Bisbee, Arizona: 67, 68, 118

Bjorklund, Lorence F.: 56, 57

Black Bart: 15, 57, 61, 66, 75, 109, 120, 129, 155, 169, 216

Blackburn, Dunc: 136

Black Hills: The Land of Legend: 173

Black Sheep, The: 138

Blake, Tulsa Jack: 56, 57, 61, 109, 118, 136, 216

Blazer's Mill: 13, 16, 21, 53, 54, 59, 95, 117, 146, 155, 177, 196, 199, 211, 224, 233

Blazing Frontier, The: 224

Blocker, Ab: 112

Bloodletters and Badmen: 155

Blue Duck: 15, 33, 56, 61, 62, 95, 129, 136, 138, 141, 148, 194, 198, 211, 216

Bobbitt, Gus: 37, 52, 100

Bonanza West, The: 82

Book of the West, The: 34

Boom Town Boy in Old Creede, Colorado: 10

Boone County and Its People: 176

Boot, Joe: 77, 141, 155

Booth, John Wilkes: 191

Border Tales: 174

Boremus, Robert: 115

Boss Cowman: 230

Bowdre, Charlie: 13, 16, 21, 30, 34, 39, 53, 54, 107–109, 117, 119, 128, 136, 146, 154, 155, 168, 196, 199, 209, 211, 215, 216

Bowler Hats and Stetsons: 179

Boy's Own Book of Frontiersmen, The: 23

Brady, Sheriff William: 13, 14, 16, 21, 39, 44, 53, 54, 83, 87, 91, 99, 109, 117, 119, 127, 128, 131, 136, 146, 155, 178, 179, 196, 200, 213, 215, 216

Brand Book of Denver Westerners: 226

Brass Checks and Red Lights: 144

Brazel, Wayne: 16, 37, 44, 45, 61, 100, 108, 109, 146, 205

Breakenridge, William (Billy): 19, 54, 61, 68, 118, 136, 190, 224

Brewer, Dick: 16, 21, 39, 44, 54, 61, 99, 109, 117, 128, 136, 146, 177, 196, 199, 211, 216, 224

Bridwell, Dick: 57, 232, 233

Broadwell, Dick: 7, 36, 56, 61, 109, 118, 156, 172, 187, 218

Brocius, Curly Bill: 4, 12, 19, 44, 45, 54, 61,

68, 114, 115, 118, 125, 128, 155, 190, 216, 224

Brooks, Billy: 14, 133, 211

Brown, Henry Newton: 21, 35, 36, 39, 53–55, 58, 128, 129, 131, 136, 141, 175, 179, 186, 187, 199, 200, 211, 224, 232

Brown, Hoodoo: 13

Brown, Neal: 19

Brown, Sam: 53

Bryant, Charlie: 56, 57, 61, 109, 118, 136, 155, 172, 216

Buck, Rufus: 56

Buckskin Frank Leslie: 180

Bullock, Seth: 122, 230

Burk, Clinton: 55

Burrel, Berry: 100

Burrow, Allen: 155

Burrow, Reuben Houston: 136, 155

Calamity Jane (Martha Jane Cannary): 6, 10, 24, 29, 31, 34, 44, 45, 48, 55, 57, 61, 66, 82–84, 89, 92, 94, 104, 105, 108, 121, 123, 127, 129, 136, 137, 141, 145, 148, 183, 190, 191, 205, 218, 230, 231

California: 120, 149

Caldwell, Kansas: 54, 56, 211, 216, 232

Call of the Range, The: 231

Campfires and Cattle Trails: 37

Cannary, Martha Jane: *see* Calamity Jane

Canton, Frank: 36, 53, 56, 57, 61, 112, 136, 155, 195

Carlisle, Jimmy: 16, 21, 87, 109, 155, 196, 199, 215, 216

Carlsbad Caverns: 80

Carver, Will: 4, 27, 54, 61, 109, 141, 206, 211, 216

Cassidy, Butch: 8, 27, 54, 61, 66, 98, 99, 109, 110, 127, 134, 141, 155, 178, 181, 191, 196, 206, 211, 216

Cattle Town, The: 60

Chacon, Augustine: 108, 109, 136, 164, 219

Chadwell, Bill: 17, 18, 56, 57, 61, 109, 118, 211, 216

Champion, Nate: 29, 48, 53, 61, 93, 99, 112, 132, 133, 191, 195, 206, 213, 230

Chapman, Huston: 53, 54, 146, 155

Cheyenne, Wyoming: 43, 141

Chisholm, Jesse: 140

Chisum, John: 13, 16, 26, 29, 34, 35, 44–46, 53, 54, 61, 81, 87, 93, 99, 102, 109, 117, 127, 128, 130, 131, 146, 154, 168, 177, 179, 181, 196, 197, 199, 200, 216, 224, 230, 232

Christian, Black Jack: 27

Christie, Ned: 56, 61, 136, 155, 164, 204, 211

Claiborne, Billy: 4, 54, 61, 68, 83, 89, 91, 108, 109, 115, 118, 120, 129, 136, 154, 190, 211, 224

Clanton, Billy: 2, 4, 14, 22, 33, 34, 54, 61, 66–68, 83, 108, 109, 115, 118, 120, 129, 133, 136, 155, 181, 190, 211, 216, 224

Clanton, Ike: 2, 4, 14, 22, 33, 34, 38, 54, 61, 67, 68, 77, 83, 108, 109, 115, 118, 120, 129, 133, 136, 155, 173, 181, 182, 185, 190, 211, 216, 224

Clanton, Phineas: 2, 19, 22, 54, 224

Clark, William A.: 191

Clay, John: 160, 231

Clayton: The Friendly Town of Union County: 209

Clements, Archibald: 17, 18, 157

Clements, Gyp: 157

Clements, Mannen: 3, 15, 44, 45, 54, 55, 61, 74, 83, 115, 125, 136, 146, 157, 178, 190

Cleveland, Jack: 57

Clifton, Dan ("Dynamite Dick"): 37, 61, 109, 136, 216

Clifton House: 61

Clum, John P.: 54, 118, 125, 127

Coe, Frank: 13, 39, 53, 54, 109, 117, 119, 128, 136, 146, 196, 199, 224

Coe, George: 13, 16, 21, 39, 53, 54, 109, 119, 128, 136, 146, 155, 196, 199, 200, 215, 224

Coe, Phil: 3, 14, 16, 23, 28, 33, 54, 55, 61–63, 71, 74, 105, 108, 109, 133, 136, 179, 186, 216

Coffeyville, Kansas: 7, 9, 34, 56, 57, 61, 104, 109, 118, 155, 172, 185, 200, 213, 218, 224

Coffins, Cactus and Cowboys: 161

Colbert, Chunk: 33, 44, 61, 98, 136, 181, 190, 202

Collins, Joel: 3, 7, 26, 28, 32–34, 38, 42, 48, 51, 61, 64, 66, 73, 84, 87, 94, 109, 113, 122, 136, 155, 164, 178, 181, 185, 188, 189, 216, 230, 231

Colorado: 5, 10, 46, 49, 102, 150, 208

Colorado: Queen of the Rockies: 5

Colorado South of the Border: 208

Come Listen to My Tale: 170

Complete and Authentic Life of Jesse James: 17

Complete and Factual Life of Billy the Kid: 21

Cook, Bill: 61, 111, 136, 211

Cooper, Andy: 125

Courier of New Mexico: 162
Courtright, Jim: 17, 54, 61, 128, 136, 169, 187, 205, 211, 216
Cowboy, The: 177
Cowboy Capital of the World: 33
Cowboy Life: 189
Cowboy Life on the Llano Estacado: 227
Cowboys: The Real Story of Cowboys and Cattlemen: 93
Cowboys and Cattleland: 87
Cowboys and Cattlemen: 222
Cowdust and Saddle Leather: 114
Cravens, Ben: 136, 213
Crawford, Foster: 134
Creede, Colorado: 10, 49, 56, 75, 141, 183
Crittenden, Thomas T.: 56, 80, 167, 191, 216, 217
Crockett, Davy: 98, 190, 211, 224
Crowe, Pat: 110
Croy, Homer: 17
Cummins, Jim: 17, 18, 136
Curry, Flatnose George: 8, 27, 61, 99, 109, 216
Curry, Kid: 8, 54, 61, 66, 99, 103, 109, 141, 181, 206, 216
Curry, Lonnie: 8

Dalton, Bill: 52, 56, 57, 61, 62, 66, 79, 109, 118, 129, 136, 152, 155, 156, 169, 172, 185, 187, 216
Dalton, Bob: 7, 36, 40, 56, 57, 61, 66, 79, 109, 118, 127, 129, 136, 152, 155, 156, 169, 172, 185, 187, 213, 216, 218, 224
Dalton, Emmett: 7, 9, 40, 56, 57, 61, 66, 79, 104, 109, 118, 127, 129, 136, 152, 155, 156, 169, 172, 185, 187, 213, 216–18, 224
Dalton, Frank: 17, 79, 172
Dalton, Grat: 7, 36, 57, 61, 66, 79, 109, 118, 127, 129, 136, 152, 155, 156, 169, 172, 182, 187, 213, 216, 218, 224
Dalton, J. Frank: 71, 172, 191, 214, 217
Dalton Gang, The: 172
Dart, Isom: 109, 140
Daugherty, Arkansas Tom: 1, 56, 57, 109, 136, 216
Davis, George: 21
Davis, Jack: 3, 26, 28, 34, 42, 48, 61, 84, 109, 136, 231
Deadwood, South Dakota: 3, 23, 34, 42, 57, 63, 82, 94, 105, 141, 148, 190, 191, 210
Developing the West: 122
Dig Here!: 164

Dodge, Fred: 118
Dodge City, Kansas: 19, 29, 33, 34, 38, 43, 54, 56, 61, 62, 66, 88, 89, 92, 93, 95, 115, 129, 131, 140, 141, 148, 155, 157, 169, 185, 190, 191, 205, 213, 216, 218, 231
Dodge City Story, The: 88
Dolan, James J.: 13, 53, 54, 61, 99, 128, 131, 146, 196, 199, 213, 215, 222
Doolin, Bill: 17, 52, 56, 57, 61, 91, 108, 109, 111, 118, 136, 141, 147, 152, 155, 169, 172, 185, 191, 214, 216
Dorsey, Frank: 19
Dow, Les: 27, 146
Dowd, Dan: 13
Downing, Bill: 36, 181
Dunn, Rose: *see* Rose of Cimarron
Dutch Henry (Born): 53, 136
Dynamite and Six-Shooters: 27

Early Day History of Rome City: 124
Earp, James: 12, 44, 61, 83, 136, 179, 190, 224
Earp, Morgan: 2, 4, 9, 12, 14, 19, 25, 33, 36, 44, 45, 54, 55, 57, 67, 68, 83, 94, 98, 99, 108, 109, 115, 118–20, 129, 133, 136, 155, 157, 190, 213, 215, 216, 223, 224
Earp, Virgil: 2, 4, 9, 12, 14, 19, 25, 33, 36, 44, 45, 54, 61, 67, 68, 83, 94, 98, 99, 108, 109, 115, 118, 119, 120, 129, 133, 136, 155, 157, 190, 213, 215, 216, 223, 224
Earp, Warren: 12, 61, 68, 83, 118, 190, 216, 223
Earp, Wyatt: 2, 4, 9, 12, 14, 19, 22, 25, 28, 29, 33, 34, 36, 41, 43–45, 54–56, 58, 59, 61, 62, 66–68, 80, 83, 88, 89, 94, 98, 99, 102, 108, 109, 115, 118–20, 122, 125, 127–29, 133, 136, 139–41, 147, 148, 155, 157, 161, 163, 169, 179, 181, 186, 187, 190, 205, 208, 211, 213, 215, 218, 223, 230
East, James: 16, 53, 54, 131, 215, 216, 224, 233
Echoes of the Past: 171
Edison, Thomas: 191
Edwards, Belle Fenley: 70
Ellsworth, Kansas: 28, 33, 34, 55, 56, 93, 115, 129, 155, 190, 216, 224, 231
El Paso, Texas: 86, 146, 161, 211, 216
Enter Without Knocking: 151
Escapades of Frank and Jesse James: 18
Espinosa, Felipe: 136
Espinosa, Vivian: 136
Evans, Chris: 61, 120, 136

Evans, Jesse: 16, 53, 54, 61, 109, 117, 128, 136, 146, 199, 215, 216
Everheart, Sheriff William: 73, 84

Fallon, Rattlesnake Jake: 53, 109, 136
Fallwell, Gene: 84
Famous Figures of the Old West: 45
Famous Guns from Famous Collections: 14
Famous Lawmen of the Old West: 108
Farr, Sheriff Edward: 8, 61, 102, 196, 209, 216, 221
Far Southwest, The: 119
Fiddlefooted: 111
Fifty Years on the Owl Hoot Trail: 36
Fifty Years on the Trail: 158
Fired in Anger: 62
First Cowboys and Those Who Followed, The: 233
Fisher, Big Nose Kate: 19, 33, 34, 53, 68, 89, 109, 118, 129, 136, 141, 155, 157, 218
Fisher, King: 3, 28, 36, 42, 44, 45, 54, 61, 80, 89, 113, 134, 136, 159, 179, 190, 213, 216
Flagg, Jack: 53, 93, 112, 195, 230
Fletcher, Baylis John: 189
Fly-Speck Billy: 158
Folklore of the American Land: 64
Folklore of Romantic Arkansas: 1
Following the Frontier with F. Jay Haynes: 210
Ford, Charlie: 17, 18, 41, 44, 45, 49, 50, 53, 56, 57, 61, 109, 127, 136, 155, 181, 201, 213, 216
Ford, Robert: 10, 17, 18, 20, 29, 30, 41, 44, 45, 49, 50, 53, 56, 57, 61, 64, 75, 89, 98, 109, 124, 127, 129, 136, 141, 145, 150, 155, 167, 172, 179, 181, 201, 213, 216–18, 220
Fort Griffin: 34
Fort Stanton: 16, 119, 199
Fort Sumner: 16, 117, 119, 128, 146, 155, 168, 181, 199, 200, 216
Foster, Tom: 19
Fountain, Albert Jennings: 4, 54, 85, 86, 146, 196, 203
Four Men Hanging: 100
Four State Chisholm Trail, The: 35
Fowler, Joel: 99, 196
Franks, G. W.: 196
Frantz, Joe B.: 132
Franch, Jim: 13, 56, 129, 148, 196
Frontier Violence: 99
Frontier Ways: 47

Gallagher, Pat: 120
Galleher, Jack: 53, 57, 61, 77, 101, 108, 109, 136
Garcia, Three-Finger Jack: 57, 61, 120, 149, 216
Gard, Wayne: 73, 80
Garrett, Buck: 7
Garrett, Pat: 2, 4, 9, 11, 13, 15, 16, 19, 21, 29, 35, 37, 44, 45, 50, 54, 61, 66, 70, 80, 83, 85–87, 93, 99, 100, 102, 107–109, 117, 119, 127–29, 131, 136, 139, 146, 155, 168, 169, 178, 180, 181, 186, 191, 196, 199, 205, 208, 209, 211, 213, 215, 216, 218, 224, 227
Gates, Bet-a-Million: 191
Gathering the Past: 69
Gause, Godfrey: 21, 54, 70
Geisinger, Marion: 61
Gentle Tamers, The: 24
Ghost Town Album: 75
Ghost Towns and Mining Camps of New Mexico: 196
Ghost Towns of New Mexico: 107
Ghost Towns of Texas: 116
Gillett, James: 3, 11, 26, 54, 113, 114, 134, 136, 169, 192
Gilliland, James: 146, 196
Give Me Room!: 102
Glamorous Days: 28
Golden Days in the Black Hills: 121
Goldblatt, Kenneth A.: 86
Gold Hunter: 13
Goldsby, Crawford ("Cherokee Bill"): 7, 15, 56, 57, 59, 61, 62, 135, 136, 155, 185
Gonzaullas, M. T. ("Lone Wolf"): 134, 192
Graham-Tewksbury Feud: 19, 54, 93
Grant, Joe: 21, 61, 136, 146, 155, 199, 200, 216
Graves, Whiskey Bill: 57, 109, 136
Greathouse, Jim: 87, 196, 199
Great Lawmen of the West: 19
Great North Trail, The: 44
Great Range Wars, The: 53
Great Taos Bank Robbery, The: 97
Great Trails of the West: 58
Greigo, Pancho: 98, 136, 190
Grimes, A. W.: 3, 9, 84, 134, 138, 216, 229
Grounds, Billy: 68
Gunfighter, The: Man or Myth?: 186
Gunfighters, The: 190
Gunfighters, The: 213
Gunman's Territory: 7
Gunnison Country: 220

Hand, Dora: 54, 55
Hall, Lee: 113, 134
Hamer, Frank: 113, 142, 192, 218
Hardin, John Wesley: 3, 14, 26, 28, 35–37, 42, 44, 53–55, 60–63, 66, 74, 80, 96, 99, 109, 113, 116, 131, 134, 136, 138, 139, 142, 146, 155, 161, 169, 178, 181, 190, 193, 207, 211, 213, 216, 218, 224
Harkey, Dee: 27
Harpe, Wiley: 211
Harpe, Wilham: 211
Harrington, Frank: 27, 114, 175, 209, 216
Harris, Jack: 3
Hart, Pearl: 61, 77, 106, 127, 136, 141, 148, 151, 155
Haunted Highways: 128
Hays City, Kansas: 14, 62, 63, 71, 89, 108, 139
Heart Full of Horses: 70
Heath, John: 67, 68, 118, 136
Heffridge, Bill: 3, 17, 26, 42, 48, 57, 61, 73, 84, 109, 122, 138, 164, 178, 189, 216, 230, 231
Hell Hole, The: 22
Hell Holes and Hangings: 91
Helm, Boone: 6, 53, 57, 66, 77, 101, 109, 136, 179
Helms, Jack: 136
Henry, O.: 19
Herndon, Albert: 3, 26
Hero Stories from Missouri History: 41
Herstrom, Guy M.: 226
Hickok, James Butler ("Wild Bill"): 1, 3, 13, 14, 19, 23, 28, 29, 33, 34, 37, 38, 41, 44, 45, 48, 54–58, 61–63, 66, 71, 74, 77, 82–84, 89, 92–94, 99, 102, 104, 105, 108, 109, 121, 122, 127, 129, 133, 136, 139, 141, 148, 155, 159, 166, 169, 172, 173, 183, 185, 186, 188, 189, 191, 195, 205, 210, 211, 215, 216, 218, 224, 230, 233
Hildebrand, Sam: 176
Hill, Tom: 21, 54, 117, 196
Hindman, George: 13, 16, 21, 44, 54, 61, 83, 87, 109, 117, 128, 155, 178, 196, 199, 213, 215, 216, 224
Historical Background Setting and Synopsis of Jesse James, The: 167
History of Central Texas, A: 9
History of Kern County, California: 149
History of Nowata County: 79
Hite, Clarence: 17, 56, 57
Hite, Wood: 56, 57, 216

Hodges, Thomas D.: 136, 141
Hole-in-the-Wall: 8, 27
Holliday, John H. ("Doc"): 4, 12, 19, 22, 33, 34, 36, 37, 53, 54, 66–68, 75, 88, 89, 94, 98, 99, 108, 109, 115, 118, 120, 127, 129, 133, 136, 139–41, 147, 157, 163, 181, 190, 193, 211, 213, 215, 216
Hooks, Bone: 59
Horn, Tom: 53, 54, 59, 61, 77, 109, 112, 136, 139, 155, 159, 160, 169, 205, 211, 213
Houston, Temple: 135, 136, 205, 207, 213
Howard, Tex: 68, 136
Hoy, George: 19, 54
Hughes, John R.: 192
Hundred and One Ranch, The: 40
Hunt, Zwing: 54, 68, 107, 136

I Killed to Live: 43
I Knew Jesse James: 214
Illustrated History of the Texas Rangers, An: 113
Imprints of Pioneer Trails: 137
Indian Territory (Oklahoma): 7, 31, 36, 44, 52, 56, 61, 91, 152, 153, 204
Ingalls, Kansas: 52, 56, 61, 172
Iron Men: 135
Ives, George: 53, 57, 77, 99, 108, 109, 179, 216

Jackson, Frank: 3, 9, 11, 26, 36, 51, 64, 69, 73, 84, 109, 113, 136, 138, 181, 207, 229, 230
James, Frank: 1, 9, 10, 17–20, 29, 30, 34, 36, 38, 41, 44, 45, 50, 51, 56–58, 61, 66, 80, 83, 89, 90, 95, 96, 99, 109, 113, 116, 122, 124, 127, 129, 135, 136, 150, 152, 155, 167, 172, 178, 179, 190, 191, 194, 198, 201, 211, 213, 214, 216–18, 230
James, Jesse: 1, 9, 10, 17–20, 29, 30, 34–36, 38, 41, 44, 45, 49, 50, 53, 54, 56–58, 61, 64, 66, 71, 75, 80, 83, 89, 90, 95, 96, 98, 99, 105, 109, 116, 122, 124, 127, 129, 135, 136, 141, 150, 152, 155, 167, 172, 178, 179, 181, 185, 190, 191, 194, 198, 201, 211, 213, 214, 216, 217, 218, 230
James, W. S.: 189
Jennings, Al: 7, 56, 57, 109, 135, 136, 147, 152, 155
Jennings, Frank: 57, 109, 152
Jesse James Was One of His Names: 191
Johnson, Arkansas: 3, 28, 62, 171, 172
Johnson County War: 29, 48, 53, 54, 61, 93,

99, 109, 112, 129, 132, 133, 179, 191, 195, 206, 213

John Wesley Hardin: Texas Gunfighter: 74

Jones, Morice: 111

July, Jim: 7, 15, 55–57, 61, 109, 127, 129, 148, 194, 216

Kansas: 43, 54, 63, 88, 115, 156, 185, 225

Kelly, Dan: 62, 136

Kelly, Edward O.: 10, 17, 49, 64, 75, 89, 98, 109, 145, 181, 183, 216, 220

Kelly, James H. ("Dog"): 118, 190

Kemp, J. A.: 19

Kernbeger, Karl: 107

Ketchum, Ami: 59, 231

Ketchum, Sam: 8, 27, 61, 98, 136, 155, 164, 196, 206, 209, 211, 216, 227

Ketchum, Tom ("Black Jack"): 8, 27, 36, 61, 81, 89, 97–99, 102, 107, 114, 136, 139, 143, 155, 164, 175, 181, 196, 200, 206, 209, 211, 216, 221, 226, 227

Killeen, May: 106

Killeen, Mike: 106

Killing of Bass Outlaw, The: 103

Kilpatrick, Ben: 8, 27, 54, 61, 109, 114, 136, 178, 181, 186, 192, 206, 213

King, Sergeant Melvin: 44, 45, 61, 108, 136, 179, 207, 208, 211, 215

King, Sandy: 4, 68, 75–77, 107, 128, 164, 181, 196

Kingston Story, The: 203

Kinney, John: 16, 53, 54, 203

Kosterlitsky, Emilio: 4, 118

Lake, Stuart N.: 54, 88, 115, 118

La Lutz I Remember, The: 85

Landusky, Pike: 8, 27, 54, 66, 109, 136, 216

Lane, Club-Foot George: 57, 77, 101, 136

Langford, H. H.: 19

Larn, John: 3, 53, 146, 169

Last Cherokee Warriors: Zeke Proctor, Ned Christie: 204

Last of the Great Western Train Robbers: 221

Las Vegas: 30

Las Vegas, New Mexico: 16, 30, 34, 154

Las Vegas and Uncle Joe: 154

Lay, Elza: 8, 27, 54, 61, 98, 109, 136, 196, 209, 216

Ledbetter, Bud: 7, 56, 57, 118, 152

Lee, Bob: 54

Lee, Oliver: 107, 146, 196

Leech, M. P.: 32, 48, 73, 138, 231

Lefores, Joe: 112

Legend Makers, The: 54

Leslie, Buckskin Frank: 4, 19, 22, 68, 89, 91, 106, 118, 136, 151, 180, 211, 213

Lewis, Kid: 19, 134, 152

Liberty, Missouri: 17, 18, 56, 95, 179, 194, 198, 213

Liddill, Dick: 17, 41, 56, 57, 61, 98, 127, 129, 136, 155, 213, 216

Life and Adventures of Harry Tracy: 110

Lincoln County War: 13, 16, 29, 34, 39, 44, 53, 54, 61, 81, 87, 93, 99, 109, 117, 119, 128–30, 146, 168, 177, 179, 196, 199, 200, 209, 211, 213, 215, 216, 222, 224, 227

Littrell, Marion: 102

Locke, Raymond Friday: 127

Logan, Harvey: 8, 27, 54, 136, 206, 216, 221

Logan, Lonnie: 8, 54, 61, 206

Longabaugh, Harry (Sundance Kid): 4, 8, 27, 29, 54, 66, 89, 98, 99, 109, 127, 136, 141, 178, 181, 206, 211, 213, 216, 221

Longhorns North of the Arkansas: 112

Longley, Bill: 61, 80, 96, 136, 155, 181, 191, 211, 213, 216

Love, Harry: 89

Love Song of the Plains: 188

Lowe, Rowdy Joe: 28, 55, 136, 148, 155

Lowe, Rowdy Kate: 148

Lyon, Haze: 53, 57, 77, 101, 109, 136

McCall, Jack: 14, 19, 23, 36, 48, 55, 57, 61–63, 71, 77, 82, 83, 92, 104, 105, 108, 129, 136, 148, 155, 190, 191, 216, 218, 231

McCanles, Dave: 19, 23, 58, 61–63, 66, 83, 92, 105, 108, 129, 166, 188, 190, 193, 216, 230

McCarty, Bill: 213, 216

McCarty, Joe: 16, 144

McCarty, Tom: 8, 216

McCloskey, William: 16, 53, 61, 128, 196, 200

McCoy, Joseph: 58, 84, 129, 140, 189, 190, 224, 225

McDonald, William: 19, 134, 192

McDouglet, Cattle Annie: 109, 141, 205, 218

McIntire, Jim: 54, 136

McKemmie, Reddy: 38, 122, 230

McKinney, Kip: 16, 131, 146, 168, 186, 199, 200

McKittrick, Joe: 103

McLaury, Frank: 2, 4, 14, 25, 33, 34, 36, 61, 68, 99, 109, 115, 118, 120, 127, 129, 133, 136, 157, 181, 190, 211, 213, 224

McLaury, Tom: 2, 4, 14, 25, 33, 34, 36, 61, 68, 99, 109, 115, 118, 120, 127, 129, 133, 136, 157, 181, 190, 211, 213, 224

McNab, Frank: 16, 53, 61, 117, 136, 199, 215, 216

McNew, William: 107

McSween, Alexander A.: 13, 44, 53, 54, 61, 81, 91, 93, 99, 102, 109, 117, 119, 146, 155, 177, 178, 199, 213, 215, 216, 222, 224, 232

Madsen, Chris: 19, 56, 57, 61, 80, 118, 136, 152, 169, 172, 205, 213, 216

Marlow, Alfred: 87, 152

Marlow, Charles: 87, 152

Marlow, George: 87, 152

Marlow, Llewellyn: 87, 152

Marshal Without a Gun: 225

Mason, Barney: 199

Mason, David C.: 76

Masterson, Bat: 2, 3, 10, 13, 14, 19, 28, 29, 33, 34, 36, 37, 40, 41, 43–45, 48, 49, 51, 53–56, 58, 59, 61, 62, 66, 68, 80, 88, 94, 99, 102, 108, 109, 113, 115, 118, 122, 125, 127, 129, 133, 136, 140, 141, 147, 148, 160, 169, 175, 179, 181, 187, 190, 205, 207, 208, 211, 213, 215, 216, 218, 224

Masterson, Ed: 14, 19, 33, 56, 57, 108, 115, 129, 136, 175, 186, 208, 216

Masterson, Jim: 54, 56, 108, 190, 213

Mathers, Mysterious Dave: 94, 108, 136, 147, 155, 190, 213, 224

Matthews, Billy: 13, 21, 155, 179

Maverick Tales: 181

Maverick Town: 131

Maxwell, John Alan: 134

Maxwell, Pete: 16, 44, 45, 54, 61, 70, 119, 127, 146, 155, 168, 200, 224

May, Boone: 122, 230

Medicine Lodge: 232

Medicine Lodge, Kansas: 21, 66, 175, 187, 200, 211, 232

Merrill, Dave: 110, 216

Mesilla, New Mexico: 16, 181

Metcalf, Lennie ("Little Breeches"): 56, 109, 141, 205, 218

Michael, Maurice: 156

Middleton, Doc: 32, 158, 231

Middleton, John: 13, 16, 39, 53–57, 61, 95, 99, 109, 127–29, 131, 146, 148, 194, 196, 199, 200, 211, 216

Mighty Land, The: 66

Military Posts and Camps in Oklahoma: 153

Miller, Clell: 17, 18, 41, 56, 57, 61, 127, 136, 155, 191, 211, 213, 216

Miller, Jim: 3, 37, 45, 52, 54, 74, 80, 89, 100, 113, 146, 199, 211, 213

Milton, Jeff: 27, 54, 61, 74, 136, 161, 181

Miner, Jim: 109, 155

Miracle of the Chisholm Trail: 105

Missouri: 11, 18, 20, 41, 124, 167

Mitchell, Luther: 59, 231

Montana: 53, 66, 101, 104, 112

Montana Vigilantes: 77, 101, 112, 211

Moore, Maurice: 9, 134, 229

Morris, John T.: 15, 45, 56, 62, 194

Morton, Billy: 13, 16, 21, 39, 44, 53, 54, 83, 95, 109, 117, 155, 177, 199, 200, 211, 213, 216, 224, 226

Mossman, Burton: 19, 67, 108, 109, 112, 136, 182, 213, 219, 233

Muir, Mrs. Emma: 77

Murder on the Palo Duro: 215

Murieta, Joaquin: 57, 61, 75, 89, 109, 120, 129, 136, 149, 155, 169, 216, 228

Murphy, Jim: 3, 9, 26, 36, 50, 51, 61, 64, 73, 84, 109, 113, 138, 155, 164, 170, 181, 207, 216, 229, 230

Murphy, L. G.: 34, 59, 93, 102, 117, 128, 177, 196, 215, 216, 222, 224

Murrell, John: 1, 58

Musgrove, George: 136

My Girlhood Among Outlaws: 117

My Life in the Southwest: 86

My Seventy-five Years Along the Mexican Border: 125

Mysterious West, The: 228

Nebraska: 31, 51, 105, 112, 231

Nebraska Folklore: 31

Negro Cowboys, The: 59

Nevermore Cimarron Nevermore: 98

Newcomb, Bitter Creek George: 33, 56, 61, 109, 141, 172, 211, 213, 216

New Eldorado, The: 49

New Frontier: 184

New Mexico: 4, 8, 16, 27, 44, 53, 70, 72, 76, 78, 81, 85–87, 89, 91, 97, 98, 102, 107, 117, 133, 146, 162, 168, 181, 196, 199, 203, 209, 211, 215, 226, 227

New Mexico and Texas Ghost Towns: 76

Nix, Everitt Dumas: 56, 57, 61, 152

Nixon, Tom: 42, 48, 61, 84, 155, 216, 230

Northfield Bank Robbery: 17, 44, 50, 56, 66, 80, 95, 109, 135, 167, 178, 191, 194, 213, 216, 218
North Kansas City: 150
Notorious Ladies of the Frontier: 55

O'Day, Tom: 8, 61, 109, 136, 206
Off the Beaten Trail: 207
O'Folliard, Tom: 13, 16, 21, 37, 53, 54, 108, 109, 117, 131, 136, 146, 168, 196, 200, 209, 215, 216, 224
O K Corral Fight: 2, 4, 14, 25, 33, 34, 61, 66–68, 75, 80, 93, 98, 99, 108, 109, 115, 118–20, 125, 129, 133, 145, 155, 181, 190, 213, 216, 218, 224
Oklahoma: 40, 56, 80, 87, 100, 143, 153, 211
Oklahoma Panhandle: 143
Old West, The: 89
Old West in Fact, The: 11
Olinger, Bob: 2, 16, 21, 34, 39, 46, 54, 70, 80, 108, 109, 117, 127, 128, 136, 146, 154, 155, 168, 178, 199, 215, 216, 222, 224
Olinger, Wallace: 117
Olive, Print: 55, 136, 231
Once in the Saddle: 195
O'Neal, Bucky: 112, 136, 169
One Hundred and One Ranch, The: 40
One Man's Montana: 104
O'Roark, Johnny-Behind-the-Deuce: 2, 12, 45, 54, 115, 118, 125, 136
Outlaw, Bass: 74, 103, 113, 136, 161, 179
Outlaw Album: 145
Outlaw Queen: 198
Outlawry and Justice in Old Arizona: 2
Outlaws, The: 126
Outlaws on Horseback: 56
Owens, Commodore Perry: 19, 53, 108, 109, 125, 136, 182, 205

Packer, Alferd: 49, 75, 136, 155, 220
Parker, Robert Leroy: *see* Butch Cassidy
Parker, Isaac: 7, 15, 56, 57, 118, 153, 172, 191, 204, 205, 211, 216
Parrotti, Big Nose George: 18, 61
Pat Garrett: The Story of a Western Lawman: 146
Peak, June: 3, 170, 171
Peppin, George: 13, 16, 21, 39, 53, 109, 117, 119, 199, 224
Peterson, Harrold L.: 62
Phelps, Jesse: 49
Philpot, Bud: 4, 33, 54, 68, 108, 190

Pickett, Tom: 16, 30, 53, 131, 136, 168, 182, 190, 199, 216
Pictorial History of the Texas Rangers, A: 192
Pierce, Charlie: 56, 136, 172, 216
Pioneer Days in Jackson County: 20
Pipes, Gerald: 201
Pipes, Sam: 3, 17, 26
Pitts, Charlie: 17, 56, 109, 136, 155, 178, 213, 216
Place, Etta: 61, 206, 213
Pleasant Valley War: 19, 53, 99, 125
Plummer, Henry: 6, 53, 61, 77, 94, 99, 101, 104, 108, 109, 136, 155, 169, 179, 211, 216
Poe, John W.: 16, 37, 54, 108, 109, 117, 131, 146, 168, 181, 186, 199
Pony Express Trail, The: 166
Powell, Dick: 7
Powers, Bill: 56, 57, 61, 109, 118, 136, 156, 172, 216, 218
Proctor, Zeke: 204

Quantrill, William Clarke: 1, 17, 20, 56, 57, 61, 89, 126, 127, 136, 153, 172, 194, 201, 213

Raidler, Little Bill: 19, 56, 57, 61, 109, 136, 172, 216
Ranch on the Ruidoso: 39
Rangers of Texas: 229
Ray, Ned: 57, 101, 108, 136, 179
Ray, Nick: 48, 93, 112, 132, 133, 191, 195, 206, 213, 230
Reed, Ed: 7, 56, 129, 194, 216, 217
Reed, Jim: 7, 15, 17, 44, 45, 55–57, 61, 62, 109, 123, 127, 129, 136, 148, 191, 194, 198, 216, 217
Reedstrom, Ernest L.: 190, 218
Reminiscences of Fort Huachua: 163
Reminiscences of Roswell Pioneers: 197
Reminiscences of Senator William H. Stewart of Nevada: 25
Reni, Jules: 58, 66, 83, 155, 158, 186, 212
Reno, John: 57, 61, 109, 155
Ringo, Johnny: 2, 4, 54, 61, 68, 117, 118, 127, 136, 155, 172, 181, 211, 216, 224
River of No Return: 6
Road Agents and Train Robbers: 57
Robbers' Roost: 8, 109, 216
Roberts, Andrew ("Buckshot"): 13, 21, 39, 44, 53, 54, 109, 117, 146, 155, 179, 199, 200, 211, 216, 224

Rock Creek Station: 23, 61, 71, 83, 92, 105, 108, 166
Rogers, Ike: 135, 230
Rose of Cimarron: 24, 57, 61, 109, 136, 141, 216
Roswell: A Fond Look Back: 168
Round Rock, Texas: 9, 28, 42, 51, 62, 64, 69, 73, 84, 89, 113, 114, 116, 134, 138, 139, 164, 170, 185, 207, 211, 229, 231
Rudabaugh Dave: 16, 30, 34, 49, 53, 54, 75, 102, 109, 129, 136, 146, 168, 182, 183, 190, 199, 200, 215, 216
Russell, Charlie: 47, 59, 127, 131
Russian Bill: 4, 12, 68, 75–77, 100, 107, 128, 156, 164, 181, 196
Rynning, Tom: 36, 169

Saga of the Colts Six-Shooter: 218
Sample, Red: 68, 118
Samuel, Dr. Reuben: 17, 41, 57, 167, 201
Scarborough, George: 3, 14, 27, 54, 61, 103, 113, 130, 161, 181, 216, 221
Scurlock, Doc: 16, 54, 117, 119, 146, 199, 224
Segale, Blandina: 208
Selman, John: 3, 14, 16, 35, 39, 53, 61, 74, 103, 104, 113, 117, 136, 146, 161, 179, 190, 207, 211, 216, 218, 221
Sermon in Wax, A: 184
Shady Ladies of the West: 148
Shakespeare, New Mexico: 4, 75–77, 100, 128, 164, 196
Shaw, Charles: 211
Shepherd, George: 201, 213
Shepherd, Oll: 17, 201
Shields, Sheriff Rhome: 164
Shirley, Ed: 15, 24, 56, 194
Shirley, John: 15, 56, 191, 194
Shirley, Preston: 15, 56, 194
Short, Ed: 56, 57, 61, 109, 118, 155, 172, 216
Short, Luke: 2, 14, 17, 29, 36, 54, 61, 68, 118, 122, 129, 136, 140, 141, 155, 169, 187, 190, 208, 211, 213, 215, 216, 230
Showdown: Western Gunfighters in Moments of Truth: 211
Silva, Vicente: 58
Siringo, Charles: 11, 37, 61, 66, 87, 108, 136, 146, 189, 205, 206, 213, 215
Sirdoksky, Sam: 120
Skinner, George: 57
Skinner, Cyrus: 109

Slade, Joseph: 38, 53, 57, 58, 61, 66, 83, 101, 104, 109, 122, 136, 155, 158, 169, 212, 230
Slaughter, John: 4, 54, 61, 67, 114, 117, 118, 122, 129, 136, 169, 172, 190, 211, 230, 233
Slaughter, Johnny: 38, 57, 61, 112, 122
Smith, Soapy: 10, 49, 55, 61, 75, 82, 110, 155, 183
Smith, Tom: 19, 54, 105, 108, 129, 133, 140, 141, 169, 195, 205, 211, 213, 225
Soapy Smith: King of the Frontier Con Men: 183
Socorro, New Mexico: 75, 76
Sontag, George: 61, 120, 155
South Dakota: 63, 112, 121, 122, 173
Southwestern Historical Wax Museum: 80
Southwest Heritage: 139
Spaniard, Jack: 129, 148
Sparks from Many Camp Fires: 101
Spegelberg, Flora: 72
Spell of the Turf: 96
Spence, Pete: 54, 213
Spottswood, Tom: 3
Stage Robbery: 5, 48, 56, 112, 118, 122
Starr, Belle: 1, 7, 14, 15, 17, 24, 29, 33, 36, 44, 45, 55–57, 61, 62, 80, 89–91, 95, 109, 121, 123, 127, 129, 136, 138, 141, 148, 152, 153, 155, 172, 185, 191, 194, 198, 204, 211, 213, 216–18
Starr, Henry: 1, 7, 15, 36, 40, 56, 57, 61, 89, 109, 136, 152, 155, 176, 185, 194, 208, 213
Starr, Pearl: 7, 15, 55, 57, 61, 109, 127, 138, 141, 148, 172, 194, 213, 216, 217
Starr, Sam: 1, 7, 15, 17, 33, 55, 56, 61, 90, 91, 95, 109, 123, 127, 129, 136, 141, 148, 155, 172, 194, 213, 216, 218
Starr, Tom: 33, 56, 61, 90, 136, 194
Stiles, Billy: 36, 57, 108, 136, 191, 211, 219
Stillwell, Frank: 19, 61, 89, 108, 109, 118, 136, 186, 190, 216
Stinking Springs: 16, 30, 34, 44, 45, 54, 107, 119, 146, 154, 199, 218, 224
Stinson, Buck: 53, 101, 108, 109, 136, 179
Stockton, Ike: 128, 199
Storms, Charlie: 68
Stoudenmire, Dallas: 3, 54, 74, 114, 136, 155, 161, 169, 211
Such Outlaws as Jesse James: 193
Sumner County Story, The: 181

Tales of California: 120
Tales of the Frontier: 48
Tales the Western Tombstones Tell: 77

Tame the Restless Wind: 84

Tascosa, Texas: 16, 54, 95, 129, 131, 146, 165, 207, 211, 215, 216, 232

Taylor-Sutton Feud: 3, 44, 61, 116, 229

Ten Tall Texans: 134

Territory Tales: 52

Texans, Guns and History: 3

Texas: 8, 9, 24, 26, 28, 42, 44, 51, 56, 61, 65, 86, 87, 103, 112–14, 116, 134, 142, 171, 192, 205, 207, 211, 215, 216, 227, 229

Texas Ben Thompson: 159

Texas Jack: 56, 124

Texas Rangers: 3, 11, 26, 29, 33, 42, 54, 61, 73, 74, 89, 103, 108, 109, 113, 114, 118, 134, 142, 181, 192, 205, 211, 216, 229

Texas Rangers, The: 42

Texas Rangers, The: 65

Texas Rangers, The: 142

Them Were the Days: 182

There Must Be a Lone Ranger: 29

This Is Frank James: 217

This Is Three Forks Country: 90

Thomas, Heck: 7, 56, 57, 61, 62, 135, 136, 147, 152, 172, 186, 204, 205, 211, 216

Thompson, Ben: 3, 9, 19, 28, 33, 34, 44, 45, 54, 55, 61, 62, 66, 80, 108, 109, 113, 115, 136, 147, 155, 159, 169, 172, 179, 186, 190, 211, 213, 215, 216

Thompson, William (Bill): 9, 28, 33, 34, 61, 108, 109, 115, 159, 172, 186, 190, 213, 215

Tilghman, Bill: 19, 55–57, 61, 66, 80, 108, 109, 118, 135, 141, 147, 155, 169, 172, 181, 205, 213, 216, 218, 233

Tipple, Anson: 190

Tombstone, Arizona: 2, 4, 12, 19, 22, 33, 34, 36, 44, 61, 68, 89, 99, 115, 118, 129, 141, 151, 157, 163, 190, 211, 213, 216, 223

Tombstone, Arizona: 12

Tombstone: Myth and Reality: 68

Tombstone Story, The: 223

Tom Horn: Man of the West: 160

Towle, Frank: 38

Tracy, Harry: 61, 110, 136, 216

Train Robbery: 17, 18, 27, 32, 48, 56, 61, 66, 81, 97, 98, 102, 113, 118, 175, 178, 205, 296, 209, 211, 216

Trousdale, Daniel: 206

True Wild West Stories: 83

Tucson, Arizona: 68, 89, 106

Tunstall, John: 13, 16, 21, 29, 39, 44, 53, 54, 61, 83, 91, 93, 99, 102, 109, 117, 131, 139, 146, 155, 177, 196, 199, 200, 211, 213, 215, 216, 224, 230

Turbulent Taos: 78

Tutt, Dave: 129

Under Cover for Wells Fargo: 118

Underwood, Henry: 3, 26, 48, 61, 109, 137, 216, 231

Union Pacific: Hell on Wheels: 32

Union Pacific Train Robbery: 3, 26, 28, 32, 34, 42, 48, 61, 64, 73, 84, 94, 113, 134, 138, 145, 161, 170

Updegraff, Al: 129

Upson, Ash: 16, 21, 61, 117, 178, 188, 199, 200, 213, 216, 230, 231

Up the Trail in '79: 73

Utah: 8

Varnes, Johnny: 38

Vásquez, Tiburcio: 57, 61, 136, 149, 155

Vaughn, Joe: 217

Vigilante Woman: 212

Wagner, Dutch John: 108, 109, 136, 186

Wagner, Jack: 33, 54, 190, 208, 216

Waite, Fred: 199

Walker, Alfred: 33, 54, 186, 190, 208, 215, 216

Ware, Dick: 3, 26, 28, 73, 114, 179, 181, 211

Warner, Matt: 8, 61, 206

Watson, Cattle Kate: 24, 31, 55, 61, 66, 112, 132, 136, 141, 148, 155, 177, 178, 211, 213, 221

Watson, Edgar: 7, 15, 44, 45, 56, 57, 95, 127, 129, 216

Webb, Joshua: 16

Weightman, Red Buck: 57, 61, 109, 141, 155, 216

Welcome to Tombstone: 157

West, Jesse: 100

West, John: 56, 95

West, Little Dick: 7, 56, 57, 61, 109, 136, 213, 216

Western Badmen: 109

Western Lawmen: 205

Western Outlaws: 178

Western Peace Officer, The: 169

West That's Gone, The: 175

Wheeler, Ben: 21, 54, 61, 175, 179, 187, 200, 211, 213, 232

Whiskey and Wild Women: 141

White, Fred: 12, 19, 44, 45, 61, 68, 115, 190, 224

Wichita, Kansas: 19, 33, 34, 56, 83, 115, 125, 157

Wichita Falls, Texas: 19, 56

Wichita Mountains, The: 152

Widenmann, Robert: 16, 39, 53, 99, 109, 117, 119, 196, 200

Wild and Woolly: 136

Wild Bunch: 8, 29, 54, 61, 66, 108, 109, 134, 155, 181, 196, 206, 213

Wild Bunch, The: 206

Wild Bunch at Robbers' Roost, The: 8

Bild Bill and Deadwood: 71

Wild Bill Hickok: 63

Wild, Wild West, The: 129

William S. Hart on Wild Bill Hickok: 92

Williams, Mike: 14, 62, 108, 133, 186, 190

Wilson, Billy: 16, 30, 53, 109, 117, 136, 146, 168, 199, 215

Wilson, Floyd: 61

Wilson, Kid: 15, 56, 61, 208

Wire That Fenced the West, The: 130

Women of the West: 123

Woodruff, Len: 37

Wyatt Earp: 115

Wyatt, Zip: 136

Wyoming: 8, 43, 77, 93, 99, 112, 132

Yeager, Red: 53, 57, 109, 136, 179, 211

Young, Harry: 62, 63, 190

Younger, Bruce: 191

Younger, Cole: 7, 9, 15, 17, 18, 20, 24, 29, 36, 49, 50, 55–57, 61, 66, 80, 83, 89, 90, 95, 109, 116, 127, 129, 136, 138, 141, 155, 167, 172, 176, 191, 194, 198, 201, 211, 213, 216, 218

Younger, James: 17, 18, 36, 50, 55–57, 61, 66, 83, 89, 90, 95, 109, 116, 129, 136, 167, 172, 176, 191, 194, 198, 201, 211, 213, 216, 218

Younger, John: 17, 29, 61, 109, 129, 136, 155, 167, 172, 176, 191, 194, 198, 201, 213, 216

Younger, Pearl: 15, 55, 57, 109, 138, 148, 172

Younger, Robert: 15, 17, 18, 29, 36, 50, 55–57, 61, 66, 83, 89, 90, 95, 109, 116, 136, 155, 167, 172, 176, 191, 194, 198, 201, 211, 213, 216, 218

Younger, Scout: 194

Younger's Bend: 7, 90, 129, 194, 216

Yountis, Oliver: 57, 61, 109, 136, 172

Yuma, Arizona: 106, 151

Zachary, Robert: 109, 136